THE CAPE BRETON FIDDLE

MAKING AND MAINTAINING TRADITION

GLENN GRAHAM

THE
CAPE BRETON FIDDLE

MAKING AND MAINTAINING TRADITION

GLENN GRAHAM

CAPE BRETON UNIVERSITY PRESS
SYDNEY, NS, CANADA

Cape Breton University Press recognizes the support of the Province of Nova Scotia, through the Department of Tourism, Culture and Heritage. We are pleased to work in partnership with the Culture Division to develop and promote our cultural resources for Nova Scotians.

NOVA SCOTIA
Tourism, Culture and Heritage

Cover Design: Cathy MacLean, Pleasant Bay, NS
Layout: Gail Jones, Sydney, NS
Printing by Kromar Printing Ltd., Winnipeg, MB

Library and Archives Canada Cataloguing in Publication

Graham, Glenn, 1974-
The Cape Breton fiddle: making and maintaining tradition / Glenn Graham.

Originally presented as the author's thesis (M.A.--Saint Mary's University) under the title: Cape Breton fiddle music.
ISBN 1-897009-09-7

1. Fiddling. 2. Fiddlers--Nova Scotia--Cape Breton Island. 3. Celtic music--Nova Scotia--Cape Breton Island. I. Title.

ML863.7.N8G739 2006   787.2'162'0097169   C2006-904068-0

Cape Breton University Press
PO Box 5300
Sydney, NS B1P 6L2
Canada

THE CAPE BRETON FIDDLE
MAKING AND MAINTAINING TRADITION

TABLE OF CONTENTS

ACKNOWLEDGEMENTS

I had the privilege of attending Saint Mary's University in Halifax for my Master of Arts degree in Atlantic Canada Studies, which helped me to gain an understanding of the socio-political and cultural landscapes of Atlantic Canada, its diversity and the importance of its local histories. I was attracted to the Atlantic Canada Studies program because of its openness to having students write their theses about almost anything of relevance to the region. Topical choice was not narrowly focused. Traditional Cape Breton music is one of my dearest passions and I thank Saint Mary's for providing me the opportunity to write my thesis about it. This book flows from that thesis.

Allow me to acknowledge a few individuals who were instrumental in guiding me through both the thesis and the book. I would like to thank my thesis advisor, Dr. Ken MacKinnon, for the many hours that he generously put into the project. I sense and admire Ken's wealth of knowledge and passion for Gaelic culture. Writing about a relatively unexplored topic with limited resources is a daunting task. Notably, Ken was helpful in "filling in the gaps" with regard to the state of the music and culture of Cape Breton in two early time periods discussed in this book: pre-confederation and 1867-1914. I feel like calling Ken a co-writer, for helping me with those difficult early time periods and I am grateful for his expertise.

I must also thank my thesis examining committee: Dr. Margaret Harry, Dr. Pádraig Ó Siadhail, and Dr. Richard Twomey for all of their constructive comments and criticisms that strengthened the final product. Richard Twomey was not only a fine professor through this, but was a friend and confidence builder when I needed it most. Deserving of thanks are researchers Allister MacGillivray, Mike Kennedy, Liz Doherty, Jackie Dunn-MacIsaac, Ian MacKinnon, Kate Dunlay and David Greenberg for early studies on Cape Breton fiddling—their work was a foundation for my writing. I also thank Joey Beaton for having the foresight to compile interviews with influential fiddlers in the 1990s that were very useful for this book. These and his other interviews will be important to generations of researchers and musicians.

Additionally, I thank the Judique Celtic Music Interpretive Centre, the Beaton Institute and Saint Mary's, St. FX and Dalhousie university libraries for their facilities, materials and equipment. Sincere thanks also go to the musicians and the late musicians' family members who generously allowed me to use their music for the accompanying CD. May their memory live on with the publishing of this book.

I thank Dave MacIsaac for inviting me into his home and discussing his experiences with and knowledge of Cape Breton and other music. I hope his wealth of encyclopedic knowledge and home archives of all things Cape Breton music will continually be recognized and utilized by more musicians and researchers. I also thank David Gillis for helping me gather photos for the book and home recordings for the accompanying CD. David's photos and music collection are invaluable to the Cape Breton musical tradition. I extend a heartfelt thanks to Kinnon and Betty Beaton for inspiring me and helping me throughout my music career and to Kinnon and John Donald Cameron for their assistance in identifying tune titles for the accompanying CD.

Thanks to Jamie Foulds at Soundpark Studios, Sydney, for engineering the CD. Mike Hunter and CBU Press also deserve a special thank you for all of their help and for realizing the importance of publishing works representing Cape Breton's living Gaelic culture. Finally, an ultimate loving thank you goes to my extended family: my brother Dustin, sisters Eileen, Amy and family, and supportive parents Danny and Mary, for always being there for me throughout my music career and the completion of this book.

Glenn

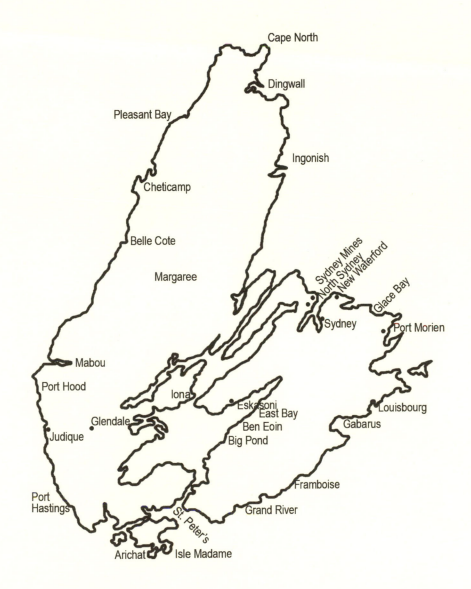

ONE

AN INTRODUCTION

When I was seven years old, two of my first memories of the Cape Breton fiddle were planted. They remain there today, fixed; whenever conjured up, they bring forth a sense of pride, tradition and responsibility. These memories—though slightly faded, like an old manuscript—remain cherished more than twenty years later. They are of my grandfather, Donald Angus Beaton, who by this time had lived, breathed and exuded a tradition that he and my family began to offer to me at that tender age. Just as I fondly remember learning Gaelic words from my father at the age of four, the image of receiving my first fiddle from Donald Angus at the age of seven remains embedded in my psyche. Although I was too young to know the history behind such a gift (and I mean more than just the instrument itself), I still recall the warmth in the room at this particular family gathering at my grandfather's house as I received this fiddle. The instrument itself was not an expensive piece of handcrafted glory. It was a fine, half-sized learner's fiddle, carefully "set up" by Donald Angus for his grandson, who he hoped, and must have "felt," would carry on the traditional Cape Breton fiddle style that he held so dearly. I can clearly remember him playing only once—and I believe it was that evening—but it was enough to implant a sense of curiosity and musical enjoyment that would foster musical growth within me in later years.

Other musical awakenings still come to mind: picking at "Lord Lovat's Lament" and the "Black Hoe Jig" at an early age, gathering with my cousins to learn our first tunes from our uncle Kinnon Beaton, and playing those tunes at our first public performances in Glendale and Mabou, Cape Breton. There were also low musical points: the frustration of "perfecting" early tunes and a lull of virtually no playing while I concerned myself with other childhood preoccupations such as baseball and hockey. Tradition, though—a living tradition, many in Cape Breton would describe it—constantly beckons and burns within the heart. That is why, at the age of fifteen, I rediscovered what my grandfather, grandmother, other relatives and, most importantly, parents had probably hoped and known would be a part of me. During that spring, I began listening to old "homemade" recordings of music played by members of the Beaton Family: Donald Angus, Kinnon, my grandmother Elizabeth and my uncle Joey. At this point of musical exposure, I began to learn the special sounds and rhythms that made this music and culture so rich. I then knew why my mother played those tapes over and over again, probably hoping a musical osmosis would take place between those recordings and her children. I finally realized why my parents were so eager to share and teach, but not to force, this musical tradition upon me. It was for me to discover and for them to reveal and guide me through.

During these earlier teen years I began to discover and understand that there was something different about this music. It was set apart from any other. It was more than just musical notes taken from a notated page and played on the violin. It was quite structured and complicated, played in a way that spoke about the oral Gaelic culture from which it emerged. As Rev. Hugh A. MacDonald has noted, "Cape Breton fiddle music ... reflects the zest and vitality of the life of the Scottish pioneer. And the pioneer was able, noble, robust, humorous, strong, ingenious, and at times, steeped in sentiment."[1] Having gained experience in playing, listening to and analyzing this music, I can appreciate his comments because the way that this type of music has been and continues to be played, is noticeably different when contrasted stylistically with all other types of music.

This book attempts to address the living tradition that I have just discussed. I intend to show that Cape Breton's geographic isolation has been a primary contributing factor in the preservation, yet cautious evolution, of its fiddling tradition. However, of at least equal importance is that Cape Breton fiddling has evolved with the careful guidance of family and the local community and a general acceptance and support by local, and predominantly Catholic, clergy.

This is not to suggest that the Cape Breton fiddling tradition is similarly fostered in all families throughout the island. In fact, it is safe to say that experiences similar to mine are rare, probably during the last half-century at least. I think that I *can* safely say that experiences like mine are common to certain families that have extensive musical lineages and are noted as "musical families" throughout the island. This does not mean to exclude Cape Breton fiddlers without large family musical legacies. However, I do suggest that in most instances, the Cape Breton fiddle tradition has been passed down over generations of Gaelic descendants in a local, family-centred fashion similar to the personal experiences described earlier.

I intend to expand on this personal example by describing where Cape Breton fiddle music came from, how it has evolved, and where it is going. Exploration of larger cultural concepts would help to better understand the art form. For instance, as my plan is to provide an analysis of traditional artistic expression within a cultural group, it may be helpful to look at features of cultures in general and how aspects within those cultures, in a sense, evolve. Also, since I will be discussing the making and maintaining of fiddle traditions among rural Gaels, it seems fitting to trace the origins of their communities and the reasons for their relocation to Nova Scotia. This way, we can better understand the people and the musicians who came to Cape Breton. Careful attention to both the cultural inheritance of the Scottish Gaels and the difficult circumstances surrounding their emigration takes us back three centuries, but it is a necessary prelude to learning about their transplanted Gaelic society and the strength of their musical heritage. It is also useful to understand the subsequent socio-economic and cultural development of the rural society created by the descendants of Gaelic settlers, for it is the story of their struggle with their Cape Breton circumstances which most effectively contextualizes the preservation and evolution of the island's lively music and dance traditions. Just as economic difficulties had an impact on Gaelic culture in the era of the Highland Clearances, so too the cultural traditions of the Cape Breton Gaels have been maintained against a backdrop of continuing economic struggle.

Whether maintainers of a cultural tradition succeed or fail in managing their economic affairs, it must be understood that this kind of daily struggle always has repercussions for their art forms. Also, to grasp the evolution of artistic expression, direct information from those within the tradition—the musicians themselves—can also help complete and test theories surrounding the art form. An overview of the ensuing chapters will put the above ideas into perspective.

The matter of context is addressed immediately: the next chapter is "A Social History of the Cape Breton Fiddle Tradition." Here, the question is asked, "Where did Cape Breton fiddling come from?" In response, the general origins of the music will be traced to the Gaelic Highlands and islands of Scotland. Further, we can ask, "What is Cape Breton fiddling?" For even the term is a relatively new development in the long history of the Gaelic fiddling tradition.

"Cape Breton fiddling," as recently as the early 1980s, was often referred to as "Scottish fiddling" or "Cape Breton Scottish music." Arguably, the term is a mid-evolutionary classification of the traditional music of the island, tied more to identifying with the place of Cape Breton than the place of Scotland. As the passing generations became less attached to the old country, and their feelings of identification and origin came finally to lean more toward their native soil of Cape Breton, the term "Cape Breton fiddling" became more common. Our global community has become more accessible, given that international contact and communication has increased. Perhaps with growth in air travel, technology and communications, Cape Breton musicians and music fans have grown to see differences, or at least enough differences, between their music and Scottish, Irish and other music, to deem it acceptable to call their traditional music by its own name. No longer is a Cape Breton musician required to be called a Scottish fiddler, or an Irish player. Now—and less confusingly—they are referred to as Cape Breton fiddlers. However, influences from other styles still exist or continue to be imported, exchanged, and adapted to the general—and well-guarded—Cape Breton traditional style. The newer "Cape Breton fiddler" is also a more accurate and respectful description, as there are a number of talented French Acadian and Mi'kmaq players with similar playing styles on the island.

The social history in the chapter will include references to fiddle music in Scotland before the mid-19th century and background information on emigration from Scotland. Additionally, other Scottish-influenced fiddle styles in Canada will be explored, noting their evolutionary contrasts with the Cape Breton style, as well as evolution and conditions of the music in four periods: 1800-1867, 1868-1914, 1915-1955 and 1956-2004. In an attempt to provide the first reasonably elaborated social history overview of Cape Breton fiddling, the chapter builds on the earlier work of Allister MacGillivray, as in *The Cape Breton Fiddler.*[2]

Topics that directly apply to the evolution of fiddling as an art form focus the third chapter, "Cape Breton Fiddlers and Recent Decades of Change." A wide range of traditional influences on fiddling can no longer be taken for granted. Perhaps the most volatile subject, whether in terms of impact on the music or on debate about the future of the music, is the relationship between the maintenance of the Gaelic sound in the playing style and the accelerated decline of Gaelic language during the last couple of decades. Thus, long-standing influences such as the Gaelic language, bagpiping, dance and the Gaelic style of fiddling will be examined, as well as the development of accompaniment in the tradition. Additionally, the evolving participation of women and of ethnic minorities such as Acadians and Mi'kmaqs will be explored. In order to bring the chapter to a grassroots level, I refer to the results of a survey completed by eighteen Cape Breton musicians, and I use interviews (most of them conducted by Joey Beaton of Mabou in the 1990s) of seven prominent Cape Breton fiddlers.

The survey is a questionnaire covering a wide range of topics addressing the island's traditional music (see Appendix I). I don't contend that the survey is a comprehensive study representing Cape Breton's musicians. It is not intended to be a scientific analysis. Although I was certainly not able to predict what answers and insights the respondents would offer, I have found that the survey supports some preconceived views on the tradition, as well as a new and fresh perspective from musicians who are well-informed about their craft. The information it supplied is valuable and was helpful to me in elaborating my arguments throughout the ensuing pages. Moreover, it delivers immediate views by those who live the tradition, as opposed to perspectives often articulated in isolation by most academic studies. The survey respondents range in age from sixteen to eighty-five. Some play or have played the fiddle professionally, while others perform simply because it is or was an enjoyable part of their daily lives. Of the eighteen respondents, eight are male, ten female, at least one has Acadian roots. All are Roman Catholic and live in Inverness County, the predominant fiddling county of the island. As Ian McKinnon notes, "The centre of Gaelic culture has always been Inverness County—the area where many feel also lies the heart of the Scottish fiddle music tradition."[3]

My aim is to make this above all a musician's outlook. By this I do not mean that it will exclude other perspectives, but that it is meant to be a full statement of my own view of Cape Breton fiddling and the views of other players as practitioners who have a stake in the viability of its future. In other words, it will address the need for fiddlers to have an up-to-date perspective on their music, elaborated in the context of origins, culture, language, emigration and evolution. History is part of that background and so are academic views of various issues, like the role of Gaelic or accompaniment or step-dance in the music. This purpose is reflected in my use of the survey which, frankly, gives a high priority to seeking the involvement and opinions of players who are among the most highly engaged and experienced participants in the music. The surveyed feelings and convictions of fiddlers and the interviews are meant to convey a unique view of Cape Breton fiddling from inside the tradition. While such a picture is not the only one we should seek, it is a fact that the voices and viewpoints of the players are seldom heard in public discussions about the music and its context.

Activists for Gaelic and Gaelic culture often have common cause with Gaelic fiddlers; this book also draws from some of their work: the most notable example of constructive cultural activism in recent years is Michael Kennedy's *Gaelic Nova Scotia: An Economic, Cultural, and Social Impact Study* (2002), one of the most in-depth works ever compiled on the province's Gaelic culture. Kennedy's report treats fiddling with other related traditions like piping and step dancing, and he is alert to the educational, business and tourism contexts of these art forms. The work of *Am Bràighe*, a Cape Breton-based quarterly paper commenting on and advocating for Gaelic culture, is a valuable resource which I have also drawn from.

Academic interest in fiddling has a place too, even though the output is small. Some of it is by fiddlers who have written in an academic context. For instance, Jackie Dunn's 1991 undergraduate thesis, *"Tha Blas na Gàidhlig Air a h-Uile Fidhleir"* (The Sound of Gaelic is in the Fiddler's Music), provides a detailed analysis of the connection between the Gaelic language and the music, while Kate Dunlay and David Greenberg's *Traditional Celtic Violin Music of Cape Breton: The Dungreen Collection* (1996) summarizes the music's history, has transcriptions of traditional tunes played by various fiddlers and gives detailed analysis of playing style techniques. I draw from the views of Dunlay and Greenberg from time to time, and from other ethnomusicologists like Burt Feintuch and Cliff McGann. Irish fiddler Elizabeth Doherty skillfully covers Cape Breton fiddling as an evolving art form from the 1920s until the early 1990s in her 1996 dissertation, "The Paradox of the Periphery: Evolution of the Cape Breton Fiddle Tradition." The views of local and international music scholars and of musicians other than fiddlers have also proved to be useful from time to time.

The few academics who focus mainly on the Gaelic language and its linguistic traditions and who comment occasionally on the music must also be considered. Because their views of the relationship between the fragile situation of Gaelic and the future of Gaelic fiddling are generally less optimistic than those of musicians, and since there is controversy over the importance of the language to the music, it is perhaps best that I deal immediately with the basic positions that are generally put forward by Gaelic language scholars. In the late 1980s John Shaw, then a resident of Cape Breton and who later became a professor in the Celtic department at Aberdeen University, interviewed various older Nova Scotia Gaelic speakers about the effect on fiddling of the loss of Gaelic. In an article published a little later, he reported their fears for the future of the Gaelic sound. After a presentation of the views of his informants, Shaw concluded: "In the light of the foregoing comments by traditional Gaels, the younger, non-Gaelic speaking generation of fiddle players may be understood to practise a post-Gaelic style, rather than being situated within the traditional Gaelic realm of *ceòl ceart*."[4] (*Ceòl ceart* is a Gaelic phrase for correct playing. "Correctness" in playing will be discussed in Chapter 4.) While Shaw's informants were known Gaelic tradition bearers, only one was a fiddler. Moreover, his comments seem more based on a deduction that since Gaelic is fading, so too is the Gaelic flavour in the music of younger players. We must note, however, that he provides no evidence in his article that his comments are based upon his own direct observed performance of representative players. It is rather an argument based on the opinions of informed witnesses and Gaelic advocates who know the language well, which of course suggests the necessity of bringing forward counterbalancing testimony from those who know the music intimately. Thus, we need to hear as well from the Inverness County music community—that is, from the voices which find expression in my survey.

I do not deny that there is a strong connection between the music and the language. It is generally agreed that in Gaelic tradition the fiddling, piping, dancing and language are intertwined. The use of my survey will provide new and alternative insights with regard to the controversial subject of the Gaelic influence on the music. Approaching the Gaelic issue with the acknowledgement that the language has affected and influenced the music, I propose a more positive view that the Gaelic sound will be retained in a post-Gaelic Cape Breton if certain conditions are met by both the musicians and the local communities. This idea contrasts with well-known views of scholars like Shaw who leave us with the impression that one must speak the language or have an intimate understanding of it to be able to play an instrument in the Gaelic way. I must caution here that there are fluent or nearly fluent non-native Gaelic speakers (both resident and non-resident Cape Bretoners) who do not have a strong command of Gaelic rhythms and accentual nuances. In other words, a native Gaelic speaker would easily notice the lack of flavour to the conversational speech or even Gaelic singing of such individuals even though they have mastered vocabulary, syntax, grammar and so on. Would it be beneficial for a musician to learn Gaelic song melodies from these speakers? I suggest that the resulting rhythmic/accentual interpretation would lack the authentic flavour. Perhaps if the language does almost disappear, it will be best for such speakers to capture the Gaelic rhythm and accent found in the music by listening to the competent fiddlers who have learned the music in the traditional aural fashion. As scholars utilize opinions from local native speakers to support their stance on the Gaelic-music issue, I felt it fitting to do the same thing and search out the views of other locals—the musicians. Since opinions on the music side of the issue are discussed in Chapter 3, it is appropriate to acknowledge here more voices on the language side of the topic.

John Shaw, Michael Newton, Mike Kennedy, Frances MacEachen, Allan MacDonald, Craig Cockburn and Francis Collinson have all spoken and written about the Gaelic language-music connection. Most language advocates see a continuum between the rhythms of the spoken language and Gaelic singing, and the way they are both mimicked to produce a Gaelic sound and flavour in instrumental music. Their stance on this matter is more "conservative" than that of most musicians, however, especially about the degree of familiarity with Gaelic song and speech needed for fiddle playing. In this book, I propose that a Gaelic sound in the music is achieved mainly through aural musical interpretation based on applying rhythms and ornamentations on the instrument, and also being exposed to a family and community environment influenced by Gaelic culture. Frances MacEachen, the prime mover behind the influential publication *Am Bràighe*, accepts Shaw's arguments without qualification in an essay, "Cape Breton Fiddling," featured on the paper's website:

> The intimate connection between the Gaelic language and music has been written [about] by scholars such as Allan MacDonald, Dr. Shaw and Francis Collinson and infers a dramatic change in the music played by those who do not have an intimate knowledge of the language. Gaelic is a rhythmic language with long and slender vowels, when these stresses are not heard or understood, the song or tune can become distorted from the original Gaelic interpretation.... What suffers is often the tempo, as the tune becomes "smoothed out" without regard for the longer vowel stresses that were part of the Gaelic song.[5]

My discussion of music tempo in Chapter 4 indicates that despite conventional wisdom, some Gaelic-speaking fiddlers play faster than some non-Gaelic speakers. Recalling my earlier caution—Gaelic-style fiddlers learning song and melody from non-native Gaelic speakers, whether they have fluency or are classified as learners—is a slippery slope.

Cockburn seems to require fiddlers to have advanced fluency when he notes the connection between fiddle playing and *puirt-a-beul* (literally "tunes from the mouth" or "mouth music"—Gaelic words and vocables sung as tune melodies). Cockburn either exaggerates or falsely assumes that: "In Cape Breton, the Gaelic speaking fiddlers all know the words to the songs they play." He shows that *puirt-a-beul* and tune melodies are interwoven, although he neglects to deal with the fact that some tunes don't have *puirt-a-beul* or predated their *puirt-a-beul* version:

> For these musicians, *puirt-a-beul* is not a substitute for fiddling but an inseparable component of it. For you can't know a tune properly (i.e., with its inherent Gaelic rhythm intact) unless you know the words which give it that rhythm. This is why many fear for the future of Cape Breton fiddling, which seems so strong with so many talented young fiddlers around.[6]

Michael Newton's informative essay, "An Introduction to the Gaelic Music Tradition," presents a stance similar to Cockburn's. He notes that Gaelic has a "time significant vowel system." In the language's vowel system is "the obligatory initial syllable stress" that "forces speech utterances to conform to a particular rhythmic pattern. This contributes to Gaelic's characteristic cadences and speech rhythms." He also speaks of vocables as not being random, but as being important in correctly interpreting and remembering rhythm and melody. Since "Gaelic words so accurately represented the rhythms of the tunes with which they were associated, Gaelic songs could be used to teach and remember tunes." He quotes an unnamed source:

> Because the song style and the musical style are so closely related, it has been observed that proficiency in the Gaelic language is almost a prerequisite for ... mastering the genuine Highland musical style:
>
> > One endearing charm of our Scottish music lies in the fact that the words associated with each particular air are inseparably interwoven with them. It is a common belief that no piper who cannot speak Gaelic can ever acquire any efficiency on the instrument.

Of course, Newton should consider that tunes can also be recalled through melodic/rhythmic memory and applied to the instrument without knowing applicable Gaelic words. His position differs from mine in this regard. Musicians' views will also present a very different perspective from Newton's in later chapters.

Contradicting part of his own argument, Newton first cites "a nineteenth century song collector" who tells his readers that "Every old reel and strathspey, being originally a *puirt-a-beul*, has its own words. Now, if you wish to play with genuine taste, keep singing the words in your mind when you are playing the tune"; but Newton later tells us:

> This does not mean, however, that all tunes necessarily have associated words, only that the idiom has in its origins a close association between natural speech rhythms and musical style. Someone who is well versed in this idiom can still compose music in it without being a Gaelic speaker him or herself.[7]

If one can interpret rhythm well enough to compose a melody, could he or she not interpret rhythm sufficiently to play it properly on the instrument? Musical interpretations are explored extensively here, contesting the views of Newton and Cockburn.

Mike Kennedy's thoughts on the language issue are similar to Newton's and Cockburn's:

The connection between speaking Gaelic and achieving a certain flavour in the music may be an old one but is not well understood today. While studies on the influence of language on rhythmic sensibilities suggest that the language link is more important than has long been widely realized, the important point here is a simple one: at the base of the instrumental folk tradition is song. At the base of the Gaelic instrumental tradition is Gaelic song. Without Gaelic, there is no Gaelic song, and without Gaelic song, there is no longer the Gaelic base beneath the fiddling tradition, no matter how vigorous it may otherwise be. With the loss of Gaelic, the fiddling tradition now rests on a different musical foundation.

That different musical foundation, however, is still rooted in a Gaelic cultural environment that promotes aural learning. Strong family and community musical environments guiding tune and musical interpretations help retain the old sound, or "the Gaelic," in the music. We must realize that although there are tunes played that have applicable Gaelic words, an even greater number (including new compositions) now exist that have a Gaelic "feel" and through interpretation are played the "Gaelic way," which helps retain Gaelic integrity.

On another point Kennedy seems to counter Newton and Cockburn:

> What is at issue is not so much what language people speak as what language they *listen* to, especially what types of songs, and, as a result, what sorts of musical scales, modes, rhythms, and ornamentation they find appealing. Teaching people to speak Gaelic is unlikely to have much, if any, impact on how they play the fiddle on its own, but it can reopen the world of Gaelic song and its associated rhythms, which is becoming increasingly closed to the younger generation of fiddlers. The closing of that door may have a far more profound effect down the road than is currently realized.[8]

I suggest and agree that hearing Gaelic through song would help with a fiddler's interpretation. The fiddler does not necessarily need to hear a tune or air *sung*, however, but *played* by a Gaelic-style fiddler (perhaps on an old recording), as those language-based rhythms, scales, modes, ornamentations would be present. The Gaelic issue is controversial. In Chapter 3 we shall see that some commentators—who have a well-grounded fear about the dismal future of the language as the basis for a local speech community—express a negative outlook about the future of Gaelic fiddle music. However, they need to put more credence and faith in the musicians' abilities to interpret and apply rhythm and ornamentations to the instrument. A more open discussion is needed so that local musicians, their families and communities can get on with the business of passing along the old style in an aural fashion, whether in a recorded or live setting.

I carefully chose interviews of fiddlers to report on, in a manner that would represent the large social composition of musicians on the island. For instance, I chose John Donald Cameron and Alex Francis MacKay, who would both now be considered "older" players in the tradition. Donnie LeBlanc, a middle-aged player, represents Acadian fiddlers in the musical tradition, while Lee Cremo and Wilfred Prosper represent Mi'kmaq or First Nations participation. John Morris Rankin also represents a small group of fiddlers (among whom I would include LeBlanc, Kinnon Beaton, Brenda Stubbert and a few others) who carried on the music at a time when its popularity was dwindling. Natalie MacMaster's interview reveals the strong presence of women in the Cape Breton fiddle tradition while Ashley MacIsaac represents, along with Natalie, a new wave of musicians who carried the tradition forward at a time when the music was experiencing mass media appeal.

These interviews were conducted at a time that fiddler/ethnomusicologist David Greenberg describes as a possible second "Golden Age" of Cape Breton Scottish music (the "Golden Age" is discussed in Chapter 2) when the popularity of Cape Breton and other Celtic music was possibly at its peak internationally.[9] This would coincide with this chapter's additional discussion of revivals and revitalizations and those that may have occurred in Cape Breton. Related subject matter in Chapter 3 includes discussion of interpreting traditional Gaelic culture with regard to invented traditions and pseudo-Scottish culture and a view of how Cape Breton, for the most part, didn't lose its sense of "Gaelicness" through such influences. Out-migration and resulting cultural interchanges are discussed, as well as the influences of specific individuals on the tradition, revealing characteristics of the music and how it may have changed and adapted to various social settings and influences over the years.

In Chapter 4, "Cape Breton Fiddlers and Their Influences," my aim is to connect long-established cultural concepts with the phenomenon of how Cape Breton traditional music has been passed along over generations. Those concepts have to do with stability and continuity within cultures and include exploration of enculturation, diffusion, acculturation and innovation. Interviews by Joey Beaton are also reflected, as well as responses and musicians' insights from my survey; they provide a hands-on approach to exploring influences in the tradition. A wide range of topics is discussed: learning to play, and influences that lead to playing; fiddling families and communities of fiddlers; the Master fiddler/fiddling great and the kitchen fiddler; teaching and learning; fiddling techniques; other musical influences; and views of fiddlers on the Cape Breton fiddle style today and where it is headed. I will also show that various types of change have occurred within Cape Breton cultures, and with them the fiddle style.

Chapter 5, "The Economics and Business of Cape Breton Fiddling and the State of the Art Form," acknowledges that the economy of a region has a decisive impact on cultures within its geographic boundaries—and possibly beyond, if there is an immigration-emigration dynamic occurring. Hence, changes within those cultures are bound to happen. The economy continues to challenge Cape Breton: the island struggles to survive financially as the population continues to decrease. What effect does this have on its culture and music? Are Cape Breton fiddlers' connection to and knowledge of the music's history, presentation and stylistic application as strong today as in previous years? Indeed, over the generations, underdevelopment in the Atlantic Provinces has had a strong impact on Gaelic and other local cultures. Yet the music of Cape Breton has survived, regardless of a massive exodus of people and persistent underdevelopment. This chapter attempts to address the notion that there has been a balanced evolution of Cape Breton fiddling in conjunction with capitalism as it has become more global; that is, increased exposure to Western popular culture and a profit-driven music industry has not greatly affected the continued making and maintaining of the Cape Breton fiddle tradition. A consequence of globalization is that all cultural forms are subject to commodification; Cape Breton fiddling is no exception.

Commercialization of Cape Breton fiddling has gone on since its arrival and will continue, and it is not as "dangerous" to its healthy existence as some may suggest. Political initiatives and their effects on culture and cultural perceptions will also be covered. Comments from commercially successful Cape Breton musicians will reveal that maintenance of a cultural art form in a commercialized setting is possible, and that it has occurred with Cape Breton traditional music. Joey Beaton's interviews with John Morris Rankin, Natalie MacMaster and Ashley MacIsaac are particularly useful because at the time of the interviews these performers were three of the most well-travelled and internationally recognized fiddlers from Cape Breton. Their viewpoints help indicate the effects of cultural exchange and importation/exportation as well as commercialization in those years of prominence for the tradition during the 1990s. Views from the survey are used to expand even more upon the business of fiddling, as well as the state of the art form today and where it may be going in the future.

Where is Cape Breton music heading in the 21st century? Will it and can it survive new challenges in its fast-changing global and local settings? Some feel that the pace of culture, in a general sense, is accelerating phenomenally compared to the past.[10] In a time of internet and satellite communication, cultures are absorbing and adopting cues from a growing Americanized mass media. Those cues could involve fashion, technology, lifestyle, or musical trends that could quickly be adopted, altering long-standing practices and traditions in cultures and replacing older ways more rapidly than they may have in a less technological age. Does this acceleration of change apply to Cape Breton fiddling? Basically, this book tries to answer that question, giving an overview of where the music stands today, through the surveys and discussions with Cape Breton style fiddlers in the early years of the twenty-first century.

It is my hope that with the addition of my survey as a resource, the direct views of contemporary musicians—especially the helpful interview comments made by Dave MacIsaac—will enhance my analysis and contribute to a further interest in the continuing phenomenon of Cape Breton traditional fiddle music. In addition, existing viewpoints by historians, ethnomusicologists, scholars, enthusiasts, and musicians will be explored and at times challenged, with the intention of provoking discussion and interest in evaluating the present state of fiddling as an evolving art form.

Fig. 1. Donald Angus Beaton. Photo by: Unknown, n.d. Courtesy of family.

TWO

A SOCIAL HISTORY
OF THE CAPE BRETON FIDDLE TRADITION

The arrival of the 21st century witnessed a high point with regard to the popularity of Cape Breton fiddling. This living traditional art form has garnered international attention and deserves an in-depth historical analysis. Past studies of Gaelic fiddling are few and, though valid and valuable, many of those have been narrowly focused. Even rarer are serious articles on the development and cultural contexts of Canadian Gaelic music. This chapter attempts to build on the limited earlier work of scholars like Anne Lederman, a scholar of Canadian fiddling generally, and Allister MacGillivray, author of the valuable study *The Cape Breton Fiddler*. An overall cultural and social history of Cape Breton fiddling is long overdue.

As descendants of Scottish Gaels, Cape Breton fiddlers have been able to preserve their Highland fiddle style through a strong form of aural transmission, a result of being the dominant local culture in the majority of the isolated rural communities of Cape Breton Island. Even though the music developed under stressful economic conditions over several generations, the Cape Breton Highland fiddle style has survived with integrity of continuity and remains a flourishing art form through a local and familial cultural transmission that emphasizes an open-ended attitude favouring self-expression. Traditional musical forms, like Cape Breton Scottish Gaelic fiddling, evolve over time within changing societies. Arguably, a balanced evolution, in contrast to stasis on the one hand and disruptive change on the other, contributes to keeping a traditional art form appealing, alive and vital.

In approaching the Scottish roots of the Cape Breton fiddling tradition, it will be useful to focus on basic techniques and approaches of prominent influential players and composers in 18th- and early 19th-century Scotland. Attention to the basics that helped those fiddlers create a distinct tradition will assist in tracking the music as it moves from Jacobite-era Scotland to colonial British America and on to contemporary Cape Breton. These basics have provided a musical cornerstone for the musicians who have followed in the traditional vein, both in Scotland and in Cape Breton. The history of the music will then be taken to Cape Breton where more than 30,000 Scottish Gaels relocated, mostly in the early-to-mid 1800s. The Scottish influence on various styles throughout Canada will be discussed and they will be contrasted with the Cape Breton style and how it has evolved. I will then trace the history of Cape Breton's fiddle tradition from 1800 to 2004.

FIDDLE MUSIC IN SCOTLAND BEFORE J. SCOTT SKINNER

Through most of the 17th century, the bagpipe was the most prominent instrument in the Highlands and Islands of Scotland, lending its spirited sounds and merriment to military life and the local social gatherings of the common person. Viols were also prominent instruments at that time,[11] enjoying the height of its popularity between 1500 and the mid-1700s. It was not until around 1670 that the violin would arrive in Scotland:[12]

> The violin was first introduced in the Highlands in the late seventeenth century by Scottish lords who hoped to bring new culture to the area. It also became a force for social change. The Highland chieftains traditionally employed harpers and pipers to entertain them in the mead hall or to lead them to battle. The new class of anglicized lords, however, were eager to replace this older culture with something more acceptable to their cosmopolitan tastes. Little did they realize that the violin they preferred would be so enthusiastically embraced by the natives, who would make it an instrument of native Scottish music rather than of imported Italian music.[13]

Early proponents of this music contributed strongly to its development and expanding popularity. One of the first known Scottish composers of reels, John Ridell (1718-95), publicized his *Collection of Scots Reels and Country Dances* in 1766.[14] Daniel Dow (1732-83) followed with *Thirty-Seven New Reels and Strathspeys* in 1775.[15] The "strathspey" originated around this time, described as a type of reel born in the strath (valley) of the River Spey.[16] It is said that the playing style application of strathspeys, unique now to Cape Breton playing (and its proponents), is reminiscent of that of the late 17th- to 18th-century Scottish Highlands.

While the early composers were notable, the most famous of Scottish player-composers of the time period was Niel Gow. Gow (1727-1807) and his son Nathaniel (1763-1831) were revered for their performances and compositions. Though Nathaniel was reportedly better "schooled" in theory and composition, Niel's legendary style and bowing techniques have been widely considered the epitome of Highland Scottish fiddle-playing in his era. His famous "up-driven bow" technique "has been handed down from player to player, for over two hundred years."[17] Alan Bruford credits William Marshall (1748-1833) with improving the strathspey and originating "the graceful slow strathspey for listening, not dancing, to"[18]—a direction indicative of the changing times.

During the evangelical revival in northern and western Scotland at the dawn of the 19th century, a restrictive Calvinistic Presbyterianism was becoming ascendant; this led after mid-century to the predominance of the Free Church (which remains a force in places like the isles of Lewis and Harris even today). Calvinism, which had always frowned upon dancing, became more influential than never before in the Highlands and Islands. The trend away from dance was accelerated when a number of leading rural fiddlers of the period found "successful careers mainly in Edinburgh as players and composers." "They too," notes Bruford, "helped establish the classical Scots style continued by Skinner...."[19]

The influence of James Scott Skinner (1843-1927), originally a Deeside dance fiddler who later attained great virtuosity through formal musical education, established the highly-accented style of the northeast as the Lowland classical standard, understood by the modern world as Scottish fiddling. Skinner, who was also a prolific composer, was known as the "Strathspey King." Many of his best compositions included slow strathspeys, while his orientation was to play in a clean, classically inclined style and to present tunes as recital pieces in a concert-hall tradition which soon came to hold sway in Scotland—and pretty much everywhere in the Scots diaspora, except Cape Breton.

Henry Farmer, in his 1947 study, laments the loss of certain essential techniques after the late 18th-century "Golden Age" of Scottish fiddling:

> Perhaps the cunning of digital and bow technique had lost its best exponents as the years rolled on, and that simpler and less energetic forms ensued in consequence. All this bareness and lack of inspiration in the later strathspeys and reels might easily have been due to such causes, as well as to the demands for simplicity by the Lowland public.[20]

However, Highland fiddlers who immigrated to Cape Breton Island would maintain the up-driven bow and other techniques exemplified by Gow, and pass them on to following generations aurally—a transmission relied upon even into the 21st century. In rural Cape Breton Island, expatriate Gaels were able to preserve their Highland style through a strong need to continue both their aurally transmitted dance music and their predominantly oral cultural forms. These old and interdependent traditions were readily transplanted as the basis of local entertainment. Over several generations they came to provide relief not just from isolation and long winters, but from the heavy labour associated with a challenging environment as well. Even though in recent times much of the original Gaelic culture has been in steep decline, the music has continued to flourish. While a healthy evolution of the form is evident despite radical changes in linguistic, social and economic conditions after 1955—when the Canso Causeway opened—Gaelic fiddling has survived intact.

HIGHLAND IMMIGRATION TO CAPE BRETON

A paradox is evident in the "progress" of industrialization and advanced capitalism and the anguish and hardship that resulted, exemplified by the Highland Clearances. Many Gaels suffered home loss, violence and starvation at the hands of wealthy landlords who wanted larger profits from their lands. After their final attempt to restore the Stuart monarchy and the infamous defeat at Culloden Moor in 1746, the Scottish Gaels found themselves at the mercy of the Hanoverian dynasty and a rapidly developing capitalist system.[21] The old style tenant system became increasingly inefficient for clan chiefs and landlords. Cattle and later sheep became guarantors of economic prosperity for the chiefs while higher rents and "the merging of small holdings into large single units under one tenant increased the numbers of landless men."[22]

The process whereby thousands of Gaels were removed from the Islands and Highlands of Scotland has been discussed by historians in detail, and therefore need not be discussed in detail here. It appears that the exodus occurred in two phases, the first being led by the clan lieutenants (called tacksmen) and tenants "more wealthy" than the rest. J. M. Bumsted describes this phase as the "people's clearance,"[23] which affected the Maritimes from the 1770s to the 1820s. The second phase, generally known as the "Highland Clearances," began with the Sutherland Clearances of 1818—forced emigration guided by landlords with the cooperation of government. This lasted until around 1860, affecting the Maritimes and Cape Breton especially, but also Ontario, Australia and New Zealand. The communities and the Gaelic culture that were transplanted to Cape Breton, brought the traditional fiddle style of the Highlands and Islands with them.

Based upon Gaelic-language evidence, Mike Kennedy observes that "descriptions of community emigration do not depict a helpless people swept out of Scotland against their will, but an active people making a positive decision to start a new life." One sees, Kennedy argues, especially in the earlier migrations, a sense of hope and excitement in the Highland people as a new life of promise beckoned beyond the increasingly anglicized culture being imposed by elites in the old country. His work counters the mythology common among the majority of emigration scholars who—in working from "an anglocentric perspective"—frequently quote "atypical" viewpoints of Highlanders "to fit the stereotype of melancholy and nostalgia."[24]

Kennedy's view, that the Gaels were looking forward to a promising new life where they could maintain their culture, supports the theory—heard from Father John Angus Rankin—that the basic spirit of the music in the New World was one of "defiance and exhilaration," seemingly more upbeat and "lively" than that evolving in Scotland:[25]

> For longer than any other Scottish settlement the people of Inverness County continued to live as they might have lived in Scotland. Moving back into the hills and glens and following the water routes they established their basically family communities giving them the names of their clans or their places of origin in the old world: Rankinville, Campbellton, Stewartdale, Kiltarlity, Mull River, Skye Glen, Glencoe, MacDonald's Glen, MacKinnon's Brook. They built their homes on the highest hills as if in dreams they anticipated attacks from a rival clan. Almost invariably they painted the houses white. They maintained their strong religious beliefs, their fascination with the supernatural, their interest in folk tales, their love of dancing and Scottish music, their delight in the Ceilidh, their respect for education, their fondness for animals and the basic emotionalism of their nature. They maintained also their lilting language. The language that the English had so long considered barbaric and unprogressive and spoke of contemptuously as the "Irish Tongue."[26]

In his historical geography of Cape Breton in the 19th century, Stephen Hornsby examines the economic background to Highland emigration in the early decades of the century. He observes that though some rural Gaels moved to industrial towns in Lowland Scotland, a far greater number emigrated overseas. This fact suggests that, since music was at that time integral to even the smallest of Highland communities, a significant number of musicians would have migrated to urban Scotland, but even more are likely to have emigrated overseas. Since, "at the height of the migration, during the 1820s and early 1830s, more Highland Scots were moving to Cape Breton than to anywhere else in North America," and since this was still a time when fiddle and dance traditions retained their considerable strength in the high-migration areas of Gaelic Scotland, it is probable that a great number of good players would have immigrated to Cape Breton.

As a result of the Highland influx at this period, Scots on the island came to outnumber Irish, Acadian, and Loyalist families by two to one. Hornsby concludes that, for a time in the 19th century, settlement in Cape Breton provided Scottish Gaels "a meagre rural niche in a rapidly industrializing world." The island gave them "an opportunity denied them in Scotland: to make an independent living on the land. Gaelic language and culture were given an extended lease on life."[27]

Ultimately, Cape Breton became ethnically dominated by the Scottish Gael and a haven for a distinctive mould of fiddle music, steeped in a Gaelic tradition resembling the style of antecedents like Niel Gow, and seemingly mimicking the Highland bagpipe sound of Scotland.

Fig. 2. *Bagpiper and woman with spinning wheel. Photo by: Unknown, n.d. Beaton Institute, Cape Breton University. 97-620-28468.*

French and Mi'kmaq villages would even become attracted to this lively and contagious style of dance music.[28] Retention of relative traditional purity is, as mentioned, partly due to the geographic isolation of Cape Breton Island and especially its rural communities:

> The early settlers left Scotland toward the end of the heyday of Scottish fiddling, the so-called "Golden Age," a time in which there was widespread appreciation for traditional music in Scotland. While the fiddle music suffered a decline in Scotland after that era, the music flourished in its new home across the ocean. Conditions in nineteenth-century Cape Breton were ideal for the preservation and development of the transplanted Gaelic culture. The displaced Scots found freedom and potential in the unexploited land of Cape Breton. Because they had a common background and were by far the major ethnic group on the island, their traditions and lifestyles were maintained. For many years the island remained isolated enough from outside influences to require virtual self-sufficiency in almost every aspect of life, including entertainment.[29]

Aside from Cape Breton's geographic isolation, the main reasons this traditional style remains a living artistic expression has been familial and local aural transmission. Admittedly, Cape Breton fiddling is not the only style brought over with the Scottish exodus. It seems, however, that it is the closest in resemblance to the Highland style of Gow's "Golden Age" of Scottish fiddling.

SCOTTISH AND GAELIC FIDDLING IN CANADA

The fiddling found in Cape Breton is not the only style influenced by or originating from the Scottish tradition. In fact records of the Hudson's Bay company show that in 1749 there were three fiddlers playing at Moose Factory during an evening party of tunes, singing and dancing. Anne Lederman tells of the Scottish musical influence in different areas in those days of the fur trade:

> Scottish employees of the Hudson's Bay Company brought many violins to Canada, and with them a repertoire of dance music that was carried throughout much of the country by the company's fur traders. The "fur trade" repertoire of the 18th and 19th centuries seems to have been based largely on Scottish reels, jigs, and hornpipes, subject to French, Native, and American influences.[30]

Lederman's final words in this statement help support a point that although other styles found in Canada have been introduced or influenced by the Highland Scottish style, they have been more vulnerable to change and "style blending" because of a greater proximity to outside, other local and other ethnic influences. Even into the 21st century, Cape Breton's population has remained predominantly a Highland Scottish Gaelic one.

While Scottish immigration and influences are traceable in every province and territory, some regions come to mind more readily than others when we think of Scottish heritage in this country. Besides Nova Scotia and Prince Edward Island, we associate it with Glengarry and adjoining areas in eastern Ontario, Red River settlements in Manitoba and the impact of the Scots as a result of their activities in the fur trade. While some areas of "English" Canada have had more Lowland than Highland influence, regions like Glengarry that had a predominance of early Gaelic settlers are where we look to make comparisons with Cape Breton.

Before discussing Glengarry or other Scottish fiddling outside the Maritimes, it is important to note that it has generally been customary to make reference to Prince Edward Island's fiddling whenever there is an extended discussion of the Cape Breton scene, for good reason. At least in parts of PEI, observers either see the playing as basically Scottish or they regard many players as under Cape Breton influence. This observation is also made of fiddlers from the eastern Nova Scotia mainland. At one time there existed for generations in the eastern Maritimes the largest contiguous Gàidhealtachd outside Scotland and Ireland: Gaelic was spoken community-wide in places like Earltown and other parts of Colchester County, NS, and in Pictou, Antigonish and Guysborough counties, in large areas of central and eastern Prince Edward Island and, of course, in Cape Breton. By the second and third decades of the 20th century this contiguous territory had, for all intents and purposes, shrunk to Antigonish and Cape Breton; by the 1960s the Maritime Gàidhealtachd had become a Cape Breton one. Now, although even the Gaelic-speaking areas of Cape Breton are isolated from each other, and habitat for the language exists more in families than in communities, the island remains the symbol and rallying point for Gaelic linguistic revival and cultural survival in North America.

Like Cape Breton and Glengarry, Prince Edward Island in colonial times was another haven for Scottish Gaelic settlers, so it is natural to look for signs that its music has been carried forward to the present. Although some fiddle players there have been influenced by the "Down-East" style of the famous Don Messer (who will be discussed later), only his repertoire has been widely adopted. Ken Perlman observes that in PEI "his fiddling style was never highly regarded." Local players "felt he played too fast and too 'straight-ahead', with none of the complexity and drive so prized in Island playing." This preference suggests that where playing in PEI is similar to that in Cape Breton Gaelic communities, it is rooted in a tradition that has persisted from earlier generations. The Chaisson family from Souris, PEI, exhibit a musical legacy that displays a version of the Highland Scottish one, moulding a unique sound, yet one similar to that of the players of Cape Breton Island. Perlman, in his 1996 study of Prince Edward Island fiddle music, characterizes the fiddlers from the northeast sector of Kings County centring on Souris and Rollo Bay as playing "an ornate, hard driving style heavily influenced by the Scottish-oriented fiddlers of Cape Breton."

One solution to the debate whether the northeast Kings style is a retained tradition or a recent influence is to ask whether it might not be a blend of both. While outlining six distinct regional playing styles on the Island, Perlman contends that "there is nevertheless a distinctive 'sound' that is characteristic of nearly all Island players."[31] Because he sees at least some Scottish influence in all but the most westerly region, it is possible that something from the Scottish idiom has been a vital element in the distinctive Island sound. Like their Cape Breton counterparts, Island players are noted for expressing their personal individuality regardless of regional tradition influencing them. The two islands have also shared a long-time aversion to fiddle contests. A detailed study clearly needs to be made of both historic and present-day PEI fiddling in relation to Scottish and Cape Breton fiddle traditions.

Kate Dunlay, who is far more schooled than Perlman in Scottish music, is categorical: "Prince Edward Island fiddlers play essentially in the Cape Breton style, whereas Glengarry fiddlers have been influenced by the Northeast Scottish style." As already suggested, what is now acknowledged as the Scottish style is the style of Scotland's northeast, the region centring around Aberdeen, and this fiddling has been enormously influenced by the long career of Skinner, who came to prominence in the later decades of the 19th century. He was firmly grounded in and vehemently promoted a classical style, downplaying older techniques. His legacy most likely led to the development of the newer, choppier, less spirited style of strathspey playing found in Scotland today, as well as an academic playing style well-removed from dancing.[32] The Skinner influence could well have come into certain areas of Canada as a result of army veterans drawing on influences acquired from informal cultural exchanges they had while overseas during the Great War of 1914-18. Undoubtedly, some fiddlers came back "fearing their own tradition was not truly Scottish,"[33] but there is no evidence that the Skinner style affected that of Cape Breton, although his compositions have enjoyed popularity on the island and elsewhere for at least the last half-century.

Other areas of Scottish settlement in Canada did not retain Gaelic culture as robustly as PEI and Cape Breton. By the end of the 19th century, Canada had become more ethnically diverse with an inevitable blending of cultures. Throughout, a variety of fiddle styles were either established or taking shape. Lederman summarizes this development:

> By the late 1800s, then, four distinct fiddle traditions had become established: French-Canadian in Quebec and Acadia; Native and Métis in the northwest, northern Ontario and northern Quebec; Scottish in Cape Breton and other Gaelic speaking areas; and Anglo-Canadian—the mixture of Scottish, Irish, English, German and U.S. tunes popular in English-speaking Canada. Although the four traditions would continue to interact, each was recognizable in style and repertoire, albeit with many local variations.
>
> A new wave of immigration in the 1890s brought Eastern European, and, especially Ukrainian, influences to the Anglo-Canadian and Métis dance music on the prairies.[34]

Seemingly, the Cape Breton fiddle tradition was escaping any noteworthy diffusive adoptions from other styles because of the Gaelic dominance in geographic isolation. Other Highland Gaelic settlements would find their culture more easily exposed and in greater proximity to influences of other cultures. Let us look at the case of Glengarry County, Ontario.

Immigration came to the Glengarry Scottish settlements of Ontario, in three waves. The first were the British-American Loyalists: the Loyalists who settled Glengarry after the War of Independence were recent Highland emigrants from Scotland who had first settled in the Mohawk Valley of the province of New York. They were soon followed by the second and third immigrations, both of them large; the second directly from Scotland, and the third constituting an entire Highland regiment of soldiers in 1802.[35] A Scottish visitor wrote home in 1814 that the Glengarry region had "from 1100 to 1200 families, two thirds of them MacDonalds": "You might travel the whole of the county and by far the greater part of Stormont, without hearing a word spoken but the good Gaelic."[36]

In 1976 George S. Emmerson wrote that Glengarry County kept the music and dance of Scotland. He suggested similarities with Nova Scotia traditions: "It would startle any Scot today to walk into a hall in Maxville, Ontario, or Sydney or Halifax, Nova Scotia, and find a score of fiddlers who had never seen Scotland, crowding onto a platform to play reels, hornpipes, jigs and strathspeys with all the love and fervour in the world."

Despite Emmerson's enthusiasm, however, there are stylistic differences between Cape Breton and Glengarry players. Arguably, the Glengarry style exudes a classical flavour, lacking bowing and ornamentational intricacies of the Highland-sounding Cape Breton style. Emmerson adds that Scottish dance music "remains a living tradition and nowhere more so than in the regions of Gaelic settlement in Canada, particularly in Cape Breton, Glengarry, and the Ottawa River Valley."[37] His suggestion that each region had developed its own unique style is not quite accurate. The Cape Breton style has, to a large extent, maintained similarity to the old Highland style while the Glengarry and Ottawa River Valley playing, for instance, have diverged from their origins. In general, the latter has been more susceptible to classical, Down-East (Don Messer), Irish, French, German and other ethnic sounds, some of it resulting from interaction and music sharing between lumber camp fiddlers over the years.[38] The possibility of French influences also being found in Glengarry fiddling should not be underestimated either, as Shanna Jones and Ken Steffenson note:

> By the early nineteenth century Glengarry's population was almost exclusively Scottish. Gradually this began to change. A shortage of land in the populated areas of the neighboring Quebec townships induced French Canadians to move into Glengarry. Some of the Scots, in turn, moved to settle elsewhere. Today the population of the county is about half French and half English.[39]

Besides increased ethnic diversity in the county, exposure to and inheritance of formalized military and contest piping will have had an effect, stylistically, in the Glengarry fiddling instance. I think that there are a few benefits of musical competitions, such as money incentives and increased social interactions between—and interactive support among—fiddlers and interested listeners. There are also risks, however, if there is interest in maintaining individualized expression (at least with regard to ornamentation and regional/familial bowing applications).

This situation, perhaps combined with a focus on competition-friendly or pre-required tunes, contributes to a limiting of stylistic freedom. The result can be style homogenization and a change from an original style. Rhythmic dynamics and tasty tune variations may be undervalued and played down in the continued competition settings found outside Cape Breton Island. Noting the above, and seeing the fact that fiddling competitions across the country have taken place primarily since the 1950s, and in noticeably less Gaelic areas of the country than Cape Breton, I suggest that more exposure to strict competitive playing has perhaps "streamlined" the Glengarry, Ottawa River Valley, and other Scottish-influenced styles. These styles have simply been more susceptible to Anglo-Canadian culture and cultural adoptions in terms of geographic proximity and closeness to Anglo/urban vicinities. One such cultural adoption was fiddle competitions. Kennedy cautions that competitions—referring to pipe competitions—can negatively affect traditional folk music. The same can be stated of fiddle styles:

> Some aspects of the tradition that were once considered supremely important, such as rhythm and were readily learned through the more interactive system of folk education are inherently difficult to define (especially in writing) and inherently difficult to teach using a bureaucratic system. The emphasis on competition in the bureaucratic approach also leads to narrowing of the presentations against one another unless they all play the same tunes—even down to using exactly the same ornamentation. It is also easier to notice a specific mistake in melody than in rhythm since the latter quality suffuses the entire performance, making it more difficult to make quick and quantitative judgements concerning rhythmic presentation, while scoring a performance. The tendency in such cases is simply to accord the challenging facet of musical expression in question less importance among performances. At its extreme ... normal facets of a healthy musical tradition can come to be seen as quite foreign and intrusive, provoking suspicion and hostility when they appear.[40]

Given the fact that fiddling competitions were never prominent and now virtually extinct in Cape Breton, the above stylistic ramifications have not occurred there.

As a fiddle instructor, I have taught a few students who do take part in fiddle contests. In one instance, I was informed that, yes, the student was entering a competition and she was required to present to the judges in advance the sheet music of the tunes she was going to play. This requirement intrigued me. Couldn't they see how well she was playing by watching and using their ears, as is common in the Gaelic folk tradition of Cape Breton fiddling? What would happen if she decided to play a variation of the music or add grace notes where they weren't indicated in the sheet music? What if she decided, as I actually did suggest to her, that she try bowing a few notes a little differently from those the publisher of the music indicated? This limiting of expression concerned me and made me realize that the lack of a competition context in Cape Breton has allowed players there to remain different from each other. As a result, Cape Breton fiddlers are also distinct from those who emphasize or are a major part of organized competitive fiddling—the latter being the fiddling that would be more widely seen in Ontario and much of the rest of Canada.

Returning to Glengarry and Ottawa Valley fiddling, it is worth conjecture that military bagpiping there disrupted the sort of symbiotic relationship that existed in Cape Breton between folk piping and fiddle music. Because Glengarry and adjacent regions of Scottish settlement originally had strong elements of ex-soldiers and were under threat of American invasion before, during and after the War of 1812,[41] the region was more readily co-opted through active local militia into British Empire military conventions of the 19th-century, like martial pipe music. As elsewhere, it was easy for military piping to overwhelm local traditions. It is possible that the resultant exposure to the power of formalized military and contest piping could also have had an effect, stylistically, in moving the playing away from older music in both the pipes and the violin. This is not to say that one style is superior to another: it is better to say that the conditions were right for the Cape Breton style to maintain the authentic Golden Age Highland sound. In other Scottish-Canadian settlements, fiddling was susceptible more to outside influences than internal strength: this may have been in part because Gaels in places like Glengarry faced more pressure to assimilate into the majority culture than they did in Cape Breton. In other areas of Scottish settlement besides Cape Breton, the pressure to conform to anglicizing cultural practices was greater and it came earlier. Glengarry did not long escape the force of this trend; with an earlier and more rapid loss of the Gaelic language, the conditions were perhaps too well set for a faster reformation or transformation of its fiddle style.

Alistair MacLeod's 1977 essay, "Inverness County: From Highland to Highland and Island to Island," illustrates this erosion of culture. Like the Highlanders in Scotland, Cape Breton settlers were also challenged by poor land, bad weather and remote access to markets. Unlike the Scottish Gaels, however, they had secure tenure on the land and this gave them not only food and life's necessities, it allowed their culture to survive many former struggles and to make it vibrant. Meanwhile, the Highlanders who settled in Canadian towns, however small the towns were at first, not only remained landless, they were soon under pressure to engage with rapid change, a burgeoning market economy and an urbanizing culture. MacLeod provides us with an example of Gaelic settlers in the town of Dundas (located adjacent to Hamilton at what would later become the apex of the "Golden Horseshoe" at the western end of Lake Ontario). Inverness settlers faced much hardship but nothing like the "culture shock" experienced in Dundas:

> They were not in the position of the bewildered Highlanders of Dundas, for example. People without land and without food, clad in kilts and speaking only Gaelic to a resident population that did not understand them.

Individual prosperity might have been achieved more easily than in Cape Breton, but whether the Scots immigrants became rich or remained poor, Gaelic identity had to be abandoned:

> To the Highlander in Dundas, his clothes, his music, his language, his "culture", if you will, were obvious handicaps to be gotten rid of as soon as possible if he were not only to prosper but even to survive in the new world. It happened very rapidly. In those settlements which were near larger industrial centres the breakdown occurred often within a generation.[42]

By contrast, Inverness county settlers "did not come to a land heavily populated by people other than themselves" and for a long time in their isolation they felt "no immediate need to adjust to any system of life or values other than their own."

Glengarry, though not far from Montreal and Ottawa, has never been as central to an industrial development corridor as Dundas, which was incorporated into the City of Hamilton in 2001. And though it remains true that Glengarry County maintains a rural atmosphere, one can see that cultural traditions have struggled for protection there. It is safe to say that in Glengarry the degree of "ruralness," isolation from large towns and ethnic singleness, does not come close to the situation in Cape Breton, where I suggest traditions can still be more easily fostered, protected and continued with less urban influence than most places in North America.

Besides the above, in many Scottish areas of British America in the decades after the War of 1812 a sense of Scottish heritage began to be promoted by elites who feared that the settlers would rapidly become Americanized; a number of elite-created fraternal organizations began to appear and gradually to absorb energies that many colonists had been putting into maintaining their traditional modes of cultural expression. This kind of self-consciously "Scottish" cultural construction by elites within Highland societies and Caledonian clubs, such as those in colonial Glengarry, may actually have contributed to the loss of the Highland fiddle style. Highland societies in the New World were founded by and composed of both Highland and Lowland gentry, "receiving their Charters from the Highland Society of London, which had been founded in 1778." These societies were not Gaelic in spirit. Like Halifax's North British Society (founded 1768), they were the product of British-influenced elites, promoting a "new" Scotsman, loyal to the British Crown and government and articulating a newly-constructed social identity based on "improvement" and "commercial values."

Rusty Bitterman notes that there was a web of connections between notable family elites of the Old World and the colonial owner class; in both instances, the new Scottish construction was shared. This was strongly evident in linkages between the old and New World, Glengarry and the Maritimes, as Bitterman adds:

> Many Highland immigrants to the Maritimes, like their counterparts who moved to Eastern Ontario, would find property and power concentrated in the hands of the descendants of the upper ranks of the Highland society they had recently left. Did those at the bottom accede to the construction of Highland identity that was being crafted by these elites? Did they readily adopt a version of Highland identity that embraced commercial values and improvement?[43]

There seems little doubt that the strong influence of the Highland societies had an effect on many aspects of Gaelic culture in Glengarry and Ontario and even on that of the Maritimes and Nova Scotia. Examples of change included the move to newer competitive piping and the newer, soft-shoed Highland dancing that is wrongly considered by some to be the traditional dance of Scotland (step-dancing predated the "slippered" genteel modern Highland dance in Gaelic Scotland and Nova Scotia). The added fact that Maxville, in Glengarry County, is home to the largest Highland Games of its kind in North America also points to its adherence to more newly-formed Scottish (non-Gaelic) traditions that were constructed by Scottish lowland elites. Conclusively, while speeches at St. Andrew's dinners often sang the praises of Gaelic bards, there was never any commitment expressed that included the preservation of the Gaelic fiddle style, perhaps even the Gaelic language.

But we need to be cautious on this point as well. While these societies certainly had influence, we ought not to blame them for everything in the decay of tradition. When the details of how Gaelic fiddling in Eastern Ontario developed are in the future researched and published, we shall probably see a fairly complex picture which we now can only guess at. All we can now say with confidence is that under the cultural system that came to prevail in greater Glengarry and in most Scottish-Canadian districts during the great age of British Imperialism, it is not surprising that Gaelic tradition declined when the conditions that supported it disappeared.

CREE, METIS AND NON-CAPE BRETON NATIVE FIDDLING

As shown earlier, Scottish fur traders brought violins with them to Canada, often introducing their music and violins to various Native peoples. This occurred, for instance, in the late 17th century when some Scottish traders from the Orkney Islands brought their music to the Cree of James Bay. A 1980 National Film Board of Canada documentary, *The Fiddlers of James Bay*, discusses this by focusing on Cree fiddlers Bob McLeod and Ray Spencers, who travel back to the Orkneys to share the fiddle music that was passed down by their fathers and grandfathers, long after the fur traders had left James Bay. In the film the men perform and display the tunes and style that had been passed down to them in a localized, aural fashion by their forbears. Watching the film, even though there was a clear similarity of tunes between Cree and Cape Breton fiddling, I noted a definite difference in style. One noticeable difference was that the Cape Breton style exhibited more left-hand ornamentation. How can this be explained? While I cannot provide the necessary detailed historical facts here, I can make suggestions. First of all, the Scottish Gaelic presence wouldn't have been as strong in that community in terms of ethnic dominance over a long period of time, as it would have been in Cape Breton. That could have left more room for a Native tradition, whether through interpretation of melody or tune structure, to cause a deviation in style.

Perhaps there was less bagpipe music played there, the lesser ornamentational influence of the pipes contributing to the stylistic difference. Also easy to miss here is that much of the music that influenced the Cree was from the Orkneys, a group of islands that are, along with the Shetlands, in relatively close proximity to Scandinavia. It is widely known that Scandinavian culture (more specifically that of Norway), including its fiddling, has had a great influence on that of the Orkneys and Shetlands. Jim Scarff notes that, "The music from Shetland and Orkney contains more Norwegian influence and less Gaelic influence than that found elsewhere in Scotland; the difference is particularly noticeable comparing the music of the Western Highlands and Outer Hebrides."[44] The style that came over to the James Bay area then, was most likely affected by a Scandinavian influence as much or more than that of Highland Scots and would help to explain why Cree "Scottish" fiddling sounds different from that found in Cape Breton.

Lederman notes that other styles and ethnic backgrounds blended in the fiddle traditions of Canada:

> Apart from Native society, these two inter-related cultures—Métis (the mixture of Native, French and Scottish traditions) and French-Canadian—were predominant until the early 1800s. Beginning in the late 1700s, however, immigrants of Scottish, Irish, British and German background began to arrive in number. Scottish music and dance traditions were reinforced by an influx of Gaelic speaking Highlanders to Cape Breton, Prince Edward Island, and Glengarry County and other parts of Ontario. Irish traditions took hold particularly in Newfoundland, in the Mirimachi area of New Brunswick, in the Ottawa Valley, and in parts of Quebec, but Irish fiddle tunes were assimilated into the repertoire of both francophone and Anglophone communities throughout Canada.

THE DOWN-EAST STYLE

Another supposedly Scottish-influenced style to be discussed is the "Down-East" style. As mentioned, fiddle styles have been affected and formed in Canada by a blending of many tunes coming from Scottish, Irish, German and U.S. traditions popular in predominantly English-speaking areas of Canada. It seems that purveyors of this Anglo-Canadian style were generally most open to the influence of Messer, whose CBC radio show (and fiddle style) would be heard across the country beginning in 1944:

> Messer's influence on Canadian fiddling has been profound, particularly in areas where the Anglo-Canadian tradition prevailed. As a result of its wide exposure on radio, records, and later, TV, Messer's style—smoother and less ornamented than the older French, Scots-Irish, and indeed Anglo-Canadian traditions—gradually became synonymous in much of English Canada with the idea of Canadian "old time fiddling."
>
> ... The down-east style has been popularized further by the many contests which have adopted it as their standard.... Contests in old-time style have come to be held in every province.... [45]

We have already noted that while conducting a study of Prince Edward Island fiddlers in the 1990s, Perlman learned that Messer's "fiddling style was never very highly-regarded" by Island fiddlers. This despite the fact that for two decades Messer's orchestra was PEI based. The fiddlers' views were not dismissive; they just considered the difference between his style and theirs and they preferred their own. It is not hard to see in their critique of Messer that his smooth stylings could appeal to a listening audience, but in the dance tradition still alive on PEI there remains a strong taste for or bias toward the Scottish style.

GAELIC TRADITION AND MUSIC
IN THE CONTEXT OF ISOLATION

An inland place that is considered remote today would have been extremely remote two hundred years ago. In earlier times, if a community or region was geographically isolated, or isolated from major changes occurring in the larger society, its culture changed very slowly. It took the Reformation nearly three centuries to change the culture of the Scottish Highlands; we can imagine how remote such a bastion of Gaelic culture once was from the dominant culture in Scotland. In fact, it took radical economic and political change to undermine Gaelic society enough that the stern messages of 16th-century Calvinism could have influence. By the time that happened, much of the population, including a proportionate share of tradition bearers, had emigrated in response to the aforementioned disruptive changes in economic and social relationships.

When one group of émigrés from any particular old-country locality communicated the viability of a new colonial settlement to those left behind, there was a tendency for friends and relations to follow. The more immigrants who went to the new destination the more viable it became as place to settle. This pattern of chain migration became almost the rule in the Highlands and Islands. Where immigrants were able to continue to be neighbours, not just with fellow Gaels but with their own kith and kin, the old-world culture could take root and re-grow. In some areas like Glengarry and Pictou counties and much of Prince Edward Island, the culture was successfully transplanted, but it had a hard time flourishing in the post-Confederation years. In places like Antigonish County and rural Cape Breton where the culture was both isolated and locally dominant, Gaeldom continued to thrive into the 20th century. In his 1953 classic study *Highland Settler: A Portrait of the Scottish Gael in Nova Scotia*, which focuses on Cape Breton's maintenance of Gaelic, Charles Dunn celebrates this resilience when he names his central chapters "The Folk-Culture Transplanted" and "The Old Tradition Flourishes."[46]

The remoteness of colonial-era Cape Breton is always assumed, but we might learn something about the evolution of the island's fiddling by elaborating on the cultural context of isolation which then existed. Not only was Cape Breton located adjacent to the eastern tip of a peninsula that extended from the continental mainland, and therefore quite remote by overland travel, it was also to the east of many major transatlantic immigration landfalls. After landfall, immigrants not settling locally usually kept heading west. If colonists did not first arrive in Cape Breton, they went there only if they were from Newfoundland or if they felt unwelcome in Pictou or Prince Edward Island. Catholic immigrants who arrived at Pictou invariably went or were sent east to Antigonish or Cape Breton. PEI tenant farmers who resented landlords could shed the misery of distraint by land agents and escape forever from rent by removing their families to Cape Breton's hills and rocky soils, a rather different but probably a preferred challenge.

If geography helped make and keep Cape Breton Scottish, travel difficulty over non-existent roads between the early settlements encouraged the immigrants to retain their habits of self-sufficient living under primitive conditions, a legacy from centuries of marginal survival in Scotland. Appalled by the settlers' lack of creature comforts, travellers from outside the culture often assumed or concluded that such people were simple, unsophisticated and unworldly. Their rich and ancient oral culture usually went unnoticed by observers not only hostile to their language, but quite unaware of the viability of the Gael's traditional orientation. Focused on themselves and the intricacies of their extended families, therefore the settlers both entertained themselves and enriched each other's appreciation of all the facets of the culture that were shared communally. Alistair MacLeod sees in the Cape Breton Island experience a repetition of an earlier Celtic pattern of cultural evolution through isolation:

> For centuries [Celts] ... inhabited regions which geographically cut them off from people unlike themselves.... Isolation causes an intensification and a refinement of that which already exists and is familiar....
>
> Cape Breton Highlanders ... came to land that was hauntingly familiar [in environment]....
>
> Living and developing, again in isolation, the people of Inverness County were able to continue the intensification and refinement of what they had brought with them and considered so important.

Noting that the Gaels "settled largely in family groups," MacLeod sees kinship working to make separate aspects of the culture shared and interdependent. In regard to violin music, the result of this intensification of island life was becoming "part and parcel of almost every household and those who are not musicians and dancers were highly appreciative listeners."[47]

While music was originally diffused everywhere through the island's Scottish settlements, over time certain districts became more associated than others with fiddling. In his 1981 book, MacGillivray noted some of the more well-known of these:

> There existed isolated pockets of music—such as Mabou, Iona, Queensville and Margaree—and the poor conditions of early roads prevented much communication between these villages. Thus, until the early part of this century, each region preserved a pure strain of ancient Highland Gaelic, piping and fiddling.[48]

This purity of style could be maintained because the close-knit family groups that made up each village or district were the descendants of the original settlers. Furthermore, the modes of fiddle playing and dancing went back to the period when much of the immigration to the island was community-based.[49] The near wholesale transfer of communities overseas would ensure the literal transfer of a local kinship-based Gaelic culture, including fiddling styles. Mac-Gillivray's fine brief historical essay "The Cape Breton Scot and His Music," which opens *The Cape Breton Fiddler*, elaborates interesting detail about the performance contexts, the dependence of the music idiom on Gaelic, and the varieties of accompaniment available in the early years of settlement. While his essay takes us chronologically from the earliest times to the 1980s, it is clear that it would be worthwhile to try and clarify how shifting circumstances can mark definite periods in the evolution of the Cape Breton fiddle. By defining periods we may get a better feel for the way that the music has always been able to respond creatively to social change, change that after Confederation often came on fast despite the island's much remarked-upon isolation.

THE COLONIAL PERIOD
SCOTTISH FIDDLING BEFORE CONFEDERATION

From 1800 to 1867, when most immigration from the Old World occurred and Confederation was established, there is little or no written material about the music tradition. However, reasonable postulations can be assumed. Mac-Gillivray sticks closely to Cape Breton sources, and they are mostly 20th-century views and traditions regarding the conditions of music in the first decades of settlement. While these accounts seem credible enough, we are without much direct documentation. This is to be expected: few accounts exist in English and aside from verse, little was written in Gaelic, which at the time was still primarily an oral language. But accounts do exist in English from other parts of the Maritime Gàidhealtachd, and since the Cape Breton

Gaelic culture today is the greatly contracted remnant of that larger cultural region, these sources do illuminate the place of the fiddle in the pioneering phase of east coast Scottish and Irish settlements.

It seems that Gaelic song and the music of the fiddle and pipes have always been means of entertainment, even facilitating forms of work for certain of the Highland descendants. The Gaels did not neglect the artistic merit of their folk-art forms and accepted them as normal and vital parts of their everyday lives. This, of course, would be especially true before 1900 when there weren't other distracting forms of entertainment with which to compete. Thus, family gatherings, kitchen parties, housewarmings and house dances would have been normal entertainment settings after the day's work was done. Compared to the next centuries, when the fiddling gradually came to the fore, the 1800s would have seen a more prominent presence of the bagpipe at gatherings. In his *Highland Settler* study, Charles Dunn suggests a division of labour between the two instruments:

> The pipes were considered suitable, and indeed almost indispensable, at any occasion, trivial or serious, solemn or hilarious; the everyday visit, the baptism, the engagement party, the wedding, the funeral were all graced by the piper's skill.

> The fiddle was also produced at any gathering, large or small. It was especially favoured at moments of quiet relaxation.... Thus the diverse folk-culture of the Highlander served in many ways to cheer the heart of the settler.... Their long hours of toil and their few well-deserved moments of leisure were always the occasion for laughter and story and song and music.[50]

Proctor and Miller quote an eyewitness in support of their claim that as early as 1833 the violin was in demand as the instrument of choice for the Canadian Scottish settler, as was the trend in the old country:

> Scottish settlements invariably had a bagpiper but at their dances within doors they ... generally prefer the old Highland fiddler, or the young one who has learnt the same music, which is at all times played with the spirit and rapidity of which the Scotch reels and strathspeys are so eminently susceptible.[51]

The 1830s observer, in mentioning the young person who has learned the music from the Highlander before him, provides early documentary evidence of the tradition not just continuing, but thriving in the period after the settlers' arrival. The learning referred to here was, of course, aural (not focused on tune books and note reading), for most musicians weren't musically literate or formally educated.

It is because of aural learning that the older style has been retained. In a 1981 interview in Cape Breton's Magazine, Allister MacGillivray singles out how Mary MacDonald—a revered Gaelic fiddler born in 1897 at MacKinnon's Brook in Mabou Coal Mines—learned her playing style aurally from Alexander Beaton, a pioneer settler:

> Mary MacDonald—a great violin player—she was originally from Mabou ... she was explaining ... the method she was using to learn tunes [listening and learning by ear] from an old man called Alexander J. Beaton, who was born in the 1830s. His father was born in the 1700s. And Mary had it in two hops from the 1700s.... That to me typifies the type of approach that the players had in those days. So much reliance on the ear—it came through the 1800s. There was very little book reading among the Cape Breton populace because often they weren't even literate in their language, let alone in their music.... So, although we didn't have a high degree of education, we did have this great fidelity to aural transmission. And the music that we were playing in Cape Breton, especially in the early 1900s, it probably sounded very much what you would have heard in the early 1800s. Because of the isolation in Cape Breton and the reliance on the correctness and flavour that was passed on, that couldn't have been passed on by book.[52]

Returning to the comments of the 1833 observer, it is remarkable that he describes the fiddling of the young players of colonial birth as "the same music" which the older fiddler learned in Scotland. We may note too that what he describes is spirited Gaelic music for dancing, which does not reflect the slower strathspey playing being introduced during this period in Lowland Scotland. The observer is John MacGregor (1797-1857), who had emigrated with his parents from Lewis at the age of six, grew up in a Gaelic community in Prince Edward Island and who, after a brief career at home, travelled widely to become a political economy writer on colonial and imperial affairs.[53] In an 1828 sketch of his home province, MacGregor's remarks on the conservative character of the Gaelic settlers parallel those in Dunn's 1953 account of colonial-era Cape Breton in his Highland Settler chapter "The Folk-Culture Transplanted":

> I have observed, that wherever the Highlanders form distinct settlements, their habits, their system of husbandry, disregard for comfort in their houses, their ancient hospitable customs and their language, undergo no sensible change. They frequently pass their winter evenings reciting traditionary poems, in Gaelic, which have been transmitted to them by their forefathers....

In addition, dancing and festive customs were carried on as in the Scotland the settlers left behind: "Dances on many occasions are common, families visit each other at Christmas and New Year's Day, and almost all that is peculiar to Scotland at the season of 'Halloween' is repeated here."[54] Although MacGregor does not use the Gaelic term for the traditional house visit,

Fig. 3. A spinning frolic at Englishtown. Photo by: Unknown, n.d. Beaton Institute, Cape Breton University. 86-148-16245.

the ceilidh, it is clearly being referred to here. But the ceilidh was not the only occasion for dance: wives with an abundance of wool or flax to spin invited other women to a spinning frolic where they would "remain all day at work" and then "remain to dance for some part of the night." In the evening, men turned up—likewise the women would join the men for dancing after "chopping frolics." Macqueen reports how at a PEI milling frolic the dance tradition could thrive just with puirt-a-beul: "Following the thickening [of the cloth], the evening was spent in step dancing and reels. When instrumental music was lacking a jigger chanted his wavering melody to the amusement and great delight of the whole party."[55]

In his comments on rural travel in winter, MacGregor makes a useful point that running cabrioles and sleighs on river ice made districts more accessible to each other than in summer. "Picnic parties," and picnic excursions

Fig. 4. An eight-hand reel in Englishtown. Photo by: Unknown, 1922. Beaton Institute, Cape Breton University. 86-123-16221.

which were then "much in vogue all over America," were enjoyed even more in winter because of the fun of being driven. His brief account of Cape Breton (also in 1828) seems based on his experience in warm weather: "From want of roads, and the consequent difficulty of travelling, that intercourse which is so common in Canada, Nova Scotia and Prince Edward Island, between the inhabitants of one settlement and another, does not exist in Cape Breton...." But, since we can safely assume what he says about the winter picnic elsewhere probably applied to Cape Breton as well: "Soon after [the meal], a country dance is announced; the music strikes up, and the party 'tripping it off' on the light fantastic toe, seldom break up before day-light the following morning."[56]

As in the old country, weddings continued to be an obvious time for dance music, whether of the pipes or of the fiddle. At such times, the celebratory mood often gave the bagpiper the advantage, especially when the music had to be heard outdoors. But there was room for the fiddler too. MacGillivray notes the lack of accompaniment other than the use of a second fiddler:

> Players would often team up, and, to gain more volume, would occasionally use (1) special tunings, such as "high counter and bass" and "low bass", and (2) a technique called "first and second violin" in which one fiddler utilized the back strings while another concentrated on the front to create octave harmonies around the melody line. Sometimes a woman would tap her knitting needles on the neck or body of the violin to provide a rhythm, and some men played along with the spoons, Jew's harps, or merely "kept bass" with their voices by humming through cupped hands, thus creating a novel form of chording.[57]

The circumstances of the colonial-era music context were indeed modest, but that hardly prevented people from having a good time. Proctor and Miller tell us that music for dancing was "the most popular form of entertainment. Many of the instruments were home made."[58] Charles Dunn reports: "Since they could only get a set of pipes from Scotland at great expense, some settlers made their own."[59] The venues of entertainment, like those of religion, were modest. Both Catholic and Protestant religious services were held in the people's homes until settlement was well progressed. The settlers' houses and barns, however humble, were the only indoor music and dance venues. While to this day, people's kitchens and homes remain as lively gathering places for stories, music and dancing, it is only in recent years that the céilidh—Gaelic for visit—has had much attention from the wider world. While it still applies to a house party, the term ceilidh has now been appropriated by tourism and events promoters to advertise Celtic-oriented music performances in public spaces.

The high value of the traditional Gaelic-language ceilidh in the lives and culture of the settlers can be glimpsed in this 1928 recollection from Margaret MacLeod (born about 1840), the daughter of a PEI pioneer from Skye:

Although times were hard our wants were few and simple, and I do not recall that we had to deny ourselves more than we do today. It may be that not knowing luxuries we never craved them. The only pleasure women engaged in were the "ceilidhs," which I suppose correspond to the modern "teas." The neighbouring men and women gathered at each other's homes. The Highlanders were all fond of singing and music. The flute, the fiddle and mouth organ were the usual musical instruments. There was always someone with an ear for music.[60]

Writing about Gaelic culture in Cape Breton, Hector MacNeil cites the older form of house ceilidh as "the main social institution that provided a venue for the transmission of tradition":

A Ceilidh-house was a favoured gathering place in a community and each ceilidh-house would be known locally for its particular form of entertainment. This would most often be determined by the talents of the occupants of the house. A man or woman known for their singing abilities would attract other singers and those who enjoyed songs to that particular house. Hence, singing would be the main entertainment with story-telling, music and dance mixed in. Another house might be known primarily for story-telling, and yet another for music and dance....

Often performance was followed by discussion. The history behind a story or a song, the meaning and nuances of a particular word or line, bowing styles, fingering techniques—these and other topics might be discussed and even debated. In this way, people shared their collective knowledge, for a Gaelic audience at its best is an informed audience capable of truly appreciating the individual style and talents of the performer within the parameters of the wider tradition. Even the person who might never "perform" participates in a valuable and valued way through his or her knowledge of the tradition.

In this way, localized styles and repertoires of music, song, and story along with knowledge of tradition ... were—and still are—maintained and developed....[61]

Peter MacKenzie Campbell adds that not only knowledge and performance were shared, so too was the burden of hosting them: "The homes in the neighbourhood took turns in catering such ceilidhs."[62] Thus, in the case of fiddling, we can see how a particular blas—what we might in English call the "flavour" of the Gaelic sound—came to be preserved and developed. The music was passed on by ear through family-encouraged transmission which thrived in an informal network of interconnected families and ceilidh houses within particular districts, and it was always oriented toward the dance. These elements of positive energy, more than the merely protective circumstances of isolation, gave drive to the music and kept the late 18th-century Scottish fiddle tradition intact as it evolved into the present Cape Breton tradition.

Fig. 5. *Milling Frolic North Shore. Photo by: Owen Fitzgerald, 1984. Beaton Institute, Cape Breton University. 84-426-14526.*

Because of its mostly family-intensive venues, fiddle music coexisted with the sounds and syntax of Gaelic, with puirt-a-beul, with the drones of the pipes, with step-dance treepling and other traditional dance patterns, with the responsiveness of a knowledgeable audience, and with the Gaelic spirit of a multitude of forms of cultural expression. The rural community was materially poor in the colonial era but the ingredients of long-term integrity in cultural expression were securely planted. As Cape Breton moved into the post-confederation era there were more outward signs of advances in material culture, but new conditions also were rising up to challenge the intense support which the culture was offering its fiddle music.

FIDDLING BETWEEN CONFEDERATION AND THE FIRST WORLD WAR

As with the earlier state of the tradition, that of the 1867-1914 time-period is difficult to trace in historical detail. The music of the period wasn't recorded, so there is no concrete evidence as to how it sounded, except for the rationalizing earlier with regard to Mary MacDonald. This is not to say that all was well in the island communities. The late 1800s and early 1900s witnessed a massive exodus of people from rural areas for city life, whether it be Sydney, Halifax, the Boston area, or even places like British Columbia and California. While this mass emigration affected the Gaelic culture, there are no indicators that the fiddle music suffered to any large extent. Still, the Gaelic language and the old dance style highland piping were disappearing:

> The story that Cape Bretoners tell about their fiddle music is that the settlers brought their music to the new world, where they continued to find it beautiful and useful, while Scotland then underwent significant enough socioeconomic changes that the old music either fell into disuse or was modified. Some aspects of culture that those early settlers brought with them became increasingly marginal, barely enduring into the 21st century. For instance, the Gaelic

language, which in 1900 was the first language of about 85,000 people in Cape Breton, is now the first language of perhaps five hundred people on the island, if that. In the realm of music, the piping tradition, which once represented a freer, more dance-oriented style than modern Scottish highland piping, is nearly gone as well. But for whatever reasons, the fiddle music is thriving....[63]

While families—both nuclear and extended—were large at this time, out-migration was beginning to affect the Gaelic solidarity of family life, even of the part of the family that remained at home. With so many young people leaving home and the region, and some of them returning, at least for visits, even the most localized of families could no longer go uninfluenced by the larger world, its dominant-culture attitudes and its living standards. At the same time, despite the views of some clergy, worldliness was hardly an overt threat yet to the rural way of life.

While at this time in Scotland the work of Alexander Carmichael in his *Carmina Gadelica* (1899) was recording the ancient linkages between individual Christian practice and Gaelic tradition, among the Confederation-era rural Scots of Canada the newly-emergent cultural dominance of the churches was rapidly supplanting traditional reliance on private piety. By this period, the churches were far more strongly organized and influential than they were before. For a time, they threatened to wage a war on the fiddle: it was associated with dancing and—in an era of temperance movements—dancing was associated with excessive drinking.

At the same time, the church and community began to collaborate on the parish picnic, as MacGillivray explains:

> Sanctioned by the Church, this fund-raising event was usually held over a two-day period. It consisted of suppers, sporting events, fiddling and dancing. Bough-covered platforms were erected to accommodate the solo dancing ... with the musicians often playing on into the morning.

With improved educational infrastructure emerging, another new venue appeared at this period: "When no particular social occasion presented itself, the spontaneous joy the music created in the people soon led to the establishment of school-house dances and eventually to the construction of dance halls." The word "eventually" is appropriate: Rhodes points out that for a generation after Confederation, houses remained by far the dominant venue:

> The only alternative places for indoor dancing ... were barns and schoolrooms, for public halls were not built until the early years of this century—the first in Inverness County was built about 1900.

Among the younger people outdoor dancing was also common, the wooden bridges being particularly popular as dancing-places....

Rhodes also notes that for the two days of a community picnic "large open-air dance floors would be built."

Because the picnic presented local culture in a public space, outsiders could finally partake in, or at least observe, a dance culture that was seldom experienced or else was previously hidden from them. By the last decades of the 19th century, the Gaelic culture of Cape Breton was drawing its first attention from visiting journalists and travel writers. As the road system began to develop, Scottish fiddle music was also attracting the interest of the French and Mi'kmaq communities, possibly because by the 1890s some parish picnics had become regarded as rather grand affairs that drew people from a considerable distance.

MacGillivray notes the major changes in accompaniment that occurred in this period:

> As the pump organ became more common, it was used to provide a bagpipe-like drone behind the fiddling, and it was not unusual to see a wagon or sleigh transporting these heavy instruments to a dance. In time, the piano replaced the organ and the accompaniment became more elaborate. The piano stylings became as distinctive as the violin playing, with special bass runs and doubling of the melody being characteristic.[64]

While there was an increasing sophistication of accompaniment, more public venues and the beginnings of exposure of their culture to a wider world, the local people in each district continued their ceilidhs and maintained a year-round array of music and dance activities. This combination of change and cultural tenacity must have helped to make the children and grandchildren of the original settlers aware that their fiddle music was now evolving without sacrificing the basic character of Gaelic dance music.

If rural Cape Bretoners had much music in their daily lives, particularly during the long winter evenings, the scene in summer was changing rapidly, particularly as the local families began to host summer visitors who came either as tourists or as family members returning from away. With the coal mining industry and a railway opening up Inverness County in the 1870s, linkages to the outside world were developing.[65] While playing by ear continued to be the rule, fiddlers were now beginning to learn to read music, to collect tunes, to collect books of traditional tunes and to compose.

MacGillivray's biographical sketches in *The Cape Breton Fiddler* remind us that accounts of fine well-remembered players from this period could still be collected in 1981: "The Cape Breton fiddling community now had heroes of its own. There were prominent musical families who not only composed and played well, but also, through additions and improvisations, changed and improved the old tunes."[66]

While the names of many pre-Confederation-era Cape Breton fiddlers are known, they are not well known and not yet well-researched, even though more detail about the earliest accomplished dancers is available. The dancers are known today not only because people's memory of them was kept fresh into the post-Confederation period but also because their children were still instructing dance at that time. Frank Rhodes mentions Allan MacMillan as a celebrated dancer who kept a dancing class in Judique and Creignish, the Beatons who held classes in Inverness and South West Margaree, and John MacDougall and John Kennedy and his son, all of Broad Cove. These dancers were well remembered because they instructed both their families and their students, who also passed the tradition on. When Rhodes did his fieldwork in 1957, he was still able to interview the grandchildren of the original dancers and dance instructors.[67] Dance performance, being a popular and abiding art form, and more diffused among the population than competence at the fiddle, inspired a strong memory of its earliest exponents.

After 1870, formal education was beginning to make competence in English necessary for all commerce; monoglot Gaels were becoming rare. Formal schooling in Gaelic was never considered seriously by the provincial educational authorities. Cultural policy for Gaelic, if it could be said to exist at all, was left in the hands of a tiny literate scholarly minority who were educated in the language. Despite some conscious efforts to put the language in print, Gaelic was beginning to wane as the new century dawned. Possibly on account of the multitude of out-migrants, census figures on the numbers of speakers were dropping. Locally, however, in the rural areas, if not in the new towns emerging in the industrial region of the island, the language and its traditions seemed as strong as ever to those who spoke it.[68] Nonetheless, within a growing Anglophone constituency the superiority—or at least the dominance—of Anglo-American civilization had become unquestioned. Attitudes were hardening against Gaelic: a movement of prejudice began to stigmatize the language by associating it with a culture of poverty, laziness and a lack of ambition.

It is possible the rapid diminution by the 1890s of a milieu for Gaelic in Pictou county and much of Prince Edward Island helped some patriotic observers wake up to the threat posed by the failure of Gaelic leadership to have a plan to cope with social change. A few in the educated elite began to worry about the disappearance of Gaelic from Nova Scotia and wrote passionately against the trend to despise the language that was gaining ground in rural areas. Perhaps influenced by the Irish Gaelic Revival they began early in the 20th century to talk about how to reconnect with Gaelic Scotland and to think about how to organize a revival movement.

It may be conjectured that fiddle music was so strong, so familiar and so well-established, it tended to be taken for granted when a few Cape Breton fiddlers serving overseas in 1914-18 began to visit Scotland and to learn about how modern Scottish music differed from their own. In the years immediately following confederation, life in many rural Cape Breton areas was a bit more comfortable, but culturally hardly changed from pioneer times. By the time of the war a great multicultural industrial region had emerged in Cape Breton County, and the fiddle culture became established there. At this stage it is also likely that the prosperity of the urbanized areas was actually helping to sustain the rural areas, some of which (e.g., Port Hood and Inverness) had a small share of the industrial economy. While out-migration continued apace, it should not be seen yet as bleeding the rural districts too severely. Although these regions could hardly be considered affluent, life was probably reasonably satisfying for those who lived there. The boom years of the industrial region were still able to help many rural Cape Breton areas sustain themselves generally as viable cultural communities and specifically as the heartland of Gaelic fiddling.

It must also be noted that the Catholic clergy were recruited heavily from Gaelic-speaking families. The Church took a less than sanguine view of the loss of population from rural Cape Breton; they saw out-migration as a hemorrhaging: some clergy like Gaelic scholar Father Donald MacAdam even led a campaign to support Gaelic as one of the means to stanch the outflow of young people.

The fiddle music of Cape Breton probably evolved faster from 1914 to 1955: while there was some travel by fiddlers overseas during the two wars as well as continued out-migration to more prosperous areas of North America, another form of travel—tourism—also began to influence the music, even if only indirectly at first. More than travel influences, the introduction of radio and recordings was about to transform the awareness of all music forms in the public mind.

FIDDLING FROM THE GREAT WAR TO THE OPENING OF THE CANSO CAUSEWAY

MacGillivray's essay, "Traditional Stepdancing in Cape Breton," part of a study updating the 1957 work of Frank Rhodes, disputes the theory that the island's step-dancing was "somehow borrowed" from local "French or Irish elements":

As to the rumours of a non-Scottish origin of our dancing, Mr. Rhodes traces these to The Gaelic College of St. Ann's ... which in 1939 chose to emphasize the teaching of the more modern Scottish dances rather than the indigenous Highland stepdancing which had existed here for so long.[69]

The Gaelic College was then a new initiative projected and directed by a Scot who was not a Gaelic speaker. The College's misplaced attempt to reinvent Cape Breton dance was but a minor symptom of an inappropriate, but well-documented, cultural colonialism that plagued Nova Scotia in this period. Ian McKay has written a classic account of the inventive lengths to which "tartanism" was taken during the premiership of Angus L. Macdonald.[70]

In this era, when highway tourism began being pushed, with ethnic themes introduced to create local colour for visitors, kilts, bagpipes and tartans were given the highest visibility in marking Scottish Nova Scotia identity. If Gaelic was kept relatively hidden, except as a quaint accent in English, fiddling was given an even lower profile by the Province. Cape Breton fiddling suffered in terms of the way it was being recognized: it was becoming harder for outsiders to recognize it for what it was. First, the focus on a semi-official Scottishness had the effect of confusing everyone about the identity and status of people's actual traditions; second, the spillover of the "old-time" fiddle revival in the U.S.[71] into Canada added confusion about Gaelic music.

With large sectors of the population of Nova Scotia and Canada now moving sharply away from their ethnic origins and from languages like French, German and Gaelic, new anglophone popular culture initiatives began to fill the gap created by traditions being lost. It was during this period that heritage culture began to supplant living culture. The 1923 events at Pictou celebrating the 150th anniversary of the arrival of the emigrant ship Hector at Pictou[72] had far more public endorsement than the survival of Gaelic fiddling, one of the few things left of what the 1773 settlers brought with them. When the Gaelic College published The Canadian-American Gael in 1943, a volume with 60-plus pages of text, only a single page on Scottish fiddlers in Cape Breton was included—and the very last article at that.[73] In the era of Angus L. Macdonald a conditional message was being sent out by officialdom: if Nova Scotia was great, it was great because it was Scottish. Scottish was also British, or at least North British. Since the consensus of the day was that if the standards set for the arts were British or Anglo-American, then overcoming the province's cultural insecurity meant—for a lot of conventionally educated people—that local cultural norms and forms should comply with what was reputed to be the best from the old country. For Scottish fiddling in Canada, the northeast style had to become the norm, the correct style. Even a recent form like Scottish country dancing was seen as more authentic than the old

Gaelic step-dancing which had thrived in Cape Breton long after its Scottish demise.

Although broader cultural change in early 20th-century Canada had an impact on the status and external perception of Gaelic fiddling and culture, we need to examine as well the more immediate and local ways that Cape Breton traditions were being affected. Not only was Canada changing and perhaps getting a more distorted view of Cape Breton, local people in small communities were also now changing their view of the larger world. The Great War had taken many men overseas from rural areas; those who came back were changed. The postwar economy challenged industrial Cape Breton intensely; depressed wages and labour problems in the coalfields and the steel plant made New England, Detroit and places further afield more attractive. While out-migration ceased with the Great Depression, World War II again drew local people away from home. As the decades rolled by, rural minds, captured by the powerful events of the century, became far less isolated in outlook. The larger culture had penetrated deep into the countryside, not only with the message that small places were not exempt from world crisis, but also that their people need not be entirely passive: local talent could now participate in contributing content to the new mass-communications media.

Penetration of local culture could also be seen in the context of fiddle playing and repertoire. As noted earlier, culture and music were changing more quickly in Scotland than in Cape Breton. After the First World War, and into the 1930s, there seems to have been a move toward more note reading in the tradition than in the previous century. This move could possibly have occurred as fiddler/soldiers were exposed to music collections from Scotland during the war and may have sent or brought them back to Cape Breton with them. We know this was true of fiddler/composers Dan R. MacDonald and Gordon MacQuarrie during the Second World War. However, we do see the influence of the written note on Ned MacKinnon, a revered player from Cooper's Pond, near Christmas Island, Cape Breton:

> ...he was a terrific violin player. He'd been note-reading, playing James Scott Skinner way back then.... This Ned MacKinnon was supposedly into the Scott Skinner stuff way back then, in the '20s. And he was an outstanding player. And he just happened to be the hero in that community.[74]

Presumably, family and community guidance in Cape Breton's isolated setting kept Skinner's and others' styles from infiltrating Cape Breton to any significant extent, although musical literacy and newer non-local compositions had become more visible.

Fig. 6. Cotters Saturday Night produced for radio by a group of Sydney performers, 1935-1937. Photo by: Dodge, 1937. Beaton Institute, Cape Breton University. 77-1435-1569.

By the late 1920s, fiddlers like Hugh A. MacDonald and Colin J. Boyd were pioneering the recording of Gaelic fiddle music. Commercialization was becoming evident through radio shows and 78 rpm recordings into the 1930s. I suggest that these occurrences had a more positive effect—promoting the music for both locals and those who migrated to urban areas. In the fifty years before the Causeway opened, the Cape Breton region experienced the first radio performances, the first recordings, the first publication of original fiddle compositions, a renewed and expert contact with Scotland, the triumph of piano accompaniment and a sustained exodus, heralding noticeable decline in both Gaelic and rural communities:

> The harmful effects of this exodus from country to city on the music was [sic] somewhat counterbalanced by metropolitan radio shows such as *The Cape Breton Ceilidh*, *Kismuil Castle* and *Cotter's Saturday Night*. The first "78's" came out in the early thirties and among Cape Breton's premier recording artists were Angus Chisholm (on Decca and Celtic), Dan J. Campbell, Angus Allan Gillis (on Celtic) and "Alick" Gillis and his Inverness Serenaders (on Decca). A lesser-known group called the Columbia Scotch Band (sometimes referred to as the Caledonia Scotch Band), led by Charlie MacKinnon also released a few discs on the Columbia label. . . .

In 1940, Gordon MacQuarrie, with much help from his friend Joe Beaton, published the first collection of Cape Breton compositions. This celebrated work featured not only MacQuarrie's music, but that of Dan R. MacDonald, Dan Hughie MacEachern, "Big" Ronald MacLellan, Sandy MacLean, Alex "The Piper" MacDonald and others.[75]

These musicians, Dan R. MacDonald in particular, had a great influence on local players of that time and the years that followed.

From the early 1930s, radio stations in Sydney (CJCB) and Charlottetown (CFCY), and—from the early 1940s—Antigonish (CJFX), pumped out generous amounts of Scottish reels and strathspeys, both live and recorded, in a way they would not do later on. These new influences were a great stimulus to music and dancing. Dance halls and "rec" centres were built or updated even during depression conditions in order to accommodate the greater amount of activity.

As a result of radio and locally produced recordings—like the Celtic label out of Antigonish—lively players in the Scottish tradition, whether they were themselves of Acadian, Irish, Mi'kmaq, English, or Scottish background, became household names in the eastern Maritimes broadcast region. Don Messer's "Down-east" New Brunswick style, which became famous because of the wartime national radio broadcasts from Charlottetown, influenced fiddling across the country. It did not, however, affect the Gaelic style in Antigonish or Cape Breton even while Messer for a generation or more gave fiddling a far higher place than it ever had previously in Canadian popular culture. While the larger Canadian public may well have lumped together in a vague way all the fiddle and popular violin traditions they heard over the airways, the Cape Breton Gaelic fiddle environment had no self-identification problem whatsoever.

CJFX was also identified with the Antigonish Movement. Cape Breton is the largest part of the Roman Catholic diocese of Antigonish and the clergy, predominantly of Scottish descent, met in 1917 to discuss rural decline. One response to this call to action was the initiative of Father Donald MacAdam, a Gaelic scholar, who founded the Scottish Catholic Society at Iona in 1919. The Society started a Gaelic quarterly called *Mosgladh* (meaning "the awakening") which supported the Gaelic language and strongly supported rural renewal as a counter to out-migration.[76] The work of the Society led after 1928 to the Antigonish Movement, a cooperative approach to rural betterment facilitated by the Extension Department at St. Francis Xavier University under the direction of a Margaree-born priest, Dr. Moses Coady.[77] In 1943 CJFX was founded to enhance the work of the Extension Department; from the start it was a faithful ally of Scottish music and remains so now after the turn of the century.[78] The Catholic clergy were early to recognize the important role of music and dancing in maintaining morale in a depressed rural economy:

> The era of the parish picnic by now had begun to wane and Scottish concerts, which required less organization, took their place. Father Mike MacAdam and Father John Hugh MacEachern were among the first Cape Breton clergymen to vigorously promote such gatherings. In time, during the summer months, many parishes such as Broad Cove and Big Pond held these annual events.[79]

If parishes and radio stations could do little for Gaelic, they were helpful to the music. Most times they coexisted with and helped support the picnic, kitchen party, dances and ceilidh house settings into the 1930s and 1940s while another transition was becoming more visible: the fiddle continued to gain favour at the expense of the pipes. Allowance or acceptance of such events seemed to depend on the individual priest, as indicated by Elizabeth Beaton of Mabou Coal Mines:

> I remember dances in the Mabou hall. At that time, the priest wasn't too much in favor of dancing. The priest would be making sermons about the dances. So we missed a lot of good dances because you'd be scared to go, that you were going to get a blast for it. After that, when the different priest came, we went to them all. Picnics too. And the priests started having them themselves ... now the priests are having the dances, and they're playing themselves.... Almost everybody had a kitchen party.... You could get in for maybe twenty-five cents. You'd have to pay something to get in. Maybe sometimes they wouldn't charge anything, but most of them charged twenty-five cents to get in ... there was one room—the dancers sat there. There'd be a fiddler there, no piano player. If there was a fiddle around, Donald Angus [Elizabeth's husband] would have to play. There was one piper around, Angus Johnny Ranald. We'd be out walking, and he'd be in the field, playing the pipes. He was a good piper too. They weren't playing the pipes at the parties at that time, in the 30s.[80]

As for the traditional core of Gaelic culture, the families that kept up the language went on producing tradition bearers, albeit in declining numbers. Local entertainers continued to be in demand at ceilidhs, with fiddlers drawn heavily from musical families and the most musically active communities. Small, otherwise unnoticed places like Mabou Coal Mines continued to be the mainstay of fiddling.

From the 1940s onward, the Cape Breton style was more vulnerable to and underwent more change than in previous years, although elements changing as early as the 1920s should be considered a natural process with oral art forms. Doherty notes:

> Frequently in an oral tradition, style is in a constant state of evolution, with older elements being supplemented with and replaced by newer elements. In Cape Breton this process has been increasingly evident since the late 1920s, mirroring in musical terms the progression of the society at large.

Various individual players contributed, including Dan R. MacDonald (in terms of reinforcing the importance of the written note) and, especially Angus Chisholm and Winston Fitzgerald who exhibited "sleek" playing and high degrees of technical proficiency on the violin.

The 1940s saw a change in focus, from the fiddling being more a complement to the dance, to additionally becoming an art form for listening enjoyment.[81] These changes, especially from the 1930s up to the 1950s and even the 60s, coincided with continued out-migration from Cape Breton largely to the North-Eastern United States. Musicians lived this reality too, of course. Angus Chisholm and Winston Fitzgerald lived in the Boston area and were exposed to the music scene there. The scene, which I'll describe as "The Dudley Street Tradition," had an effect on the musical landscape of Cape Breton with a large interchange of tunes, musicians and ideas indicative of the reality of the island's musical evolution.

In the 1950s and early 1960s, despite the permanent return of Dan R. MacDonald from service in Scotland and the presence of many great older performers and the strong support of CJFX, the Cape Breton fiddle tradition was at a low ebb—not in sharp decline as the Gaelic language clearly was, but perhaps at a point where the tide needed to be turned among young people. In the last two chapters of his classic 1953 study, *Highland Settler*, Charles Dunn has provided us with a memorable portrait of the Gaelic culture of Cape Breton just as the causeway was being built: a picture of sad decline. While the economy picked up with new industries in the Strait area after the opening of the permanent link to the mainland, the Gaelic culture was in trouble. Television had arrived on the scene at the same time, as had rock and roll. In the decade after 1955, no one would have predicted that the musical community would need to come together to re-establish and revitalize the Scottish violin idiom. The modern view of music targeted fiddling as parochial and as an outdated residue of old-world tradition; the island and the world had to wait a few more years before a truly evolved Cape Breton style of fiddle music would re-emerge.

THE CAPE BRETON FIDDLE TRADITION FROM 1955 TO 2004

The Canso Causeway, connecting Cape Breton Island to the mainland of Nova Scotia, was completed in 1955, a transitional point for the culture and economy of Cape Breton. Symbolically, this event represented progress, a new stage of more efficient commerce, an opening of Cape Breton's economy and culture to the mainland of Nova Scotia and, indeed, to the rest of the world. Ironically, the world was already coming to Cape Breton at full steam. The power of technology was having its effect throughout the planet; television was replacing home-based story telling and ceilidhs on the island. The 1950s saw the birth of Cape Breton's first real "pop culture" generation. By the 1960s many young people were no longer seeing their own Gaelic fiddle music and dance as being cool. Mary Graham notes:

> Some of us were very interested but that's because we grew up with it at home. I was always interested because that's all we grew up with. There were a few other families that were still really interested but a lot of people in that age group, they became attracted to rock and roll.... When I was 15, 16, 17, Mabou still had a lot of people who were going to the dances, but then they started having Pig and Whistles; they were bar dances, and the younger ones couldn't get in, if you were under 19. So you either had to go to a square dance where there was no bar if you were lucky enough to find one that night, or now and again they'd have a rock and roll dance for the younger crew. In the early sixties the Beatles were popular with the teenage crowd and a lot of the young people liked that more than the fiddle. You always did have a bunch that were interested in the square dances, but some more wouldn't want to admit that they liked square dancing and fiddle music. With the next generations, the trend continued—into the 70s and 80s, where the interest was in rock and roll—and they [young people] went where the rest of the crowd was going. There were even fewer younger people following the fiddle music at that time than in the time of my youth.[82]

As the late 1960s and 1970s arrived, the trend that Graham mentions was threatening the survival of Cape Breton's traditional music, only a handful of young people were learning the fiddle. In 1971, the documentary *Vanishing Cape Breton Fiddler* warned that the tradition was in trouble and prompted clergy and the cultural community to revitalize the music.

Fig. 7. Massed pipe bands march for the Canso Causeway opening, August 13, 1955. Photo by: Unknown, Beaton Institute, Cape Breton University. 81-703-5783.

The music was rejuvenated and survived relatively consistently through the 1980s. The late eighties and early nineties saw an even larger growth in Cape Breton fiddling interest due to the commercial success of The Rankin Family Band, Natalie MacMaster and Ashley MacIsaac. The Gaelic language has continued to decline, Cape Breton's economy still suffers, and the island's population is declining further, but in the nineties we were in a new period in which fiddles were cool and no longer old-fashioned. From that time into the present decade, new contexts have developed; Cape Breton step-dancing and fiddle styles have gained international exposure and a share of the market for things "Celtic," postmodern tourism and globalization regenerate and simultaneously threaten culture forms, and there is serious academic and Internet discussion of Cape Breton's music and culture. What many people have not yet realized, however, is that industry attention and commercialization seems to have plateaued for the music since the late 1990s. Cape Breton fiddles are no longer as "industry cool" as may be thought. Nevertheless, in a localized context and with increased access to more people and markets with facilitated travel and internet utilization, Cape Breton's fiddle music scene seems to be strong. Feintuch agrees:

> Now of course, it's thriving, and its growth seems unbounded, as local pride, tourism, economic development, the broad interest in Celtic traditions, and the sheer exuberance of the music itself have worked together to make the music irresistible.[83]

THREE

CAPE BRETON FIDDLING
AND RECENT
DECADES OF CHANGE

While in recent decades the mainstream Cape Breton fiddling tradition flows from families descended from Scottish settlers, numerous players from other ethnic origins have come to participate without changing the course of the stream. Accompaniment has also been anything but static. Local players have emigrated, resettled where other traditions have influenced them, and then have returned home with these new influences. The "Scottish" culture of Cape Breton keeps being redefined to suit changing trends in tourism. More women are playing the fiddle now. Influential composers have pushed the boundaries of the music, and periodic resurgences of interest in the music occur, involving the young in fiddling when necessary. This chapter examines how Cape Breton fiddlers have responded to the powerful changes occurring in the musical, cultural and social world around them.

For many, both observers and players, the most profound change has been the decline of the Gaelic language, as the influence of the language on the music has always been regarded as important, or more important, than even the influence of traditional step-dancing. The purpose of this chapter is to show that although the Cape Breton fiddle tradition has in recent decades evolved in response to the above-mentioned changes, it has also remained intact, by and large retaining its distinct Gaelic sound and its vitality. I have noticed that there can sometimes be a strong difference of opinion between observers of the tradition and the players themselves over the threat to fiddling posed by Gaelic decline in the Scottish areas of rural Cape Breton.

A very important part of the research for this book involved the distribution of a survey[84] on Cape Breton fiddling to active participants in the tradition. (The complete original survey—hereafter called the Graham Survey — is included in Appendix 1). The questionnaire solicited opinions on most of the topics covered, including the influences of bagpiping and the Gaelic language on fiddling, acknowledging the importance of the relationships between them. All respondents felt that the Gaelic language

Fig. 8. John Campbell, Joey Beaton and Buddy MacMaster at the Ceilidh Trail School of Celtic Music. Photo by: David Gillis, n.d.

had an influence on Cape Breton fiddling. When asked "How?" Kenneth Joseph MacDonald and Angus Beaton indicated "through mouth music." As we have seen, mouth music, *puirt-a-beul* in Gaelic, involves the singing of Gaelic words, called vocables, to certain melodies, those often being marches, jigs, strathspeys and reels played on the pipes and the fiddle. The Gaelic vocables don't have to make sense, but they must (and always do) convey the lively qualities of Gaelic speech. If a fiddler with a good ear learned some of those melodies, obviously the rhythm of their Gaelic phrasing would affect his or her tune interpretation. Other forms of Gaelic singing were also mentioned by respondents: Elizabeth Beaton, eighty-five years old at the time of writing, felt that "maybe since Gaelic songs were sung a lot in the older days," familiarity with them could still have an impact on how they would be played on the fiddle.

Although many found it difficult to explain the notion, words such as "expression" and "rhythm" came up. For instance, renowned fiddler Buddy MacMaster stated that:

> The Gaelic sound and expression comes out in Cape Breton fiddling . . . very few if any players speak Gaelic today; the Gaelic sound has been handed down through the years. . . .

> Although the Gaelic language is dying out the Gaelic sound is in most of the Cape Breton playing.

My father, Danny Graham, who is fluent in Gaelic and plays the fiddle a bit, has always maintained:

> The rhythm and accent of the language has had an effect on the music. This makes it more easily produced by one who speaks Gaelic or who speaks English with a Gaelic accent which is often the case in Cape Breton. . . . I think this sound comes from the rhythm, ac-

cent and throaty sound of Cape Breton Gaelic and English speakers whose parents and grandparents spoke the language.

Angus Beaton points out that the Gaelic sound "has to do with the cuts/bowing style for fiddlers ... timing and accents.... It's imitating the type of accent you heard—primary influence." Here, musically speaking, we see the crux of the matter: it is *how* the application occurs on the instrument that brings out the older Gaelic sound—not whether or not the player is a Gaelic speaker. In that regard, only one respondent among the eighteen participants in my survey felt that you have to be a Gaelic speaker to have a "Gaelic" sound, and her answer was not categorical. She contended that "to some extent" you have to be a Gaelic speaker to have the sound, "although being around Gaelic speakers is very influential."

Kinnon Beaton, the island's premier dance player, sums up the Gaelic sound question when he says, "I think a combination of the language, piping and dancing all have an effect on the playing." The link between them all cannot be underestimated. As I have already shown, the music in its perfect form is mainly dance music. The pipes, which were present in the culture before fiddles, would obviously affect the way a tune was played on the fiddle. In fact, Beaton points out that "a lot of the old pipers were also fiddlers." Could the link be any closer?

Stylistically, with regard to the piping-fiddling relationship, many respondents agreed that there were noticeable sound similarities. Since in their origins in the Gaelic tradition piping and fiddling were both language-based, their sound similarities are hardly surprising. It is noticeable that the fiddling survey respondents assume the importance of retaining the sounds and identify them as both Gaelic and Gaelic-piping sounds.

Mary Elizabeth MacInnis specified that "the 'cuts' made in strathspeys and reels *sound* like they originated from the pipes." Cuts are three notes applied with bowing to mimic the same sounding digital (finger) ornamentation on the pipes. While cuts were mentioned, some felt that a lot of the same tunes are played both on the pipes and on the fiddle. A younger respondent noted that "a lot of older Cape Breton tunes were either bagpipe tunes or were written to sound like it. You'll hear a lot of tunes now played in the pipe scale." Fiddler Glen MacEachern adds that the "drones have been put into many tunes." This is in reference, for example, to a fiddler mimicking the bagpipe drone by playing an open "e" string while playing melody notes on the "a" string, or hitting an open string note simultaneously with one of equivalent value on the next higher string.

Probably the most noticeable similarities between Gaelic-style piping and fiddling are the ornamentations applied on both instruments and the dance beat applied on both instruments. The ornamentations are basically fingering techniques where one or more fingers decorate a single melody note and they are quite apparent in the old style of playing. They can be broken down into different types of "gracings" surrounding the main note. In short, there are different ways of applying the fingers to the strings on a fiddle surrounding a melody note that basically "mimic" similar approaches to playing Gaelic pipe music. The resulting "dirt" in the music gives it the Gaelic, or older, sound.

Melody Cameron says that "Highland bagpiping has influenced the Cape Breton style; you can mainly hear it when grace notes are played in the tune." Experienced Cape Breton fiddlers recognize, at least on reflection, an obvious imitation of sounds occurring in their music. That is, the way they are playing their tunes produces sounds similar to Gaelic pipe music (I refer specifically to *Gaelic* piping, not today's modern competition Scottish pipe music). Jackie Dunn-MacIsaac aptly sums up the influence of traditional Highland bagpiping on Cape Breton fiddling when she says, "The older bagpiping style (noncompetitive) is believed to be very close to our style of fiddling. The 'feel' of the music, lilt, grace notes, tempo, use of both for dancing are all examples; even shared repertoire." It is ironic that under the influence of the dominant competitive piping, Gaelic piping almost completely died out as long as a century ago in Cape Breton; pipers striving to play in the Gaelic idiom can now turn to the sounds of the Cape Breton fiddler to recapture their sound. As Scottish Gaelic piper Finn Moore told me, if you grew up playing competitive pipe music and want to play it the old Gaelic way, you must submit to relearning the instrument.[85]

Many mistakenly believe that the Gaelic style is virtually extinct among the younger players. Fiddlers under age 35 vary a great deal in their exposure to Gaelic: some never heard it at home, but have become well-acquainted with Gaelic music and song; some have had community experience of the language, while others were exposed to Gaelic speech at a young age. I, for one, claim to have "a little Gaelic," and remember having spoken Gaelic words at the age of four. Additionally, such younger players as Mairi Rankin of Mabou and Kenneth and Callum MacKenzie of Mabou Coal Mines have grown up in Gaelic-speaking households. While it might be desirable to be able to speak Gaelic, it is still possible with something less than fluency to obtain sufficient experience of the language to gain a feeling for its distinctive equivalent violin sounds. For it is the cultivation of an intuitive recognition of the language's rhythms and accents combined with digital ornamentation and bowing applications, that help to create a Gaelic sound in the fiddle, not the ability to speak it. The fiddler has to learn how to apply an interpretation musically—an individualized form of expression. Many choose to play in a certain style although they are capable of other stylistic applications. Non-musicians may find this perspective difficult to understand and I will return to this topic.

The range of attitudes that exist between the older and younger generations of players was covered in the survey. One of the questions asks, "Have you witnessed, or do you feel that, *some* older players and/or listeners have revealed negative attitudes and opinions with regard to the playing of 'younger' fiddlers? If so, is this justified or not justified?" Only one respondent answered "No." The rest answered "Yes," but there was little feedback. Most felt that sometimes negative attitudes and feelings toward younger players are justified, while other times they are not. Mary Elizabeth MacInnis commented on the question, citing concern for the tradition as a factor accounting for negative opinions and downplaying motives of jealousy:

> Yes, I have witnessed this. [...] Sometimes it might be rooted in
> jealousy but sometimes it might be that they are concerned about
> some aspect of our tradition being lost.

It was then asked whether the reverse were true also—whether "younger" players and/or listeners have revealed negative attitudes and opinions with regard to the playing of "older" fiddlers and if the opinions were justified or not. To this question, four respondents answered "yes," that younger players have revealed negative attitudes toward older ones. One answered that *some* have; two answered "not really"; one answered "very little," while the rest of the respondents answered "No." One did not answer. Most did not answer the last part of the question although a couple said that negative opinions toward older players' playing were not justified. Notably, Kinnon Beaton took an open stance, saying that in some cases the views are justified, in others, not justified. Mary Graham suggested that negative attitudes towards older players resulted from the view that young players feel downplayed. She wrote "not really, although they may feel 'slighted' because of the attitude of some that the older fiddlers are more significant." Dunn-MacIsaac, in contrast, felt that younger players must realize the importance of the older ones in keeping the tradition healthy and in check:

> For the most part I think that fiddlers of our generation (25-35
> yrs.) respect those fiddlers who came before us but I think the generation after us have not yet realized the significance and value of
> the older musicians and their place in the whole culture. It is not
> "cool" to listen to these musicians for some young players today.

So it seems that friction can and has occurred in the tradition between younger players/listeners and older ones. According to my survey, however, more felt that older players expressed negative opinions toward younger ones than vice versa. Only one respondent answered that negativity from both the young and the old players toward each other was expressed about equally.

Although not all fiddling now played in Cape Breton is still in the old style, many (if not most) fiddlers old and young, exhibit the Gaelic style. While others play a newer, smoother style, lacking a lot of ornamentations and certain distinctive bow strokes, many display a combination of both or numerous elements of one or the other. The main point is that the Gaelic style remains, while the culture has allowed for internal change or innovation, which has led to some smoother, more streamlined players, and an overall expansion of styles. This is acceptable as long as a balance remains, as Kate Dunlay aptly puts it:

> [T]he tradition was never discontinuous. Now the vitality of the tradition is at a high point and shows no sign of decline, although changes can be observed. One change, a general trend in all fiddle traditions, is the increased importance that is placed on playing smoothly and cleanly. Although this may be due somewhat to outside influences, fiddler Winston Fitzgerald (1914-1988) was a much-copied innovator who led the tradition in that direction. In Cape Breton, the grittiness and complexity of the old style may be lost except by those individuals who purposely preserve it. On the other hand, awareness of this impending loss has been growing, and some of the old tunes with their complex bowings are presently enjoying a resurgence of popularity.[86]

There is also the misconception that only older players can have a Gaelic style. Doherty, who wrote her PhD thesis on Cape Breton fiddling, refers to a common assumption that chronological age in fiddlers coincides with a newer or older sound. For instance, as she notes, Buddy MacMaster is often referred to as an old-style player, but in fact, although he is an older fiddler in age, he "stands at an intermediary point between the old and the new."[87] Kate Dunlay supports this view:

> Buddy's fiddling is the perfect link between the older and newer styles in Cape Breton. His tone is strong and his playing is clean or precise enough to satisfy modern ears, but he also retains many of the interesting characteristics found in old-style Cape Breton fiddling.[88]

Doherty adds that older players don't always exemplify the old sound and the young ones the new. Indeed, I suggest that there are younger players who exhibit an older sound than some of the older players. To expand upon this point further, and to show the ambiguity of the "chronological age" notion, it is also possible for a player to have a different "sound" at different points in his or her musical life. As a person's painting or poetic style may differ at different junctures of their lives, why couldn't a Cape Breton fiddler's musical "sound" or style change as well? I also think that critics of younger players should be open to the idea that, at age twenty, a player will not have the exact same sound, and perhaps a less "mature" sound, as when he or she is forty, fifty, or seventy years of age. I should also caution that it will not always be the case that a fiddler's sound will be "older" at an older age. Factors such as exposure to and absorption of various styles, being in "playing shape" and practice, and residence relocation could all contribute to a change in a player's sound from older to newer.

However, the concern remains among some Cape Breton fiddle enthusiasts that a loss of the old style is occurring as the majority of players in our revived music scene are from a less "Gaelicized" cultural climate:

> More serious than the uneven distribution of the rejuvenated tradition is the concern expressed over the performance itself. Unlike their forbears, the fiddlers who have taken up the bow since the 1970s have not had the same strong Gaelic community culture to draw from. These young fiddlers from the 1970s, for the most part, did not grow up with anything like the exposure to Gaelic—particularly to *puirt-a-beul* and Gaelic song—that was available to the older generation—people like Donald and Theresa MacLellan, Alex Francis MacKay, Dan Hughie MacEachern, Dan R. MacDonald, Donald Angus Beaton, Dan J. Campbell, Angus Allan Gillis, Angus Chisholm, Joe MacLean, Theresa Morrison and a large number of others, many of whom were fluent speakers of the language.[89]

While Kennedy makes a strong case, it must be emphasized that the newer form of Gaelic sound transmission—aural learning from house recordings of older players—has kept and can continue to keep the old sound alive to a certain extent. Indeed, there are younger players today who have as much a Gaelic sound as some of the aforementioned players and older ones not mentioned. However, an overall analysis of styles of various players would be a study in itself. Also, among those mentioned above, there are a couple of players, very Gaelic in fiddle style, who weren't actually fluent Gaelic speakers and who grew up at a time when

Fig. 9. Alex Francis MacKay and Betty Beaton at Glendale. Photo by: David Gillis, n.d.

or in a community where speaking and learning the language was actively discouraged.

In her essay on Cape Breton fiddling as dance music, Kate Dunlay sees today's playing as rooted in the strongly Gaelic Highland style of the eighteenth century:[90]

> It is likely that more pipe reels were played in the Highlands [than in the Lowlands] and that piping had more of an influence on the Highland style. But two other factors must have had an influence on the Highland style. One was the language difference and its effect on rhythm and phrasing on the music. The second was the difference in the styles of dancing current in the Highlands and the Lowlands.
>
> Unfortunately, scholars for the most part have neglected to consider the influence of the Gaelic language on fiddle style.

She acknowledges authorities like Allister MacGillivray who illuminated the link between Gaelic and Cape Breton playing. "In Cape Breton, droning, certain bow strokes, and techniques of ornamentation used especially by the old-style fiddlers are thought to impart a particularly 'Gaelic flavour' to the music." Dunlay makes it clear that the tradition has evolved, especially with its distinctive and innovative piano accompaniment, but also that it has remained intact—thanks in some measure to the persistence of aural transmission. As to the future, she contends that new influences "will serve to extend the bounds of Scottish music rather than dilute it." Thanks to the relatively recent discovery of Cape Breton fiddling by the larger world, Dunlay sees the Gaelic sound as one of these new influences on the international Scottish music milieu.

However, since the "Gaelic remaining in ... Scotland is probably not strong enough" to influence the fiddle revival there, hope for the diffusion and persistence of the Gaelic sound is far more likely to be realized in an indirect way from the influence of Cape Breton playing: "The Gaelic language has little direct influence on Scottish instrumental music today. There is a residual influence in Cape Breton, although the language there is almost completely lost to the present generation." Dunlay's essay notes at least three factors about the Cape Breton playing style that might help revivalists deal with the limits of their expectations, were they to look to that style and its Gaelic sound as a stimulus for Scottish music: the fact that "the tradition was never discontinuous"; the continued prominence of aural learning, which involves modelling of older players who have the sound; and the momentum of the Cape Breton style. Were a Scottish music group outside Cape Breton to adopt Cape Breton playing as an influence or an adopted style, players should first admit

Fig. 10. A Scotch Four on stage at SW Margaree Hall. Photo by: David Gillis, n.d.

frankly that their efforts would be revivalist. By contrast, Kate Dunlay says the renewal efforts in the wake of *The Vanishing Cape Breton Fiddler* telecast "were more of a revitalizing or perpetuative nature than a revivalistic one." The temporary decline in the number of young learners during the 1960s proved to be no threat to the continuity of the music. The dynamism and vigour of the tradition, which has always been fed by local community commitment to Gaelic culture and dance, has its own momentum. Dunlay notices this when she comments that although communication and exchange with a broad global world is now commonplace, the Cape Breton style is not in danger of being overwhelmed by external influences: "Styles are not likely to converge, since they have gained their own life and momentum."

In a 1996 presentation at Mabou, Dunlay mentions other factors that work toward maintaining the momentum of the Gaelic sound despite the diminishing influence of the language in Inverness County: "This is a solo tradition, usually one fiddler plays with one piano player. Listeners are intensely interested in individual styles." In reporting on the presentation, Frances MacEachen cites a corollary of the individual playing style:

> While each fiddler adds his/her flavor to a tune, Dunlay said there are 'mysterious boundaries' for what is accepted in the tradition decided by those who are part of this tradition. Fiddlers know they can go only so far.[91]

If boundaries are barriers to innovation, they also act as a brake, keeping musical taste conservative. While the content of this individual styling involves "lots of ornamentation and individual notes," the practice is counterbalanced by the fact "that there is a lot of emphasis on playing the tune correctly in Cape Breton." Individual innovation is simultaneously enjoyed and moderated by the community's sense of tradition. The Gaelic sound will survive because it is integral to Cape Breton playing, a conservative performing style which continues to evolve slowly with a well-established inner strength.

This balanced assessment by Kate Dunlay contrasts with the pessimistic view put forward by John Gibson, a bagpiping historian resident in Cape Breton: "Traditional Scottish Gaelic piping in Nova Scotia is extinct. Only an analogue remains—Scottish Gaelic fiddling in Nova Scotia—and that too is dying away. However, there are still memories of the older piping to tap."[92] Although this is a brief and unsupported remark, the comment is useful here as typical of what I would call the purist position with respect to the future of the Gaelic sound. Gibson's downbeat attitude does not take into account the several factors described above that help the music retain what Dunlay calls its residual Gaelic character.

Some younger fiddlers are recommending practical action to preserve the traditional style. While at St. Francis Xavier University, Jackie Dunn-MacIsaac devoted her 1991 undergraduate thesis to the debate about the role of Gaelic in fiddle music. Her work shows the strong connection between the language and instrumental applications. Using *puirt-a-beul* examples Dunn-MacIsaac concludes that accentual patterns and rhythmic relations can be applied on the fiddle to complement Gaelic songs and tunes: "This may possibly be what is meant by a fiddler making his fiddle 'speak' Gaelic."[93] Irish musician and scholar Doherty supports this: "The Gaelic language seems to have impressed the fiddle style in matters of rhythmic structure in that the rhythms of the language have dictated the rhythms of the tunes."[94]

Another point that must be emphasized is that musical form in Gaelic doesn't necessarily comply with theoretical musical standards; this can be seen in the tunes played by predominantly older or deceased players in the tradition. While some of their tunes follow the flow of Gaelic song and speech rhythm, Gaelic word combinations in a song do not always follow the measured time of art music. This is true of both Gaelic bagpiping and Gaelic-influenced fiddle tunes. Allan MacDonald, a Gaelic piper from Scotland, summarizes this point when he tells Kennedy about inadequate competition judging:

> The Highland Societies of London and Scotland paid people to notate music "scientifically." This involved notating the music within bar lines in time signature of 3/4, 6/8, etc., which of course implies predictable measured times. The problem is that genuine Gaelic music does not conform to strict measured time....[95]

Notes composed and played in tunes by Gaelic-influenced musicians may follow and have followed an intuitive interpretation of Gaelic vocables, rhythms and word combinations (or sense of them) as opposed to a conscious following of music theory. An example of this in fiddling would be the popular Donald Angus Beaton composition, "Tamarack'er Down" (Appendix 2). An analysis of this Gaelic-structured tune in terms of standardized musical structure would declare it a defective composition, but read in terms of an aural Gaelic rhythmic structure, it is not. Also, in the past half-century, there is a noticeable tendency toward the classical scale instead of the bagpipe scale, owing to the prominence of pianos and musicians' avoidance of "note clashes" and to the increasing number of "musically literate" musicians who are used to hearing classical scales in music every day. The challenge posed by the habits of Western art music means that fiddlers today have to be more self-conscious about the influences on their playing, and certainly more deliberately attentive to the way that matters of technique affect chosen styles.

More than twenty years ago MacGillivray's timely essay, "Cape Breton Fiddling Techniques," helped broaden awareness on the island that more reflection on method "facilitates accurate renditions of traditional-flavoured pieces."[96] Fiddlers today study the applications of style which have been traditionally used to create the distinctive sounds that derive from bagpipe and Gaelic-language influences. Ornaments and bowing techniques can be learned by younger players by listening to and watching the older players who learned to play when Gaelic was still widely spoken. Careful listening to audio tapes of Gaelic-style fiddlers aids in maintaining the Gaelic style of playing—which features ornamentations, drones and bowing that work in unison to mimic Highland pipe sounds and the accents and rhythms of the language. Dunn-MacIsaac recommends the use of this method to arrest the loss of the old style:

> [T]he "Gaelic" sound in the music most probably will die away more slowly than the language. It must also be remembered that many of the fiddlers today learn their tunes off tapes of other fiddlers. Usually, these "model" fiddlers are of older generations. As long as there are such tapes of and young fiddlers who are interested in playing the same style, the Gaelic music will not die away as fast as the language. Some of this Gaelic sound will remain in the music from the simple modeling of older players, if the younger generations remain interested in how the music was once played.

It is crucial that the younger generation of the new century, namely those under age twenty, learn tunes from older-style players and study tapes (preferably non-commercial home recordings) of old-style players, in order to maintain the Gaelic sound in the music. A supply of home recordings that enable younger players to "model" their playing is available. Because this material is so vital in maintaining the Gaelic sound for younger players, it must be made as accessible as possible.[97] To re-emphasize an earlier caution: Gaelic-style fiddlers learning song and melody from non-native Gaelic speakers, whether they have fluency or are classified as learners, is a slippery slope.

Burt Feintuch feels that the tradition has survived because its purveyors have been able to embrace change. He also suggests that an "embrace of change" could occur as a result of a single innovation becoming generally accepted in the tradition. In his view the innovations could involve a number of things: among these are the distinctive and changing piano style, repertoire from local composers, electric instruments and transducers and—something that I've been witnessing since around 1999—new skill in advanced computerized recording software like Pro-Tools, that helps to craft a desired "sound" in recordings.[98] At the same time, while new access to a global market can make it seem as if the younger players are being distracted by the technical and marketing side of enhancing the music, they are by and large well aware that it is the distinctive Gaelic sound which has provided Cape Breton fiddling with its market niche. This is the same Gaelic sound which has been so long at the core of the older playing and remains the most resilient feature among even the most innovative practitioners of the newer playing styles.

ACCOMPANIMENT
IN THE CAPE BRETON FIDDLE TRADITION

As seen above, fears continue to persist among followers of the tradition that undesired changes are occurring. Some are concerned that the old Gaelic sound is being lost while others worry about outside influences such as the Irish style and various innovations creeping into the tradition. Some fear that old tunes are being ignored, new ones lack the older sound, the music is getting faster, drums and innovative accompaniment sound foreign. It is important to note, however, that changes have always been occurring and contributing to the music's survival. Among the most notable changes are major accompaniment styles which contin-

Fig. 11. Elizabeth Beaton accompanies Morgan MacQuarrie and Willie Kennedy at a house session. Photo by: David Gillis, n.d.

ue to evolve when new instruments have been added over time. It must be stressed that this has occurred since the tradition began. One need only refer to changes since cello accompaniment in the 1740s, although I have observed that cellos do accompany some traditional music performances in Scotland.[99] In Cape Breton, before the 1930s, the pump organ was the popular choice for accompaniment among fiddlers. Earlier still, spoons, Jew's harps and knitting needles were common accompaniment methods.[100]

By the 1930s, piano was the prime companion instrument. Margaret Dunn discusses the fiddling tradition in her family noting the reference to women in the tradition:

> At the MacEachern home there was no piano or organ but Dan Hughie's sisters Kaye and Marcella provided accompaniment for the fiddle. Unfortunately, in those days the fiddle was not consid-ered to be a girl's instrument and therefore none of the six sisters play the fiddle. Sisters Kaye and Marcella would often provide this unique rhythmic accompaniment by tapping steel knitting needles on the violin strings while the brothers played.[101]

Even drums have been accompanying fiddles since at least the 1940s, begin-ning with entertainers such as Bill Lamey and Winston Fitzgerald.[102] Howev-er, new sounds *surrounding* the fiddle playing should not be the worry of con-cerned traditionalists. Modes of learning, application of style and adherence to the rhythmic nuances of step dancing are the crucial elements in checking tendencies that might lead to imbalances in the evolution of the Cape Breton fiddle tradition.

The subject of accompaniment was also discussed in the survey. In that section of the survey, the first question asks, "Do you think that accompani-ment for Cape Breton fiddle music has changed since it was first played on the island? If so, how?" The question was intended to focus on forms of accompa-niment, not how piano playing may have changed, but some respondents in-terpreted the question as referring to the latter. In her response, Jackie Dunn-MacIsaac summarizes the overall change in accompaniment:

> From organ to piano, from just piano/guitar and/or drums and/or bass and some other instruments such as flute, banjo, bouzouki, etc. A lot of the time in the past fiddle music was unaccompanied, even at dances.

Another respondent adds that the accompaniment has "probably evolved at a much faster rate than violin—A huge improvement since knitting needles."

One fiddler mentions the move and expansion from "pump organs to pia-nos to guitars, etc.," while another reiterates that now there are "more pianos; years ago it was organs." It was also noted that accompaniment has "probably gone from banging pots/spoons to organ to piano, guitar, etc. to almost any accompanying instrument today." Kinnon Beaton refers to an innovative mode of accompaniment observed in the actions of fiddler Mary MacDonald: "They don't use matches anymore to hold the keys down." Mary MacDonald, apparently, would insert match sticks into a chord formation on the piano (holding the keys down) in order to accompany herself while she played the fiddle!

Fig. 12. Clare MacDonald, Mary (Beaton) Mac-Donald and Duncan MacQuarrie. Photo by: Un-known, 1959. Beaton Institute, Cape Breton University. 78-46-1796.

The second survey question on the subject of accompaniment notes that although there were earlier forms of accompaniment for Cape Breton fiddling than the piano, it can safely be stated that the piano has been the prevailing instrument of accompaniment over time. It then asks: "Generally speaking, and understanding that no two piano players play exactly the same, is there a distinctive Cape Breton piano *sound* or *style?* If possible, provide examples and/or contrasts with other piano styles." Two of the respondents did not answer and all of the rest answered "Yes," there is a distinctive piano style, although some did not provide much feedback as to what distinguished it from other styles. Despite this, some interesting points were made. Buddy MacMaster, who has travelled abroad often, notes how he has observed that the piano styles at home are different from those in Ireland and Scotland. Cape Breton pianist Angus Beaton agrees: "A typical CB piano player sounds much different than one from Scotland for example." Guitarist Patrick Gillis, who plays a bit of piano too, says that, "In Scotland they play a lot of drop chords but they don't put any bass lines in between; they don't follow the tunes with bass lines." One respondent makes a nice contrast between Cape Breton piano style and the "down-east" style found elsewhere in Canada:

> There is an overall distinctive sound/style but as with the fiddling tradition each piano player sounds unique. As compared to "down-east" style chording, C.B. style uses more bass runs, more syncopation and more dynamic changes (accents, soft/loud, etc.)....

The next question in the survey asks if respondents feel that Cape Breton piano playing has changed over time and if so, how. I also tried to find out if respondents saw any changes as being *good*, *bad*, or perhaps a combination of *both* for the Cape Breton fiddle music tradition. Most note that they felt that the piano playing has changed. The few who answered "No" did not elaborate. However, there were some non-technical and some technical observations from the "yes" group. Kinnon Beaton, for example, says that "certainly," it has changed and that "it is not as plain as it used to be." His daughter, multi-instrumentalist Andrea Beaton adds that today's piano players add "more stuff to the tunes and play a lot more 'correctly'" Patrick Gillis describes the change well, dividing piano playing into stylistic eras:

> It has become more notationally correct. There is an old style.... The old style was very basic with not many runs between chords. They stuck to the three main roots of each key. You also have the mixture of the old and the new which is a different era all together.... The "mixture" style involved being innovative on their own, expressing more chords with the tune than was originally done, almost defining the tune with chords, more so.... The newer style—John Morris Rankin and Tracey Dares-MacNeil would be the main people that influenced today's newer style—people who read music a lot. If there were a group of certain notes, they'd break the tune down more. More moving bass lines and a big difference between the middle school and the new school is the bass hand.

Melody Cameron notes that there's "more versatility in the bass lines and chord progressions and more variations in the rhythms." Dunn-MacIsaac concurs: "[there is] a wider range of chords used, more syncopation, bass runs, more aggressive style than in previous generations."

In responding as to whether the change has been good, bad, or both for the tradition, the majority who felt that it was good for the tradition, but did not elaborate. Two did not answer because they believed there was no change, while one simply did not answer. Four respondents held that current changes in Cape Breton piano playing were both good and bad for the tradition. Basically these respondents felt that if accompaniment takes away focus from the fiddler or tunes, or if it becomes too dominant, then it is bad. For instance, Kayla Beaton asserts that it's obviously "both, depending on the listener's preference." Another young respondent remarks that, when hearing the newer style of piano accompaniment, "sometimes it is amazingly good but other times it can take away from the fiddler." Dunn-MacIsaac reports:

> Both, but more good than bad. *Good* for sure when the piano players add more "drive"/ "life" to a performance but *bad* if the piano player is too dominant and takes away from the focus of the fiddler and his/her performance.

Mary Elizabeth MacInnis agrees when she notes that it's good if the pianist can be bold "tastefully," but "bad if the piano player takes over" and becomes distracting.

Gillis brings in the subject of chord choice and suggests that the mixing of too many chords predominantly found in jazz should not seep into the traditional music genre to any large extent:

> Yes, I think it's good. I don't think any of the change has had a dramatic effect on the fiddle style itself. The only thing is that the last few years the addition of too many jazz chords, or jazz chords improperly used, has had a bad effect in terms of leading the listener towards seeing the piano as a lead instrument over the fiddle. There is a fine line between keeping the music lively and overpowering, from the perspective of the accompanist.

There is also the prospect that perhaps piano accompaniment could actually affect the fiddle style. If it does, how? Interestingly, most musicians in my survey don't lean toward how *style* is affected. Instead, many specify how the quality of musicianship of the piano player goes hand in hand with how the fiddle music will sound. Angus Beaton notes that "the better piano players definitely add to the music—often set a real good beat." Buddy MacMaster sums up the relationship:

> I don't think it [the change in piano playing] had much effect on the fiddler in terms of style. However, a good piano accompanist is a great asset to the fiddler and helps the fiddler to get in a good fiddle playing mood.

The relationship between the fiddler and accompanist could be described as symbiotic. One well-known old-style player notes that a "good Cape Breton style piano player will take the best out of a fiddler," while pianist Mary Graham remarks that "better piano playing makes for a better fiddle sound." Someone else bluntly adds, "If you have a good fiddler and a bad piano player, you don't get good music." I absolutely agree: From my experience, I would much rather play unaccompanied than with an incapable piano player.

If a piano player is playing a lot of incorrect chords, is not keeping a good beat with the right hand or is slowing down the music with a poor bass hand, there are too many musical "clashes" going on between the fiddle and the piano. The end result is music that is not aesthetically pleasing to an experienced ear. One musician makes a good point by saying that the "style has been dictated by the fiddlers themselves." Perhaps it is more an issue of "musical relationship" than style (in terms of the fiddling being affected):

It might have. If the piano player is more aggressive, then the fiddler will likely tend that way and play somewhat rougher. Also, in my little experience playing with piano players, I have noticed this effect on me along with a tendency to play faster if the piano player "takes off" on you.

Ashley MacIsaac speculates on tradition and style in relation to innovative accompaniment:

I try to combine a bit of everybody in it.... I heard someone say once—"if tradition is to remain, the new has to become tradition." [Today's Cape Breton piano playing] grew from where it was before. John Morris [Rankin].... He has his own stamp on it as well.... And just that little bit of difference keeps it interesting enough to keep people interested and keep the traditional alive.[103]

The final two questions on piano accompaniment ask respondents to name the influential piano players over the years in Cape Breton. The questio reads as follows: "This question is for piano players only. What musicians have influenced your piano style?" "If you feel that Cape Breton piano playing has changed over time, what player(s) do you think have been of the greatest influence in this change?" Out of respect for the respondents, I will not reveal the names of the influential pianists that were put forward. However, it is important to note that the majority of respondents diligently answered these questions, supporting the idea that local artistic commitment has helped to guide the evolution of Cape Breton fiddle music, piano playing included.

Fig. 13. Ashley MacIsaac performing at a community hall. Photo by: David Gillis, n.d

The next group of questions in the survey asks about guitar accompaniment and other types of accompaniment for Cape Breton fiddle music. The first question conjures up the idea that the second most predominant form of instrumental Cape Breton accompaniment in the 20th century is the guitar. Respondents were asked if they accept this instrument as a form of accompaniment. All but three said "Yes." Following this, they are asked if guitar accompaniment changed over time and, if so, how? Again, most felt that guitar accompaniment has changed over time, while the explanations as to *how* it changed were similar to the answers regarding piano accompaniment changes.

One musician simply says that the guitar playing has gotten better while another observes a move of late to a more prominent presence of the guitar, noting that earlier players' styles were more subtle, heard more in the background. This view is supported by other musicians who describe today's guitar playing as "more complex and more aggressive," "more in depth," and "more innovative as far as chording goes." Patrick Gillis, one of the most prominent and sought-after Cape Breton traditional guitar players, summarizes the changing guitar accompaniment:

> It moved from just playing bass lines to Dave MacIsaac bringing in a more percussive style and John Allan [Cameron] in the early eighties—could he get some awful ring on his twelve string! Now today young players like Gordie Sampson and myself play like a mixture of both—like a percussive instrument is the best way to say it.

MacIsaac, probably the most influential guitar accompanist for Cape Breton music, discusses how he studied piano accompanists and tried to apply elements of their styles to his guitar playing. He also sees chording knowledge and ability among accompanists as being more individually based, as opposed to being a general, evolved growth:

> GG: You're a well-recognized accompanist as well as a fiddler. Can you tell me anything you've seen changing in accompaniment over the years? Kind of how it's evolved and where you think it's going … what direction it's going in?
>
> DMI: A piano player that's been a big influence on my playing is Mary Jessie MacDonald who'd be a cousin of your own. (Her mother, "Little" Mary MacDonald was a first cousin to Donald Angus … and a great violin player, Mabou Coal Mines style). Mary Jessie's piano playing really influenced my guitar back-up. But having said that I think maybe all the piano players of Cape Breton have influenced me. When I started chording when I was ten years old, I suppose, there was nobody around here that I could watch so I just basically would try to learn, pick off what the piano players were doing on tapes and just try to mimic that … I used to listen to Buddy MacMaster's sister, Lorraine…. We had some old tapes of her and Buddy playing home and I really liked her style of playing … and her sister Betty Lou too, great piano player … and I like piano players that play chords that fit the melody of the tunes … if that doesn't happen, it's a little harder for me to listen to it. It's like when you play jazz music, if you have a jazz melody, you've got to have the right chord changes to fit that melody or else it's not going to sound right. So I guess I'm kind of a stickler for having the proper chords; the correct chords to go with the melody.

GG: Do you think it's become more involved now, piano accompaniment? Do you think there is more of knowledge of proper chords in general or …

DMI: It depends on the player.

GG: So it's more of an individualized thing.

DMI: More of an individual thing, yeah.[104]

The survey goes on to explore style in even further detail by asking if Cape Breton guitar accompaniment differs from other styles of guitar accompaniment (i.e., Irish or modern Scottish styles). Two respondents did not answer, three did not know, one replied "Probably" and twelve responded "Yes." Fortunately, two Cape Breton style guitarists elaborated on how the Cape Breton style is different from others. Differences involve tunings, chords, rhythm and method of "attack." The first guitarist, Derrick Cameron, replied:

Cape Breton guitar accompaniment is most commonly:

1) Performed with the guitar tuned either in standard or "drop D" tuning

2) Played with a pick instead of finger style

3) Played with the bass lines and chord progressions that best follow Cape Breton piano accompaniment…."Open" tunings are more commonly used in Irish and Scottish styles and they also use different chord progressions than we do.

Gillis, the second guitarist, describes the differences in guitar playing in relatively the same way. In spite of the fact that there aren't many Cape Breton traditional guitar players in contrast to the number of pianists and fiddlers, Gillis points to a consensus, at least for these two established players, about the way that Cape Breton playing differs from other styles:

They use more open tunings in Scotland and Ireland. They use "dadgad" [strings are tuned D-A-D-G-A-D] and capos, so chord progressions are quite a bit different … there's quite a bit of drone in their playing. Their beat and chords attack the tunes in a different way. They play with more "freedom" as opposed to "following" the tune.

Perhaps this "freedom" has to do with the lesser prominence of pianos in the music overseas. That is, there is probably less emphasis on the piano as being the "lead accompanying" instrument in Ireland and Scotland, as opposed to Cape Breton. In terms of "mixing" the sound with regard to instrument volumes in Cape Breton music, after the fiddle the piano takes prominence.

The guitar follows, unless the tune group being mixed is not intended to be a "traditional" selection.

The next two questions, as in the case with piano accompaniment, ask for respondents to name influential guitar players and for guitar playing respondents to mention the predecessors who influenced them. For the purpose of not offending any respondents or other musicians, again I will not mention names here. Instead I will make the point that, just as with fiddle and piano playing, it is from accomplished local players, and from those who have played in earlier times, that young traditional musicians learn to grasp their musical style.

The final part of the survey covering accompaniment deals with the addition of other instruments, genres and experimental musical exploration in the tradition. From my experience, opinions vary widely with regard to experimentation and the addition of other instruments so I felt it fitting to gather musicians' thoughts and asked, "So, is it okay to add other instruments besides the piano and guitar?"

One respondent answered "No." Buddy MacMaster answered: "I prefer piano over other instruments, guitar would be next … not so familiar with other accompaniment." Most other respondents felt that it was acceptable to use other instruments as accompaniment forms.

With regard to using instruments other than guitar and piano, Derrick Cameron raises the issue of inexperience. If the musicians playing instruments new to the tradition want to be effective accompanists, they need—but are unlikely to have—an understanding of Gaelic fiddling. He responded, "Yes, as long as the musicians have a solid grasp of the Cape Breton style of traditional music." For instance, would it be wise to ask a heavy metal drummer who has never heard the music to play along? I think not, as his idea of rhythm, dynamics, etc., would be different from that of a player who has listened to the tunes over an extensive period.

Other respondents believe it is a matter of personal preference and taste if additional instruments should or should not be used. Glen MacEachern says that banjo and mandolin sound wonderful at times with fiddle while Danny Graham adds that "as long as the fiddle remains the prominent instrument in the mix," it is okay to use other instruments. One popular dance player feels it is useful to add other instruments, but that it should depend on the venue; he'd rather see other instruments (besides piano and guitar) involved "more so at a concert style/bar event—not at dances." Again, this seems to be a matter of preference: I have heard from percussionist Matthew Foulds that fiddler Howie MacDonald enjoyed having percussion for a dance to help him acquire and feel a good rhythm. Other fiddlers, it seems, would simply rather have dancers for rhythm support. But there are risks: in poor sounding stages and in venues lacking step-dancers competent through the square sets, the rhythmic advantage can be so diminished that the fiddler could end up struggling drastically.

The next question asks, "Is it O.K. to mix other genres like jazz, rock, blues, pop, dance (techno) music, flamenco, etc., with Cape Breton fiddle music? Why or why not?" Five respondents did not answer this question. The layout of the questionnaire may have caused a blank response in a few instances. Three respondents answered "No," it is not acceptable to mix other genres. Ten felt that it was, though some attached conditions to their views. Interestingly, the three "No" respondents were older fiddlers—Kenneth Joseph MacDonald, Willie Kennedy and Buddy MacMaster, a healthy counterbalance to those who would have the music move on without holding enough to its original spirit and conventions.

Willie Kennedy answers "No" because it takes away from the traditional music, while Buddy MacMaster adds, "To me it's not okay. It no longer sounds like CB music if mixed with other genres." It seems that the concern among other respondents is one of musical categorization. They feel it is permissible to mix genres as long as the listener doesn't see it as an example of Cape Breton traditional music. Kinnon Beaton feels that mixing genres is okay but "it should be categorized as something other than Cape Breton." Dunn-MacIsaac's answer is similar when she notes, "Well, yes in good taste and in small doses in case it causes a trend and the tradition is lost." Derrick Cameron reflects the general concerns:

> I think that it would be a mistake to not allow musicians to experiment; however, the musicians have to understand that once you start blending other genres with traditional Cape Breton fiddle music, the resulting music is no longer "traditional." Also, a blend should not be presented to an audience as "traditional."

There is also the concern that this "mixing," though it can sound good, can affect younger musicians negatively: "It makes me a little nervous to see this is what is presented often. The younger players might not value the traditional music on its own."

The last accompaniment question is related to those previous, asking if it is okay for experimentation (to back up the fiddle music with jazz, blues, rock, pop and other styles) as long as the music and stylistic applications performed on the fiddle *are played strictly the "Cape Breton" way*. I also asked, why or why not? For this question, three respondents did not answer, one answered "No," and thirteen answered "Yes." Dunn-MacIsaac and Mary E. MacInnis, consider it permissible to include small, tasteful doses of experimentation which don't become the accepted "norm" or definition of what is traditional. One fiddler mentions that it is really just "up to the individual;" a couple of others note that experimentation is valid, but even the fiddle doesn't have to be played the "Cape Breton way." They simply see it as music creation—a good thing. Another suggestion is that experimentation is good in that it allows for the adding of possible enhancements and the rejection of possible hindrances to the tradition." The local Cape Breton music community seems to be able to accept what does not flow too far from the idiomatic box at any given time and is able to weed out what goes too far. Some experimentation and innovations just seem to take time to be embraced and are perhaps embraced only when a change is needed to "freshen up" the tradition. This could be in terms of new tune introductions, new chord combinations, or new instruments being added to keep and gain interest among music followers. Nevertheless, respondents concur that the interpretation of what is traditional should, in other words, be guarded and passed on correctly to both young musical participants and interested listeners in general.

WOMEN AND THE CAPE BRETON FIDDLE TRADITION

There is almost no record of women's involvement in Scottish fiddle playing in the formative years of the tradition. Male-dominated history may have exacerbated this lack. Social conventions of pioneer days were also problematic: they supported a male chauvinism which hindered women's freedom to develop and express their musical skills. In colonial times and after, the sexes lived in distinctly separate spheres. Religious attitudes worked against female entertainers. In 18th-century Scotland, while young ladies of rank were instructed in music and drawing, the musical history of that country is silent about female fiddlers.[105] Though girls and women certainly participated in social dancing, even then there were plenty of instances where their range of dance activity was circumscribed.

A few women like Mary MacDonald (1897-1983) and Tena Campbell (1899-1949), did achieve prominence as exponents of Cape Breton fiddle music. However, as Margie Dunn has noted, many felt that fiddling was not an activity suitable for women. Very few played publicly, while some secretly "took out the fiddle" within the confines of a bedroom in their homes or when home alone while their husbands "were in the fields" or "had to go to town."[106] Women were generally restricted to and expected to be seen accompanying playing, whether it be with knitting needles, pump organ or, later, the piano. Fortunately, this divisive gendering would eventually evolve into an attitude of acceptance, thanks to the initiative of MacDonald, Campbell, and later Theresa MacLellan and Theresa Morrison. Morrison, who released a recording in 1999, recalls: "There was no prejudice whatsoever against a female fiddler; so, in time, her services were requested for the numerous dances, picnics, and concerts in her locality."[107] This suggests that as early as the 1930s, acceptance of female fiddlers was becoming common; perhaps, at most, it may have been considered merely an oddity.

Margaret Chisholm and Brenda Stubbert would follow as tradition-bearers, inheriting styles from strong genetic musical lines. Stubbert is now one of Cape Breton's most respected recording artists and composers. Other recording artists include Jackie Dunn-MacIsaac, a music teacher and fiddle instructor, Stephanie Wills, Wendy MacIsaac, Kendra MacGillivray and Natalie MacMaster, Cape Breton's most well-travelled fiddler with well over one hundred thousand CDs sold during her musical career. A new wave has also begun with Mairi Rankin, who has played with a number of bands, Andrea Beaton, Shelley Campbell, Molly Rankin, Dawn and Margie Beaton, Kimberley Fraser, Leanne Aucoin, Dara Smith of Antigonish, and countless other young women. In fact, Dunn-MacIsaac has remarked that there are now more girls than boys learning Cape Breton fiddle—another indication that the tradition continues to evolve. All of the above have strong family and local influences on their playing styles.

A question in the survey discusses the subject of separate spheres in the realm of Cape Breton traditional music. The question, for female respondents only, reads as follows: "In earlier times in Cape Breton, it can safely be assumed that fiddle players were predominantly male. Do you feel 'equally' accepted in the tradition as males are or do you feel that it is still male-dominated (or possibly male-favoured)? If you do feel 'equally accepted', has this always been the case for you?" Every person answered that she felt equally accepted. The oldest respondent, pianist Elizabeth Beaton, answered that she always "felt accepted." So for most of the 20th century, it seems that women were at least accepted as participants in the tradition—in Beaton's case, as a piano player. However, this doesn't address the question as to whether or not women were accepted only as piano players as part of the tradition in the early to mid 1900s. Were fiddle-playing females feeling equally accepted? The safe conclusion would be that they were accepted, but not to the degree that they are in 2004. Today, it seems that all of the younger female players questioned say that they have always felt equally accepted. Andrea Beaton acknowledges that female players before her probably contributed to this when she says, "I feel equally accepted and always have. I guess this is because there were several female players paving the way for a few years before I started." Although this all looks promising, even as late as the 1980s there may have been a stereotype recognizing males as predominantly fiddlers/potential fiddlers and females as pianists/potential pianists. Mary Elizabeth MacInnis notes that although she feels "equally accepted ... years ago the older people would always ask my brother if he was going to play, not me."

When asked the next question—"Do you think attitudes toward female players have changed over time?"—respondents overwhelmingly responded "Yes." Buddy MacMaster answers, "I think attitudes have always been favourable toward female players. However, there are now many more female players than in former years." From here, however, we must not jump to the conclusion that there is a direct link to attitudes toward female players and the number of them playing. It may be that a more general societal change has contributed to both the transition *and* the individual freedom felt by females to participate and contribute as fiddlers.

ACADIAN AND MI'KMAQ FIDDLERS

It is worth noting that Cape Breton fiddling enthusiasts of Acadian and Mi'kmaq descent do not all seem to view the style as strictly Scottish. Acadian players, like Arthur Muise, Didace Aucoin and Donnie LeBlanc, and Mi'kmaq players like Lee Cremo, have played the music as if it is a part of their culture, not an adaptation and adoption into their ethnic communities. LeBlanc's vision of the music is evident when he said in the early 1980s (with regard to lack of Cape Breton fiddling on the radio), "It's a problem—the young people don't hear any local music to influence them. And, it should be *our* players on instead of overseas fiddlers."[108] Of course, musical exposure has been elevated since that time, but LeBlanc's personal views on his own culture's music are certainly clear. Essentially, cultural interactions have produced a universal embracing of the Cape Breton style within different ethnic communities.

Fig. 14.   J. P. Cormier, Donnie LeBlanc and Hilda Chiasson Cormier at Broad Cove Scottish Concert. Photo by: David Gillis, n.d.

Regarding the Acadians, Mi'kmaqs and Irish descendants who participate in the Scottish-Highland tradition, Dunlay notes, "Even though they may still refer to the music as Scottish, they do not need to adopt a new identity to make the music their own. Rather, the music has become the music of any Cape Bretoner."[109] In Gordon E. Smith's article, "Lee Cremo: Narratives About a MicMac Fiddler," Cremo re-emphasizes the above observation when he states the following:

> I've always been a bit nervous playing in competitions with the others (non-Natives). They don't say or do anything exactly—sometimes they just look at me and I guess they are wondering what this little Indian guy is doing playing "their" music. If that is what they are thinking then I would just like to say that it's my music too. I grew up with it like they did, and besides, I play it my own way. People don't own this music.

Lee Cremo, who died in 1999, grew up in Eskasoni First Nation, Cape Breton. He was taught to play the violin by his father, Simon Cremo (1900-1964), who learned to play by emulating and copying local Scottish fiddlers such as Winston Fitzgerald. Lee earned a collection of more than 80 awards for his fiddling. Notably, as depicted in the previous chapter, playing in competitions is not a common practice among Cape Breton fiddle players. Perhaps exposure to other styles of the fiddle competitions influenced Lee's fiddle style. Smith, after interviewing experts in the Cape Breton musical field, concluded that Lee's style was "a composite of Scottish, French, and country styles." Some see Cremo's musicianship as an adoption of outside influences, while Wilfred Prosper, another Mi'kmaq fiddler, questioned any notion of Native influences in the fiddle style that he perceived as a hybridized Scottish style. Cremo, however, felt that his interpretation of some melodies (with some embellishments) suggested a Mi'kmaq way of playing which was associated with speech and song styles and verbalism.[110] Again, this reveals a possible connection between language and playing styles. However the above is interpreted, it is clear that First Nation fiddlers have become part of the Cape Breton fiddling community.

Fig. 15. Wilfred Prosper tuning up. Photo by: David Gillis, n.d.

It seems evident, then, that the Cape Breton Scottish fiddling community has been open to players of other ethnic groups. Indeed, no group is musically or ethnically "pure." In turn, Acadian, Irish and Mi'kmaq fiddlers have taken the music of the majority and made it their own; in essence, they have adopted a child and carefully "blended" her characteristics into their own cultures. A blending of styles, whether individual, local or ethnic, would contribute to the ever-evolving music of Cape Breton, although that blend has not seemed as dramatic as has occurred with other styles throughout Canada. Mi'kmaq fiddlers such as Cremo and Wilfred Prosper have been affected in the familial and local context as much as their Scottish counterparts. Learning in the aural tradition was important in the formative years for both fiddlers. In MacGillivray's *The Cape Breton Fiddler*, Cremo notes:

> Before I was eighteen, I had figured out the best way to support the violin so that I could reach notes higher up the board. Around this time, Neil Francis MacLellan of Benacadie gave me some tips on holding the bow. Scottish and Irish music in Cape Breton music required good technique, especially the bowing. I learned a lot from listening to other players like Winston Fitzgerald and Dan Hughie MacEachern. At the dances, if I had the money, I'd go in; if not, I'd sit outside by the window and listen and learn.

Also, family and clergy played an important role for Cremo. "I was always curious about the fiddle; I knew the tunes from my father's playing. He got the fundamentals from a parish priest in Johnstown—Fr. Saulnier; after that, he was on his own."

Wilfred Prosper, whose great-grandfather was a fiddler, remembered being exposed to Cape Breton music at an early age. In his teens he began to be influenced by some of the island's fiddling greats such has Tena Campbell, Winston Fitzgerald and Angus Chisholm, Bill Lamey and "Little" Jack MacDonald. He was also exposed to some "outside" influences such as Don Messer. Of the Messer influence, he says:

> In the beginning, all I played was a few Don Messer tunes. When I was around twenty, we moved to Eskasoni—I was still immersed in the Messer style. Joe Googoo used to say, "you're playing the Scottish tunes too fast!"; he knew his music. Messer's stuff was all straight bowing, but the Scottish music presented a challenge; it was more complicated. There was such variety in Scottish—jigs, reels, strathpeys, hornpipes, clogs, etc.—that's what really turned me on!

Prosper also notes the importance of old music collections and the influence of clergy:

> Now I can take any fiddle book and play most of the tunes. Father Angus Morris just loaned me a *Capt. Simon Fraser Collection*. Other parish priests stationed on the reserve, like Fr. Raymond MacDonald, gave me tips on music.[111]

With regard to style, some interesting points are revealed in Gordon E. Smith's "Lee Cremo: Narratives about a Micmac Fiddler." Smith had inter-

Fig. 16. Jack "Little Jack" MacDonald, one of "The Five MacDonald Fiddlers." Photo by: Unknown, n.d. Beaton Institute, Cape Breton University. 80-167-4347.

viewed musicians about Lee's style of fiddling. They noted techniques within the Scottish tradition that Cremo utilized such as cuttings and the "Scotch snap," double stopping and the open fifth drone. They also suggest that his musicianship can be described as an "almost total assimilation of … outside influences." I agree with Smith when he notes that the above idea neglects any "Nativeness" in Cremo's music and his playing style should really be considered a "blending of traditions," which is a vital feature of First Nations culture.

Although Cremo sees his self-expression through extensive embellishment as a mirror of his wordy Mi'kmaq culture—surrounding single notes with left-hand ornaments to convey verboseness—Prosper leans toward the notion that "both he and Lee play 'in the Cape Breton Scottish style' and questioned whether or not there is such a thing as 'Native Influences' in the music of Micmac fiddlers." I suggest that as rhythm and accents of Gaelic contribute to the Cape Breton style, so too may the same be said about Mi'kmaq and Acadian interpretations; therefore, the result could be a "blending" towards an evolved sound in these instances.[112]

With regard to various ethnicities in the tradition, the survey questionnaire asks whether Acadian and/or Mi'kmaq players from Cape Breton have adopted the island's predominant fiddle sound and absorbed it as a part of their own cultures or if they have a fiddling tradition/sound/style all their own. Kinnon Beaton makes the point that, "I think it depends on the artist." Many players "model" their playing on what they're accustomed to hearing or on an individual artist who is aesthetically pleasing to himself or herself. This would invariably affect the style in which he or she plays. Elizabeth Beaton feels that "many of them have the general Cape Breton style," while Dunn-MacIsaac surmises that "they [Acadian and Mi'kmaq players] have incorporated the Cape Breton style into their own styles in both cases." Another musician also observes a combination of styles when she notes that, "They have some of our (Scottish) sound—some more than others. They also have a sound/style that is unique to them." Andrea Beaton reiterates this: "I guess every fiddler has a sound/style of their own. I think the Mi'kmaq and Acadian players are playing Cape Breton stuff and mixing it with their own cultures." Rodney MacDonald feels that Acadian and Mi'kmaq players have adopted our style, "although the Acadian people still have their own unique style and tunes." There were a couple of respondents who felt that the Acadians and Mi'kmaq have simply adopted our style while older fiddler Willie Kennedy feels that "they have a style of their own."

As noted earlier, style does vary from individual to individual. However, there could perhaps be a tie between the languages spoken by these ethnic groups and the rhythms and accents in (some of) their playing that slightly differs from that of Gaelic-style players. Again, even the sounds of these Acadian and Mi'kmaq players will often depend on what and who they are listening to most of the time, musically.

In Petit Etang, Cape Breton fiddler Donnie LeBlanc (b. 1955) was interviewed by Joey Beaton. LeBlanc began playing the mandolin around the age of 10 and at 14 or 15 began playing the fiddle. He mentions that "Scotty" (Winston Fitzgerald) "used to come over" and that he "used to try to imitate him and others." At first an ear player, LeBlanc later took violin lessons from Méderic Lefort and, in terms of written music books, claims to have "all the standard collections." Beaton goes on to ask about accompaniment and its influences. Of accompaniment, LeBlanc remarks that it is "just as important ... the backbone." Of fiddling influences he adds that "Arthur Muise was a real influence." Muise is a highly respected Acadian fiddler who would have been influenced by such players as the famous Angus Chisholm of Margaree.

Beaton then asks if there is an integration of cultures within the tradition with regard to the presence of French Acadians, Mi'kmaq and other ethnic groups. LeBlanc responds by saying the tradition in Cape Breton is "more open, everybody's putting in their own style."[113] Again then, the suggestion arises that style is a combination of factors; it is individualized, but influences contribute to the formation of style, regardless of a player's ethnicity.

TARTANISM AND PSEUDO-SCOTTISH CULTURE

The Cape Breton fiddle tradition has been carried on in a geographic area settled dominantly by Scottish Gaels. Surprisingly, since their arrival, interpretations of true Scottish culture representative of the Gael have been altered, perhaps even invented. The 1930s, of course, were times of great economic struggle for the world and the Maritimes. Musically, "The era from 1935-65 was a very fruitful one for Cape Breton and there were many great players and composers."[114] Meanwhile, Angus L. Macdonald, twice Premier of Nova

Scotia between 1933 and 1954, and a Gaelic-speaking Cape Bretoner, held political power through much of this period. Faced with the unenviable task of bolstering the economy, Macdonald saw tourism as a possible saviour. According to Ian McKay, the state under Macdonald enacted policies geared toward "tartanizing" Nova Scotia, a litany of signs representing a constructed "Scottish essence of Nova Scotia." Tartanism fostered a romanticized folk image of Nova Scotia, aimed at complementing the "redemptive role of tourism" in a stagnant economy. McKay summarizes Macdonald's intentions as follows:

> Premier Angus L. Macdonald, convinced of certain self-evident truths—the truths of his own particularly romantic and essentialist reading of the Scottish tradition, and the redemptive role of tourism—used the state's cultural power to fuse these two truths into one commanding commonsense. He thereby "naturalized" tartanism and made it seem to be the spontaneous expression of the province's cultural identity. In the triumph of tartanism we have an illustration of the cultural impact of tourism as it was powerfully focused by the activist 20th-century state, and of the ways in which anti-modernism influenced the vocabulary with which the Nova Scotia identity was constructed and diffused.[115]

McKay's article seems cynical. While I concede the accuracy of much that McKay points out, it is reasonable to suggest that Macdonald's intentions were at least heartfelt. Though one can look upon the invented "Scottishness" in a negative light, at least something was done, or at least attempted, to promote Scottish culture after centuries of oppression in an Anglo-centric world. Unfortunately, Macdonald's *"liberal-romantic"* view neglected the *Gaelic* part of "Scottishness"—if one promotes Highland "Scottishness," the *Gaelic* must also be promoted. The establishment of a "symbolic" Gaelic College more interested in promoting ceremonious romanticisms at that time, for instance, was not enough. (The last few decades have seen the College move toward a greater emphasis on the traditional Gaelic art forms.) Seemingly,

Fig. 17. Hon. Angus Lewis Macdonald (1890-1954). Photo by: Don MacLachlan, n.d. Beaton Institute, Cape Breton University. 77-977-1111.

a main problem with the general picture of "Scottishness" in the New World is that "one generation's invented tradition became the next generation's common-sense reality."[116]

Perhaps Macdonald and most Scots in Nova Scotia were influenced by a new Scottish order evinced by popular Highland societies organized in the Maritimes and Canada. Rusty Bitterman demonstrates that these Highland societies were structures composed of elites, interwoven between the old country and colonial society. Influenced and guided by the London social scene, these "Highland" societies seemed to ignore historical and economic realities, constructing memory and "new" Scots, loyal to British government and principles, and promoting "commercial values and improvement." In reality, they "distanced and subdued some of the themes that emerged in the Gaelic poetry of the emigration years—the elite tradition and history did not highlight agrarian transformation or the betrayal of ideals that had once placed men before gold."[117]

c. Fig. 18. Scottish Dancers. Photo by: NS Bureau of Information, c. 1920. Beaton Institute, Cape Breton University. 77-63-197.

Visions of new "Scottishness" presented contradictory ideologies with those of more realistic historical Gaelic narrative. Arguably, certain aspects of Cape Breton's community-based Gaelic culture escaped the "Scottish myth," and the Cape Breton fiddle style was relatively unscathed. On one hand, many deeply embedded elements of Scottish Gaelic culture, such as the fiddle style, were generally not directly affected by tartanism. Gaelic language, on the other hand, was virtually ignored. Actually, infrastructure developed during Angus L.'s tenure (such as the Cabot Trail and Keltic Lodge) most likely provided a larger audience of tourists for the fiddlers, indirectly making their art form financially worthwhile (albeit as a supplementary income). Ironically, Alex Francis MacKay, one of Cape Breton's only remaining Gaelic-speaking fiddlers, reflects that his first public appearance was at the opening of the Cape Breton Highlands National Park, with Premier Angus L. Macdonald in attendance.[118] Unfortunately, although his symbolic commemorative "Scottishness" likely bolstered the economy through tourism, it did little to foster the preservation of the living Gaelic culture evinced by many communities on Cape Breton Island. This was left to the local population and was (and still is) exhibited in Gaelic fiddle playing and "real" ceilidh settings at the local and family level. This is not to say that preservation of the Gaelic fiddle style has always been accepted as a "given." As we'll see later, outside influences would begin to take their toll on Cape Breton's Gaelic culture.

Fig. 19. Canadian Night, Scottish Gaelic Society, Roxbury, MA. Photo by: Glines & Slater, Boston, 1927. Beaton Institute, Cape Breton University. 79-1021-4001.

Fig. 20. The Gaelic College, St. Ann's. Premier Angus L. Macdonald seated centre, Fr. Rankin of Iona seated at far right. Photo by: Unknown, c. 1948. Beaton Institute, Cape Breton University. 86-132-16230.

OUT-MIGRATION, CULTURE AND ECONOMIC REALITIES

The effects of the economy on the culture of Cape Breton can be noted as early as the late 1800s and early 1900s. Between 1871 and 1921 almost half-a-million people left the Maritime provinces; a large number left Newfoundland as well. This out-migration would arguably be a consequence of the region failing to industrialize. However, the question of causes comes into play as well. Thornton describes two sets of economic forces at work in the process of migration; they are the "push" and the "pull" factors, which largely apply to Maritime migration studies:

> Where "push" factors at origin are strongest (such as rural poverty, low wages, and incomes, few or declining opportunities, absence of amenities, poor educational facilities and the like) then migration is less demographically and economically selective. Under these circumstances out-migration may be beneficial to the region, relieving it of surplus labour. However, where "pull" forces are strongest (such as the lure of cheap farm land, virgin forests, attractive opportunities for employment, promotion or good salaries, along with better available amenities such as schools and hospitals) then migration is usually highly selective of the young, dynamic, better-educated and more highly skilled. Under these circumstances out-migration may be depriving the region of the very people on whom self-sustained growth depends.[119]

Both "push" and "pull" factors have affected Cape Breton and the Maritimes. A major exodus of predominantly Highland Scots was evident in the rural eastern counties of Nova Scotia and Cape Breton Island in the late 1800s and beyond. For instance, there was a population decrease of more than 70 per cent between 1881 and 1931, for the rural district of Antigonish alone. One explanation for this mass out-migration involved "pull" factors such as an attraction to economic improvement, city life and a sense of "other directedness." Additionally, this exodus created new economic realities that triggered a "push" for further emigration.

The most popular destination for the emigrants was the "Boston States." At this juncture, the Boston area became a haven for Gaelic culture. Nilsen postulates that in its "heyday" as a migration destination, eastern Massachusetts would have laid claim to several thousand Gaelic speakers. In this locale, the emigrants found jobs as domestics, seamen, labourers and carpenters, while some later emigrants found employment as nurses, teachers and office workers. As the community established itself, various institutions and organizations were formed. Churches with Gaelic services were formed while dances at the Rose Croix and Hibernian halls on Dudley Street were popular attractions. The scene had "no lack of musicians," while at these dances there would be "two or three hundred Gaelic speakers."[120] Of course this activity diminished over time, but this transplantation of Gaelic culture must have had an effect on the music of Cape Breton. First, the music was brought to the Boston area where it would almost certainly influence and be influenced by other musical styles in the area. Second, the Highland Scottish communities in Cape Breton were able to continue an existence of rural isolation significant enough to maintain a continuity of fiddle style possibly unequalled anywhere else in North America. Thus, we can add emigration to the role of familial and local enculturation in combining "integrity of continuity" with openness to innovation and self-expression.

While dances were thriving on Cape Breton Island, the "Boston States" had quickly established their own dance scene, a scene that revealed both cultural exchanges and the beginnings of an evolving commercialization of the music. Performers were paid for playing, all the while sharing musical and social experiences as they travelled from one cultural haven to the other. Family musical connections remained relatively strong between those in Cape Breton and the Boston area. This observation and early evidence of commercial recordings are depicted in the words of Margaret Dunn, writing about her uncle, Dan Hughie MacEachern, a famous Cape Breton composer:

> Dan Hughie's parents did not play any instruments but they loved the music. His uncle Dan MacEachern was a fiddler and several of his children played as well. Uncle Dan's sons John R. and John Angus were good fiddlers. A third son, Dan Hughie MacEachern (known as Big Dan—first cousin by the same name) was a well known fiddler in the Boston area. In 1926 he won a fiddling contest which took place at the Intercolonial Hall in Boston. Three years later, he went to New York to make a recording with the Dan Sullivan Band.[121]

However, when rural families have to leave their rooted traditions behind and move to the city, we can see how they could readily become enculturated by urban popular culture:

> The move to urban industrialization weakens considerably the traditional and cultural influence of the extended family, the community and religion in the everyday lives of people. As a direct result, a cultural void opens up. The marketplace moves in to replace older forms of cultural activity. Culture itself is made into a commodity and is bought and sold in the marketplace.[122]

These descriptions of the activities of migrants to the "Boston States" are merely an example of the cultural responses Cape Breton Gaels made to their economic realities. The Gaelic culture and music scene remained very healthy for a number of years there. Though weekly or even monthly Cape Breton dances may still be attended in the Boston area, however, the scene is certainly not as vibrant as in earlier years.

Additionally, the exodus was also directed toward other urban centers in the Maritimes and in Central Canada. The more recent shift of out-migration toward places such as Ontario and Alberta, rather than Boston may also be more of a cause in Gaelic-cultural decline in the Boston area rather than lack of interest among its own immigrants. Although pockets of Gaelic culture and music are still visible to some degree in these urban centers, their preservation has not matched that of rural Cape Breton and depends upon migratory infusions from the musical heartland.

THE INFLUENCE OF THE DUDLEY STREET TRADITION

The Dudley Street tradition is a metaphor for what was happening in the Boston area from the 1930s onward. For decades, Boston had an influx of immigrants and visitors from places associated with music like Ireland, the Maritimes and French and Acadian Canada. Homesick and searching for social release, these immigrants would come together and celebrate and share their musical cultures in pubs on the corners of Warren and Dudley Streets, in Roxbury, otherwise known as Dudley Square. The Celtic music of New England, consequently, was a blend of Scottish (Cape Breton), French Canadian and Irish music—a cultural celebration of sharing, influencing and unifying which is still highly valid and important to this day.

House parties, pub sessions and dances were focal gatherings for cultural transmission to take place. Additionally, sessions were being recorded by such people as Cape Breton fiddler Johnnie Archie MacDonald, whose recordings "reveal a natural preference for Cape Breton Scottish music, but also include numerous recordings of Irish and French-Canadian players, many of whom were recorded on visits to Boston." These recordings are vital for two primary reasons. First, they reveal intermingling of traditional music and cultures. Second, they preserve styles that can be modelled and learned aurally by younger players. Frank Ferrel helps put the social and musical life into perspective with an interview of Joe Derrane, an accordion player:

> Just down from the corner on Warren Street was E. O'Byrne DeWitts, the Irish travel agency and music store. O'Byrne DeWitts had their own record labels, Copley and all-Ireland, featuring Boston area musicians who were regulars in the dance halls and on local radio programs…. Times were so difficult in the early thirties that at the Rose Croix they used to let the young fellows come in free because the girls had nobody to dance with, and the girls worked as cooks, and all the different jobs in the Back Bay. One of the halls was O'Connell Hall and I remember another one was Winslow Hall … the music was very, very good. Angus Chisholm and Alex Gillis and Alcide Aucoin were the real good fiddlers there, with Betty Millet at the piano there, she was real tops…."

Other Cape Breton-style fiddlers who established, ran and played for dances in the late 1940s through to the 1950s were Ranny Graham, Dan Hughie

MacEachern, Bill Lamey, and Winston "Scotty" Fitzgerald. Ferrel notes that:

> If I were asked to choose three musicians who best represented the French, Irish, and Scottish mix on Dudley Street, I'd have to say Tom Doucet, Winston Fitzgerald, and Joe Derrane. They're all classic players and I've drawn from them heavily in my own repertoire.... Winston Scotty Fitzgerald was a native Cape Bretoner, whose Scottish influenced musical style set a standard for Cape Breton fiddling. In the 1930s he worked with Hank Snow who is credited with providing the nickname, Scotty. By the late 1940s Winston was a popular radio performer with his own group, The Radio Entertainers. He made frequent trips to Boston where he would visit friends and play for local dances.[123]

Joey Beaton, a Mabou musician and composer, has stated that after extensively interviewing a great number of Cape Breton fiddlers in the early 1990s, Fitzgerald has stood out as *the* main influence of the majority.

Ferrel confirms that the Dudley Street environment encouraged interaction between the French, Irish and Cape Bretoners. Ultimately, Angus Chisholm and Winston Fitzgerald himself, having been exposed to the musical influences of Dudley Street, would have introduced new ideas, techniques and tunes to the Cape Breton repertoire which would be passed on to eager tradition bearers such as Buddy MacMaster, Jerry Holland, Howie MacDonald, Natalie MacMaster and many others.

Although the musicians were being influenced by each other at the peak of the Dudley Street period, other cultural fashions that had an effect on fiddling were being taken from the "Boston States" at an earlier time. As noted earlier, the fiddle tradition has been reflective of the dance and the dancers. Even since the early 1900s, those going back and forth from the Boston area were introducing new dance fashions to Cape Breton. Actually, these new cultural introductions prompted noticeable changes in the Cape Breton fiddle tune repertoire. Square dancing was brought into Nova Scotia and PEI by returnees from the North Eastern U.S., influenced by urban elites who brought the dances over from Lowland Scotland and other areas of Europe. Waltzes, polkas, clogs and foxtrots were also imported from Massachusetts around this time period, expanding the Cape Breton repertoire from what had originally been an almost exclusively "Gaelic" musical sphere that included mainly marches, strathspeys and reels. Kennedy laments the penetration of these "non-Gaelic" tune forms when he notes:

> A whole series of the very latest examples of big city "sophistication" were brought north to compete with the native traditions of Gaelic Nova Scotia and Prince Edward Island. New tune genres

such as polkas and waltzes, which had helped end the golden age of fiddling in Scotland a hundred years earlier, as well as Irish jigs and other forms of music now contended with the traditional Scottish strathspeys and reels in the New World environment, while a similar struggle took place in dance with the appearance of waltzes, foxtrots, and quadrilles. The supply of constantly changing fashions coming north seemed to be endless, and as Nova Scotia entered the 1950s and 60s, the Gaelic fiddling tradition, like Gaelic itself, began to noticeably fail.

With the introduction of square sets came the necessity for more jigs; thus, more jigs crossed over from the Irish tradition while Cape Breton fiddlers began composing more jigs and adding them to the Cape Breton tradition. Jigs are now considered a Cape Breton repertoire staple, although historically they have not always been. This is probably surprising to many Cape Bretoners and Cape Breton traditional musicians. Although the new forms of square dancing penetrated Cape Breton, step-dancing (doing the actual traditional dance steps) was integrated into the "Boston Quadrilles" (especially in Inverness county), keeping them "Gaelicized" and resembling dances that came over from Gaelic Scotland.[124] Maggie Moore, who has written about Scottish step-dancing, notes that Gaelic step dance in Cape Breton has remained similar to earlier times in Scotland (before the late 1800s), not as affected as Scotland was by external influences. She refers also to the evolution of the dance in Cape Breton:

> The notable exception I talked about was the introduction around the turn of the century of community halls where public dances could be held. Coupled with the importation of Quadrilles from the North-East of the United States, the old Scotch Four lost its pre-eminence at social occasions—house parties, parish picnics, weddings, and open-air concerts. In some parts of the island, the more usual way of walking through the figures [sic] but in Inverness County, the Quadrille figures were amalgamated with stepping and a wonderfully exuberant form of square dance has evolved.[125]

I should add though, that the integration of stepdancing into the square-dance figures may not have occurred, or at least have become prominently visible, until well after the square dance introduction; perhaps as late as 1940. This was noted by my grandmother, who would have been attending the dances in the 1930s and playing for them as the 1940s arrived.[126]

From the above observations, the obvious influence of the cultural exchanges between Cape Breton and areas of the "Boston States" such as Dudley Street/Square should not be dismissed as insignificant, but rather considered an important contributing factor in the evolution of Cape Breton fiddle music.

DAN RORY MACDONALD, OTHER COMPOSERS AND THE POST-WORLD WAR II PERIOD

As in the tradition of the Gows, Marshall and Dow, Cape Breton has laid claim to composers of astounding merit. One of Cape Breton's most prolific composers, Dan R. MacDonald, had a profound influence on the music of Cape Breton. Dan R. was born in the small community of Rear Judique South in Cape Breton in 1911. In his youth, he "would take two sticks of kindling, go into the building (a wagon shed) and sit on the seat of one of the wagons. There he would stay for hours singing tunes and playing his kindling fiddle, "and who knows, perhaps even composing new tunes." This was very likely not far from the truth, as Dan R. is reputed to have composed more than 20,000 tunes.

In 1940, MacDonald enlisted and found himself overseas in the Forestry Battalion. While stationed in Scotland, he befriended John Murdock Henderson, a traditional composer and player of Scottish music. The classically inclined Henderson's influence on Dan R. would be life long. Henderson, who one would assume was influenced by J. Scott Skinner before him, taught Dan R. the "finer points of composing" and critiqued his compositions, likening them to those of an earlier time, before the 20th century. One would have to agree with Cameron when he suggests that Dan R.'s approach to the music was closer to the older style than Henderson's and Scotland's—perhaps Dan R. should have been the teacher! Was there anything wrong with composing tunes reminiscent of the Gaelic tradition of which he was a part? As noted, his views toward traditional music were highly valued by his peers. It can safely be stated that Dan R.'s return from Scotland resulted in a greater focus on the written note in Cape Breton. John Donald Cameron supports both notions of the "Henderson influence" and that of others there such as Hector MacAndrew and the move towards the increased value in note reading:

> He was aware of Hector MacAndrew ... and Dan R. was told what a great player he was ... and he said, "The next CBC cheque I'm going to get, I'm going to start saving because I'm going to Scotland to listen to him play and he is going to listen to me playing...." There were some very good note readers, Red Johnnie Campbell and Dan R. used to visit him sometimes and he would play for him. He'd take out a book and start playing from that and Dan R. very much admired that and he thought that was the way to go if you wanted to further yourself in the fiddle music, you should learn to read.[127]

Dan R.'s compositions, as well as those of Dan Hughie MacEachern, Donald Angus Beaton and Gordon MacQuarrie, have become accepted universally into the Cape Breton repertoire. Their influence on younger fiddlers like Kinnon Beaton and John Morris Rankin and others has been extraordinary. Notably, Dan R. "was particularly interested in hearing new, younger players. A smile always came to his face especially if it (the tune) was his and played well." Beaton, Rankin (1959-2000), Jerry Holland and the younger Brenda Stubbert, Howie and Dougie MacDonald, have continued as the next generation of great Cape Breton composers, adding tunes to the Cape Breton repertoire. Again, this continuous flow of fresh composition suggests the evolution and continued traditional vitality of the Cape Breton fiddling tradition. Even the newest generation of young composers also shows promise and strong continuity in musical composition for Cape Breton music. I should also mention that a much overlooked composer of Cape Breton music is John MacDougall, who may have composed more tunes than any other in Scottish music history, claiming and being reputed to have composed more than 34,000 tunes. It seems though, that Dan R. was instrumental in paving the way for those that have followed:

> Of course, people like Buddy MacMaster, Dan J. Campbell, and Dan Hughie MacEachern and other prominent fiddlers all mentioned Dan R., and Alex Francis MacKay, of course, knew he was an exceptionally good composer.[128]

Dan R. was also known to be a man who enjoyed sharing his music and hearing it played by others. When he was living on Back Street in Mabou, he'd often visit the household of fiddler Donald Angus Beaton and bring up newly composed tunes for Donald Angus to play.[129] Buddy MacMaster and the Chisholms of Margaree were other players with whom Dan R. shared his dance music and whom he enjoyed hearing play his tunes.[130] Also, Dan R. often used to have a young John Morris Rankin accompany him on the piano, aiding in John Morris's musical development, while Kinnon Beaton was helped a great deal with his musical theory by Dan R.

In turn, both of these players now have a great influence on the younger players in Cape Breton. Dan R.'s influence, and that of other individual musicians, can be seen below in John Morris Rankin's interview with Joey Beaton. Beaton asks Rankin about his first instrument, the piano. Rankin speaks about his family buying a piano from Dan R.'s sister (John Allan Cameron's mother) that all of the children in his family attempted to play. Not long after that, John Morris began playing the fiddle his father had bought and "strung up." Joey Beaton then refers to Dan R. and his frequent visits to John Morris's family home, and the effect that it must have had on their music, especially Rankin's music.

> JMR: Well, you know, when you think back on things that happened early, you don't seem to at the time realize what was going

on and at that point there were a lot of influences and Dan R. was one of them and he'd come over and he'd sit sometimes for a couple of hours and played tunes that you wouldn't really.... You had to know them to get through them; so the beauty of it was that every time he'd come over, he'd play generally the same runs of tunes.... And he'd play tunes like the "Marquis of Huntley's Snuffmill" or something like that, and although it's not a difficult tune to accompany, at that time it was for a kid, so it trains you ... and it was a great experience to have a guy like that live alongside of you.... And another experience, if you'd like me to take it a little further, was that fact that we lived very close to the hall and your father, Donald Angus, used to play regular dances there ... and the window would be open behind the stage.... So the window in my bedroom in my house was very close so we used to hear that music all the time. And there was something about it, you know, I'd stick my head out the window for the longest time just listening to it.

JB: As a result of listening to the tunes and everything, I bet you were learning a lot of tunes by ear at that time.

JMR: Yeah, that's mainly what would happen. I think there are a lot of benefits to that.... It trains you to pick a lot of things up as opposed to searching something out in a book or whatever. It trains you to memorize.[131]

Dan R. stands out as one of those highly influential musicians, perhaps as much or more for his composing as his fiddle playing, although when he played at his best, he rivaled any player of his era. His stay overseas in Scotland exposed him to rare Scottish music collections non-existent in Cape Breton, which he either sent or brought home for other fiddlers. His friend Gordon MacQuarrie took advantage of this when he was over-seas during the Second World War as well.

As mentioned earlier, J. Murdock Henderson's influence probably increased Dan R.'s focus on the importance of reading music. MacQuarrie and his "musically literate" cohorts (but more specifically Dan R.) created a stronger focus on the written note from the 1940s onward. As the books from Scotland became more widespread, the interactions and opinions of Dan R., MacQuarrie and such peers as Dan Hughie MacEachern extended throughout the music community. With more books, a greater emphasis on the written note almost certainly occurred. It was seen as an important necessity in "keeping up" with others by increasing repertoire and improving musicianship. This is not to say that there was not an emphasis on note-reading in earlier times. Fiddling "greats" such as "Big" Ronald MacLellan (1880-1935) and Donald John "the tailor" Beaton (1856-1919) were also known to have knowledge of music theory (the term "fiddling great" will be discussed later).[132] They were, of course, very influential on players in their day, as well as players like Angus Chisholm, Dan R. and Fitzgerald who followed. This is a prime example of history repeating itself with Cape Breton music, although each "influencer" affected the music in his/her own way.

In the time since Dan R.'s return from the war, a greater change could be seen in the music in terms of outside pressures and an expanding technological world. Although Cape Breton's traditional music climate seemed strong leading into the 1960s, as noted with the Dudley Street tradition, television, radio and island residents' exposure to other music genres were beginning to affect Cape Breton Gaelic culture. The fiddling and Gaelic culture were quickly being let go; a revival was needed.

THE VANISHING CAPE BRETON FIDDLER

A CBC television documentary, *The Vanishing Cape Breton Fiddler*, written and narrated by Ron MacInnis late in 1971, was aired and much discussed early in 1972. The program lamented that if the younger generation did not take up the Cape Breton fiddle, the tradition was in jeopardy. Following this, the island community (under the leadership of Father John Angus Rankin) reacted by forming the Cape Breton Fiddlers' Association in 1972 and organizing a fiddling festival in Glendale in 1973 that proved to be a huge success; more than 130 fiddlers played on stage and 10,000 fans cheered them on. New interest was generated among the youth, and the fiddle music of Cape Breton was renewed with the aid of dedicated musicians, clergy and enthusiasts.[133] Since then, there are probably more youth learning Cape Breton fiddle than there have ever been.

Although this resurgence of interest in the music was a crucial factor in keeping it alive, "revivals" cannot always be considered positive occurrences. If in the strict sense a revival is the bringing of something back into existence, when an evolving thing like a tradition is revived, origins may be forgotten and there is no guarantee the recovered tradition will be authentic. Although it is generally thought that there was a "revival" in Cape Breton fiddling after the 1971 documentary, it was more of

Fig. 21. First Fiddlers' Festival, Glendale. Photo by: Unknown, 1977. Beaton Institute, Cape Breton University. 97-650-28498.

a generated awareness than anything else. Indeed, a larger "revival" (in this looser sense) may have occurred in the early 1990s with the popularity of the Rankin Family and the rise in popularity of Cape Breton fiddle artists like Ashley MacIsaac and Natalie MacMaster. Mass publicity due to the work of major record labels and band-wagon media efforts contributed to the music's visibility on a popular scale, not to mention, of course, that these musicians were very talented in their own right from the beginning. Considering that in both of these time periods, it was the raising of the profile of the music at home and abroad that led to a perception of renewal and revival, we perhaps should describe these musical growth periods as revitalizations, as opposed to revivals. If a revival is the bringing of something back into existence, then what happened in the early 1970s and the early 1990s was not a revival in the sense of recovery: the situation facing the music did not require an artificial revival of older playing in order to repair a discontinuity in the tradition.

On that note, even though revivals of interest and expansion of the market for the music are generally positive occurrences, they can also alter the cultural form that is "revived." Folklorist Cliff McGann critiques the "revival" after the 1970s by suggesting that the guiding hand of folklorists in an art form revival can affect the *direction* of that revival. In other words, the form's revival and evolution can be manipulated, so to speak, into the preferential direction of a leading figure, fiddler, or folklorist. He points out, for instance, that Cape

Fig. 22. Cape Breton Fiddlers Association at Celtic Colours International festival, Centre 200. Photo by: David Gillis, n.d.

Breton fiddler Dan R. MacDonald's return from Scotland after World War II led both the Cape Breton and Prince Edward Island fiddling traditions toward a greater emphasis on note-reading. However, McGann expands on his viewpoint by discussing the Glendale gathering of over one hundred fiddlers, in response to the *Vanishing Cape Breton Fiddler* documentary:

> During the organizing stages of the Glendale festival tune lists were handed out which all the fiddlers received prior to the mass fiddlers performance which was to take place. The emphasis in these tunes was [on] an Inverness County style of playing. While the festival didn't entirely discourage other styles of playing such as Lee Cremo's or the north side style there was a definite emphasis placed upon the Inverness repertoire. In PEI the effect of the revival upon regional variety has been something akin to the superstyle which has become commonplace in the southern United States. In PEI Acadian, Irish, and Old Time fiddling were not what Fr. MacDonald was interested in. What did occur is what caused James Hornby, in his thesis on PEI fiddling, to state that "island fiddling tradition is now being revived largely as a subsidiary of Cape Breton fiddling." What has occurred in both PEI and Cape Breton illustrates the often problematic area of revival as well as illuminates a path that I feel can illustrate the benefits that applied folklorists can have in cultural conservation.[134]

A couple of questions arise from McGann's statements. First, what did he expect would be a better way to approach the mass performance? I can understand his diplomacy in the suggestion that other styles could have been better represented. However, the event was in Glendale, a primarily Gaelic village in Inverness county, a primarily Scottish-Gaelic settled county, featuring a fiddle style descended from and more similar to that of the *majority* of immigrants and residents of the island *and* PEI—the Highland Gaelic style that was mainly featured in the *Vanishing Cape Breton Fiddler* documentary. I see McGann's point regarding equality, but I think that the "revival," if that is what it was, would basically have occurred in an Inverness County-oriented fashion regardless, as that style was more representative of the majority of Scottish-Gaelic descendants (and of what was really being lost).

Second, McGann's mention of "superstyle" development as an offshoot of fiddling revivals is interesting. One must ask why this would occur. Again, I think that "the majority rules" notion could come into play here. Perhaps, as the Inverness style was such a dominating force, and Cape Breton is in such proximity to Prince Edward Island, and PEI's Bishop Faber MacDonald (an influential priest who advocated the Cape Breton sound that was more familiar to his ears) pushed for that "sound," all such dominating factors contributed to a developed "superstyle" that included PEI with no immediately noticeable contrasting characteristics from player to player (which I think is highly questionable). We mustn't forget that the Prince Edward Island style, in its purest form, would be the same or similar to that of its Gaelic neighbour, Cape Breton. Regardless, the above suggests that perhaps a few notables, i.e., an exceptional fiddler, a domineering priest, or a respected folklorist can all contribute, in varying degrees, to both a revival *and* a notable style change (or other type of change) in an art form. Winston Fitzgerald would be one of those fiddlers. It is universally acknowledged now in Cape Breton that he was one of the main exponents of the newer, "sleeker," smoother style that has carried over to a large number of Cape Breton fiddlers.

But now we must ask two other questions: Has a "superstyle" developed in Cape Breton? Do some or most of today's generation of Cape Breton fiddlers sound the same? Carl MacKenzie, a highly respected fiddler from a prominent musical family in Washabuck, laments that this may have happened or may be happening:

> The earlier players, when I used to listen to the radio, especially CJFX, as soon as they'd play the first few notes, you could tell one from the other, like you could tell if it was Alex Francis MacKay or Theresa MacLellan, Joe MacLean, Winston, Angus Chisholm, any one of them and you could tell them very quickly. I find that the players today they play very similar, not all of them, and it takes me a while to distinguish who is playing again. No reflection on the playing, it is done very well. I would like to see a little more different style. I really miss that, the way it used to be. Maybe if people went about the books more, maybe listen to more of the older tapes, I don't know. The other thing is that back in the days of some of the older fiddlers, they didn't have so many of the influences, too, by which their music could be changed. Today there are tape recorders, CDs, TV programs, videos, etc. The fiddlers are travelling all over the globe and it's bound to change and maybe that is some of the reasons why there is not so much distinction among the players as there used to be.[135]

Some of Carl MacKenzie's remarks are valid. First, I too can often tell who is playing when I hear a recording. This is true of the older players *and* to a larger extent than MacKenzie was figuring, I can tell who of the younger players is playing when I listen to a recording. This comes, I think, with the amount of one's exposure to the various fiddlers, both old and young.

Older fiddlers who say that it is difficult to distinguish between the playing of younger players may not be listening carefully to, or listening to enough of, the various available performances to hear the stylistic idiosyncrasies in their playing. If, however, more of a "super" or "uni" style is developing, this could also be mainly due to the efforts of one or a few prominent individuals. For instance, perhaps the Fitzgerald style was generally more appealing to the majority of fiddlers in their late thirties and over (at the time of this writing), whose style in turn was favoured and emulated by the majority of the next generation, until most, perhaps, have ended up being a unified emulation of one great innovator and style purveyor. The next generation may be different. Maybe, since the 1990s revitalization, much due to the commercial success of Natalie MacMaster and Ashley MacIsaac, a majority of young players mainly exposed to Natalie's or Ashley's playing could end up modelling their playing after these individuals to the point that most in their generation could sound like MacMaster, MacIsaac and their influences.

Many other factors come into play. In addition to the few Carl MacKenzie mentions, fiddle teachers of the Cape Breton style of playing can have an effect on forming styles. If one group or generation of players are taught by one specific player, his or her stylistic applications may often be adopted and implemented by these students and eventually be accepted as the "norm" in terms of performance—if a great number of those students come to dominate the performance circuit. Admittedly, I can hear my style influence in the playing of some of my students. Too much adherence to commercial recordings by just a few artists, as opposed to the "living-culture setting" of home, ceilidh-based recordings (mentioned by MacKenzie), may also contribute to a loss of traditional repertoire and a limitation of exposure to a variety of players. Thus, a limitation in Cape Breton style influences and over-adherence by learners to those who record or who are in the limelight can also lead to a more homogenized style. Regardless of such discussion surrounding the subject of art form revival, the positive notion remains that the Cape Breton style is alive and thriving. It must also be realized that traditionally "less dominant" groups on the island have had their effect on and forged themselves into the heartbeat of the Cape Breton fiddle style.

CONCLUDING COMMENTS

This chapter has addressed various influences on the art form of Cape Breton fiddling reflecting cultural change and transmission. Adopting the universal idea that cultures change, it has been demonstrated that aspects within them must undergo change (although not always in a parallel or correlated manner). For instance, it's been acknowledged throughout that Cape Breton fiddling has evolved—but in a balanced manner. Although the Gaelic language is debilitated, the distinct Cape Breton fiddle style, steeped in a Highland Gaelic, piping and dance tradition, has continued to survive. In large part this is owing to familial, local and aural transmission of the art form through the generations with an emphasis on "integrity of continuity" and openness to self-expression. This process of enculturation, combined with other inevitable forms of transmission such as diffusion and innovation, have all contributed to a healthy result in the evolution of the art form.

Therefore, a surprising number of younger players still perform with a Gaelic sound demonstrating that chronological age does not automatically correlate to an older Gaelic sound. The Gaelic in the fiddle is derived from *stylistic application* of rhythms and accents through various ornamentations (imitating non-competitive bagpiping) and bow strokes. This is accomplished through aural learning and modelling of older players, both in a live setting and through home recordings.

This is not to say that only the old style remains. Winston Fitzgerald, likely the island's most recognized and followed innovator, has influenced many players with his smoother style. This is not a negative occurrence. Expansion of styles has been normal and balance has remained between the new and old forms of musical expression.

This chapter has also explored the evolution of Cape Breton fiddle accompaniment, as well as women and ethnic groups (other than Scottish/Irish) and their involvement in the Cape Breton fiddle tradition. Over the years, new accompanying instruments have been introduced while the piano and guitar styles have undergone some advancement in technical approach to the music. Women are more welcomed now than ever as participants while Acadians and Mi'kmaqs have adopted the style while putting individualized and possible ethnicity-related variations to the general style. Other influences, such as invented tradition/tartanism/pseudo-Scottish culture have had an effect on common cultural views of Scottishness, although the localized form of cultural transmission in the Gaelic Cape Breton fiddle tradition seems to have withstood significant negative effects. Other events and influences such as out-migration and the influence of the Dudley Street Tradition have also undeniably had an effect on Cape Breton's fiddle tradition through the exchange of techniques, tunes, dances and musicians themselves.

Musicians such as the renowned fiddler/composer Dan R. MacDonald cannot be denied their influence on the music—his contributions have demonstrated that an individual can affect the direction an art form can take. Other individuals, such as members of the clergy, were found to have been instrumental in reviving, or at least reinvigorating, fiddling in Cape Breton and PEI in the 1970s after the release of the *Vanishing Cape Breton Fiddler* documentary. The direction of the 1970s "revival" and the renowned fiddling performances in Glendale reflected what was being lost—the original

Highland Gaelic fiddle style the early settlers brought to the new Gaelic community of Cape Breton, north-eastern Nova Scotia and Prince Edward Island. The 1990s revitalization may have been even larger, in terms of popular and commercial exposure, than that of the 1970s because of the success of the Rankins, Ashley MacIsaac and Natalie MacMaster. Some older players worry that since around the time of the 1990s revitalization, a uni-style may be developing and that younger players are less and less distinguishable from one another. I argue, however, that any such possibility could be indicative of residual influences from an earlier time, from popular fiddlers like Winston Fitzgerald who played a commonly copied streamlined yet technically exceptional style. Additionally, I disagree with the notion held by some musicians and music followers that it is difficult to distinguish differences in the playing of Cape Breton's younger fiddlers. I suggest that the playing of younger players *is* distinguishable and that if we are patient and open, we can identify style differences by attending their performances and by listening to their recordings and musical maturation.

Most importantly, this chapter reveals that in the face of difficult social changes, traditional Gaelic Cape Breton fiddling has evolved soundly as an art form and its players, families and communities have also evolved to embrace and be embraced by men, women, youth, Irish descendants, Acadians, Mi'kmaq and others. In a broader context, a strong form of aural transmission based on the local community and the family has defied cultural absorption by an increasingly Anglo-centric and capitalistic society. It would be good if the limited cultural success of Cape Breton fiddling can serve as a hopeful example to other minority cultures. While the musical success is a triumph, however, the cultural success of Gaelic fiddling may be limited because the rural culture of the island has not been able to retain the language. Still, this sad possibility should not obscure our need to recognize and celebrate what an achievement in self-actualization Cape Breton fiddling represents.

FOUR

CAPE BRETON FIDDLERS
AND THEIR INFLUENCES

I n essence, Cape Breton fiddling has, up until the new century at least,
defied many odds—mass emigration, pop culture infringement, Scottish
symbolism dominating "true" Gaelic culture, urbanization, etc., have all
challenged its existence—but the power of family and community has pre-
vailed. What does the future hold? What do the island's musicians feel about
the state of the Cape Breton fiddle tradition today as the world gets closer
to being a truly global community? How have they seen it? Do they see it in
the past? How have they become a part of it? And what do they think of the
tradition as a whole? This chapter will attempt to address these questions,
exploring the views of Cape Breton traditional musicians at the beginning of
the 21st century.

The aforementioned survey will be a main source, utilizing respondents'
comments to help expand upon views, ideas and conjectures expressed in earlier chapters. Eighteen respondents completed the questionnaire. Though not
all possible respondents replied or could be included, my aim is to provide
traditional musicians and members of traditional music families the opportunity to express in detail their varied perspectives on a range of topics relevant
to fiddling. This will, hopefully, broaden views of Cape Breton fiddle music
both from within and without. I have included old and young, male and female, "commercial" and "non-commercial" respondents in order to provide a
wide spectrum of representation and viewpoints. I should also add that respondents weren't hand-picked or favoured for any other reason but conve-
nience: because their Inverness County roots are also my own, this helped me
in interpreting their often reticent comments. Moreover, this place of origin is
indisputably in the heartland of the tradition. Analysis is subjective, for I selected comments that I think stand out as reflective of the preoccupations and

interpretations that matter to musicians. Even though the survey is meant to afford those at the heart of the tradition, particularly its practitioners, the opportunity to express what they feel about the state of their art form in the new century, it will also be relevant to current and future analysts of the music precisely because the views of fiddlers are recorded in unusual detail as they respond to the cultural changes occurring in the 21st century.

LEARNING TO PLAY
AND THE INFLUENCES OF FAMILY AND LOCALS

Aside from the survey results, other useful information arose from interviews conducted by Joey Beaton, as well as from other sources. With regard to the survey questionnaire, it seemed fitting and logical to start by asking respondents about their earliest exposure to Cape Breton, Scottish and other types of music. The first question in the survey asks, "How much of (a) Cape Breton or 'Scottish' music, (b) other violin music, and (c) other kinds of music were you exposed to before taking up playing?" All respondents were exposed to Cape Breton fiddling, while most say that they had heard other kinds of music. What is notable is that most of those who answered say that they were exposed to very little or no other kinds of fiddle music. This points again, to the isolation of the island and how it helped in preserving the culture(s) of the area as well as the fiddle style. One could almost see this as the maintenance of a stylistic monopoly; there was minimal exposure to radio stations playing classical, jazz, bluegrass or Irish styles of violin music.

The next survey question asked, "Why did you learn to play the fiddle?" Informative answers again pointed to the family and local inscription. Most respondents refer to a "love" for the music while some notably say it felt "natural." Family influences are also prevalent in the responses. For instance, popular old-style player Willie Kennedy declares: "I loved listening to it and it was passed down to generations of my people." Fiddler/dancer (and presently Premier of Nova Scotia) Rodney MacDonald mentions that he "enjoyed the music," "loved to dance," that learning to play "felt natural" and that there was a "strong family influence." One respondent says that she learned "mainly because of persuasive parents, but a lot of my cousins and other family played as well." The influence of family environment can also be seen when fiddler Kinnon Beaton says, "I was hearing this music every day and knew the tunes in my head and just had this urge to learn to play." This leads me to ponder the old biological conundrum—nature versus nurture: Are the traits (other than physical ones) found in individuals genetically determined or environmentally determined? My view is that genetic predisposition should not be dismissed:

Fig. 23. Patrick, John R., Dale, Kyle and Sandra Gillis perform at SW Margaree Hall, 1990s. Photo by: David Gillis, n.d.

interestingly, respondent Mary Elizabeth MacInnis also brings up the nature/nurture idea:

> I believe the fiddling here to be a family tradition. I'm sure musical ability is inherited, to some degree. If your family is musical, you will more likely have a predisposition to being able to play. Also, if music is important to and treasured by your family, you are more likely to take an interest in it. Moreover, if you have heard the music the way family members play it, it will probably influence the way you play.

At this point, it seems fitting to discuss an interview with Mary Elizabeth's first cousin, Natalie MacMaster, one of many female players in the tradition. From a commercial viewpoint, Natalie is not only one of the most successful performers today, she is the most consistently successful of all Cape Breton fiddlers. Born in 1972, she is at the time of this work, considered a "younger" player. The importance of her family in traditional transmission goes without question. Natalie's musical roots throughout countless family connections reveal a generational web of dancers, fiddlers and Gaelic singers. She is the niece of the revered Cape Breton fiddler, Buddy MacMaster (Mary Elizabeth's father). The family connections she recites in the interview are too numerous to mention, but an excerpt reads as follows:

> [M]y uncle is Buddy MacMaster ... Archie MacMaster ... my father's grand uncle, he was a great step dancer.... [M]y grandfather's mother used to play the fiddle; she was a good fiddler.... I have a grand uncle Charlie MacMaster who died a couple of years ago in Boston; he played the fiddle a bit and he made fiddles. He used to come up to the house and one year he sent up a fiddle for

any of the MacMaster children who wanted to play it. What I remember, I went up to look at it and I liked it, and Dad showed me
"Twinkle Twinkle Little Star" and then "Space Available"; I would
have been nine-and-a-half. I started step-dancing when I was five.
I always liked it [the fiddle].... My great grandfather was from Ari-
saig; they all just loved the music, and also on that side are Alex
Francis MacKay and Dan R. [MacDonald], who was second cousin
to my father. Mom's side was quite musical as well.... My grandmother was also a great step-dancer and Mom would tell me how
she learned how to dance—Grandma would line them all up and
jig the tunes ... and teach them to step dance. My grandmother and
great grandmother's people were fiddlers and step dancers as well ...
it's kind of all connected there.

MacMaster also notes her father's influence, saying that he instructed her for
about six months and that "he's got an ear ... anytime I learn a tune or something, if there's one note wrong, he knows it and he knows how long to hold
the note and everything."[136]

Similar is clear in an interview by Joey Beaton with Ashley MacIsaac (b.
1975), who may be Cape Breton's most recognized, if infamous, fiddler. He,
too, is considered one of the "younger" players. Like Natalie MacMaster, he
has brought Cape Breton music around the world through playing and workshops, while in the process he has influenced, and been influenced by, other
musicians. MacIsaac has probably opened his music to more innovative "outside" sounds than any other fiddler to date. He has brought his traditional
art form into the realm of pop culture through trend-oriented recordings and
outrageous stage theatrics. He has accomplished this while playing his fiddle
in the traditional style, yet surrounding it with various forms of accompaniment and computer-generated samples and beats. Like Winston Fitzgerald
years before him, he is an innovator in his own way. MacIsaac was interviewed
by Joey Beaton in December of 1993, around the time of the release of his
multi-platinum recording, hi, how are you today? In his opening remarks it
is obvious that Ashley's fiddling was nourished from the beginning with a
significant family influence and musical genealogy (while the importance of
listening to tapes of older fiddlers is revealed again). Ashley's father, Angus,
and grandfather, Willie A. MacIsaac, played the fiddle, and his mother's
brothers played the pipes. Early in his life, his father would be playing tapes of
older fiddlers at home and taking Ashley to Cape Breton Fiddlers Association
practices in Baddeck and Glendale. He started step dancing at the age of five
or six.[137] Ashley's family-influenced exposure to the music is mirrored in the
experiences of other survey respondents.

Fig. 24. The MacLean family of Washabuck at Nova Scotia Highland Village. Photo by: David Gillis, n.d.

Staying on the subject of family, the survey asks respondents if they consider the fiddling form they follow to be a family tradition. Of the sixteen respondents who answered the question, every respondent said "Yes." One respondent mentioned that she felt it was a community tradition, too. Such family and community connections and influences are also depicted in the Joey Beaton interview with Alex Francis MacKay (b. 1922), of Kingsville, Inverness County. Alex Francis is recognized as an old-style Gaelic fiddler who, in contrast to most fiddlers on Cape Breton Island, speaks the Gaelic fluently.

Early in that interview, the influence of family and local musicians on Alex Francis's fiddling is revealed. His father "played a little" while his "mother was musical." Additionally, he was a cousin of Cape Breton's most celebrated composer, Dan R. MacDonald. As a youngster, MacKay notes Dan R., Gordon MacQuarrie, "Big Ronald" MacLellan and famous composer Dan Hughie MacEachern as his main influences. They in turn came from musical backgrounds.

Joey Beaton's interview with musician and composer John Morris Rankin (1959-2000) continues to reveal the importance of family and local influences and how they affect a player's absorption into the musical tradition. Aspects of enculturation, local and familial influence, diffusion, modelling and innovation are all highlighted by the following exchange:

> JMR: Through my father's side I was related to the Beatons from the (Mabou) Coal Mines. Also on my mother's side I had a grand uncle, Freddie, who played the violin.... Freddie had good timing

for a dance and I've been learning the last few years that his sister, Margaret—who'd be my grandmother—they used to travel around in the, I suppose the early 1900s and played at local dances and that sort of thing and I think Margaret, she won't admit this to me, but she played the guitar … (and piano)…. My grandfather on my father's side—his sister who's a nun—she played fiddle and I think a lot of them, especially on my father's side—they were quite apt to sing, you know, I think they were good singers from what I hear.

JB: On your father's mother's side there was music too, right?

JMR: On the Cameron side, yeah. Also Francis would be my father's uncle. And he used to play the fiddle quite a bit.

Fig. 25. Marie, Donald and Theresa MacLellan - The MacLellan Trio being introduced by Jake MacDonald at Broad Cove Scottish Concert. Photo by: David Gillis, n.d.

FIDDLING FAMILIES AND COMMUNITIES OF FIDDLERS

Mabou Coal Mines is a prime example of what are called "pockets of music," or fiddling communities, on the island. Once a thriving mining and resource-based community, this tiny coastal corner of North America has been called "the greatest cradle of Scottish culture in North America." Many Mabou-area families originate in the Lochaber district of the Scottish Highlands. The Mabou Coal Mines community became the New World home to a large segment of the musical Beaton Clan of Lochaber. Rev. Hugh A. MacDonald describes their music:

One of the unique and outstanding characteristics of the Mabou Coal Mines musical style is the Gaelic expression heard in every note.... The Coal Mines style represents an ancient traditional music that may possibly represent our best extant link to the ancient musical past of Celtic Scotland and Ireland. In this tradition, players have been trained to develop remarkably accurate musical ears in order to reproduce the old settings and arrangements ... with a complete fidelity to memory. Watching the Beatons play immediately brings to mind old paintings and engravings of the Gows and other eighteenth-century Scottish violinists. [138]

Although MacDonald's comments may be biased, they do reveal that in the instance of Mabou Coal Mines fiddling, the local transmission of style has remained very strong, perhaps unequaled by others in Cape Breton. This account, written in 1977, focuses on the late Donald Angus Beaton (1912-1982) and his son Kinnon, who in the year 2004 continues to play and compose in a style reminiscent of the old tradition, but exhibits an exciting style based upon a balanced evolution of the style. Donald Angus and Kinnon are descendants and relatives of other great fiddlers from Mabou Coal Mines, including Danny "Johnny Ranald" Beaton, Donald John "the tailor" Beaton, Johnny Ranald Beaton and Màiri Alasdair Raonuill MacDonald. Màiri Alasdair Raonuill (1897-1983) and Donald Angus's sister Janet, were two of only a noted few female players to have emerged from the earlier days of Cape Breton fiddling, although Màiri was more known for her fiddle playing. Primarily an aural

Fig. 26. The community of Mabou Coal Mines. Photo by: David Gillis, n.d.

player (ear and visual), Màiri was legendary for her style and sound. MacGillivray notes that "The bowing patterns and tune settings she mastered had their genesis in the Scotland of the 1700s, or earlier." He adds that, "the home tape recordings of 'Little' Mary have become precious property to their owners, not only because of their historical significance, but on account of the sheer joy they generate."[139]

Of course there were and are other fiddling families and communities prominently known around the island. We have to look no further than the earlier-mentioned MacMaster family from Judique that includes Buddy, Natalie, Mary Elizabeth and all of Buddy's sisters, who at one time or another would accompany him for a dance. Also, multi-instrumentalist Andrea Beaton and her step-dancing sister Allison, are Buddy's nieces, not to mention all of the relatives who came before. There are also the MacDonalds of Glendale, the Chisholms and Gillises of the Margaree and Scotsville areas, as well as the MacKenzies of Washabuck, the MacNeils of Sydney Mines, the Grahams of Judique, the MacIntyres of Inverness, the Rankins of Mabou, the MacInnises of Big Pond. The list goes on. Here we see families and communities taking pride in their culture and survival of the Cape Breton fiddle tradition.

On another note, and to broaden the definition of the term "community" in the Cape Breton fiddle tradition, a survey question asks, "Do you feel that, generally speaking, there is a sense of camaraderie and friendship among Cape Breton musicians?" All but two respondents answered and everyone responded with a resounding "Yes." This supports the notion that "community," in many senses of the word, has contributed to the continuation of Cape Breton fiddling over the years. Jackie Dunn-MacIsaac elaborates further by saying that the sense of camaraderie and friendship among Cape Breton musicians "is one part of the culture that doesn't seem to have been affected; that also contributes to the attraction and genuine nature of the music."

TEACHING AND LEARNING

One can safely assume that modes of teaching and learning have changed since the 1970s. Before then, learning the fiddle was a less formal experience. Learners were expected to watch and listen in a ceilidh or dance setting and rely on this aural approach in order to grow and develop as musicians. Of course, learners would receive pointers from experienced players in such environments. However, when the tradition was in danger of dying away in the 1970s, and the *Vanishing Cape Breton Fiddler* documentary had created increased awareness of the tradition's plight, formalized teaching and learning settings began to take prominence. This can be observed in Allister MacGillivray's interview with John MacDougall, with MacGillivray stating that, "In the early 70s, John MacDougall played a key position in aiding the resurgence of violin playing among young Cape Bretoners."[140] We see MacDougall's acknowledgement of the new teaching mode that would arise:

> Ron MacInnis woke everyone up with The Vanishing Cape Breton Fiddler.... In 1971, after the film came out, Fr. Colonel MacLeod approached me to teach; he didn't want to see this music die out! I started in February, and in July I had about thirteen children playing in a concert at Broad Cove. I was the first to start this teaching business. I taught in Inverness, Broad Cove, Mabou, Judique, Creignish, Glendale, Scotsville, Margaree Forks, and at the Gaelic College in St. Ann's. I must have taught about two hundred people—from age seven to seventy![141]

With respect to new modes of learning, a related survey question asks whether or not modes of teaching and learning Cape Breton fiddling have changed over the years and, if so, whether the results been "good" for the tradition or "bad" for the tradition? This basically refers to the setting in which someone is exposed to a traditional art form. Is the setting the newer and more formal one (a classroom), or an informal one (a ceilidh house)? Also, how is a person being taught; by written note, ear, or both modes?

Fiddler/dancer/pianist Andrea Beaton notes that teaching and learning have changed: "I'd say they changed—there are more classroom-like lessons being taught now where years ago people would have learned more on their own or by examining and hearing their elders." This more formal classroom setting, which generally brings in the written note with ear learning (as well as the instructor-student situation), was considered by most respondents as a "good thing." However, there were concerns that style and musical expression elements may be lost in the more formal setting. For example, Glen MacEachern notes that, "Any learning is 'good,' and learning has improved ... but perhaps style has been lost." This was re-stated by a high school student-player when she says of teaching and learning:

> Yes, I feel they have changed. I don't feel like it is entirely bad but they aren't that great. Now people aren't paying attention as much to how the tune is supposed to be played, but to the way it may be written.

Rodney MacDonald adds that newer teaching and learning modes are "good to some degree," but "at times there is too much emphasis on technique and not enough on what the music means ... Gaelic, dancing, etc." Mary Elizabeth MacInnis harkens back to earlier times (mentioned above), when in a "ceilidh house," during parties or visits, players could learn from listening to and watching other fiddlers. She mentions that:

They could ask questions about the tunes, composers, bowing, etc., etc. They heard their playing and observed without studio production or much accompaniment. This might have helped them to focus more intently on the art of the fiddling itself.

One should concede, however, that this can also be done in the right classroom setting, as long as the teacher and student(s) are open to a similar approach. Hopefully, this element can and will be implemented in times to come whether through formal interaction or ceilidh-type settings.

Another noticeable difference is that some enthusiasts seem to be "breaking down" the music to both teach and learn. Kinnon Beaton recognizes this as people being more analytical while Mabou-style fiddler Kenneth Joseph MacDonald describes the process as being "more scientific." Musicians/musicologists David Greenberg and Kate Dunlay have contributed a lot in this regard, much to the benefit of learners and the general public who may show an interest in the "how" of creating this style of music. However, a balance must remain—if it is overly analyzed, perhaps the "why" will be forgotten, as Rodney MacDonald has mentioned. One thing that does seem to hold true, is that talented learners will stand out regardless of the setting. As Danny Graham says, "It has been my experience that the genuinely talented ones have come to the fore both in the past and in the present regardless of teaching and learning techniques."

There were other questions in the survey that asked about modes of teaching and learning. Notably, the question, "Have you received any classical training?" yielded an overwhelming "No" from respondents (although one mentioned having received classical training on the piano). This is an obvious indication that the Cape Breton Gaelic culture has, for the most part, not allowed the classical art forms to affect its folk fiddling art form. The same is not true of Scotland, which through religious and political oppression and elitist cultural introductions, has had its fiddle style altered dramatically toward a more classically inclined sound and application. The two musical realms—folk vs. classical—have basically been kept separated, although there are certainly examples of players in Cape Breton who lean toward a classical music influence and exhibit characteristics in their playing more similar to a classical style than an "old" or Gaelic style of folk fiddling. Winnie Chafe, a well-skilled and trained musician in the classical realm, would be an example of this and, to a certain extent, Dwayne Coté. Coté is a dynamic "listening-to" violinist who can also adapt his playing to a dance setting. It is safe to say that the classical influence is less evident on the western side of Cape Breton. However, even though classical influence is not as evident stylistically, it has crept in with reference to adherence to measured times, scales and music-notated standards.

It must also be noted and reiterated, though, that many in the tradition, both younger players and older ones, have learned, and continue to learn in an aural fashion. Some have learned through a combination of the old aural way and the newer "formal lessons" approach. The realization that the Cape Breton fiddle tradition was and still is mainly an aural one stood out in the survey. For instance, in response to the question, "What, in your opinion, is more important in becoming a good Cape Breton fiddle player: having a 'good ear' or being able to read the written note?," sixteen of the seventeen who answered felt that it was more important to have a good ear while one felt that both were equally important. Notably, many Cape Breton fiddlers can both learn by ear and learn by the written note. The majority, at least until recent years, has relied on ear learning before adopting the written note as an aid. There are still teachers who recommend ear learning before the written note. For instance, I almost always teach students a tune by ear before going to the notes at the end of a session. Well-known fiddler John Donald Cameron, nephew to the late Dan R. MacDonald, was also a fiddle instructor, and does not start his students with the written note. He indicates that he tapes the music for some students: That "trains their ear; that's important."[142] Examples of aural learning, as mentioned above, come from both younger and older players, while we see the combination of newer and older learning with some of the younger ones. The importance of listening to recordings of older players should not be overlooked either. Let us look at some examples in the following.

The interview by Joey Beaton with Alex Francis MacKay reveals that MacKay began playing at the age of "fourteen or fifteen." He played at first by ear and then was tutored in reading music at the age of eighteen by "Jimmy Gillis from Margaree, a piano tuner." Soon thereafter, MacKay was playing for dances at schoolhouses and halls in Kingsville, Queensville, Glendale and Princeville, all communities near his home.

The interview with John Morris Rankin reinforces the importance of ear learning and the use of old recordings:

> JB: Tell me how your interest in Scotch music began to unfold.
>
> JMR: Well, I guess if you look back.... If you're very young and there's lots of music around the house, it's going to stick with you, I guess in most cases. When I was five years old or something, my father had tapes, reel to reel tapes, and I think when it started off, it kind of registered.
>
> JB: So the reel to reel tapes had a big impact on you?
>
> JMR: Yeah, and as well as listening to local fiddlers ... you're also exposed to other forms of traditional music, such as, you know, I

can remember listening to Clancy Brothers records … so it sort of goes from there and if you take an interest in it, it sticks.

JB: As a result of listening to the tunes and everything, I bet you were learning a lot of tunes by ear at that time.

JMR: Yeah, that's mainly what would happen. I think there are a lot of benefits to that…. It trains you to pick a lot of things up as opposed to searching something out in a book or whatever. It trains you to memorize.

Natalie MacMaster's interview reveals more of the same, but also mentions learning through formal means. For about the first year, she learned by ear before she started learning general theory from instructor-players Stan Chapman, Kinnon Beaton and Kyle MacNeil. She also refers to learning from tapes of older players:

> Yeah, now I'm getting more into listening to tapes of Angus Chisholm and Winston and Donald Angus…. And I'm getting more into that now because those are my favorite kind of tunes; you know, they've got awfully good tunes, those old ones.

The importance of old recordings in maintaining and modeling playing of traditional tunes and styles in the tradition, reiterates the continuity in learning over the generations; it shows how the older musicians have continually helped the younger players in learning and applications.

In his interview with Joey Beaton, Ashley MacIsaac reminisces about his younger years in the following (we note that Ashley, like Natalie MacMaster, was a student of Stan Chapman):

> I never picked up the fiddle before I went to Stan … I was … eight-and-a-half years old … went for two winters. Stan taught me in a way to read music … but I took piano lessons, classical, before that…. When I was eleven years old, I started listening to Buddy MacMaster a lot. The way Buddy put in his "didums" … grace notes … I could play along with a whole Buddy tape.

MacIsaac also speaks of a 1993 trip to New York where he met composer Philip Glass, another musical influence, in New York and "did music with him."

Joey Beaton redirects Ashley in the interview and the subject is turned to piano, modes of learning and styles. MacIsaac notes his previous classical lessons that helped him learn theory. At thirteen or fourteen, he "wanted to start chording" (accompanying fiddle in the Cape Breton piano style). He also states that he went to Gordon MacLean (traditional piano player) for three or four months and then "learned to chord off a tape of Joey [Beaton]." MacIsaac then speculates on tradition, style and the effects of local individual musicians on style development:

> I try to combine a bit of everybody in it ... I heard someone say once—"if tradition is to remain, the new has to become tradition." [Today's Cape Breton piano playing] grew from where it was before. John Morris [Rankin] ... he has his own stamp on it as well....
> And just that little bit of difference keeps it interesting enough to keep people interested and keep the traditional alive.

Beaton also asks MacIsaac about bowing, how he learned it, and its importance in the execution of the music. Ashley simply mentions "Buddy" (MacMaster) and his strong upward bow strokes. He adds, "I don't know if I got influenced or just did it." Many fiddlers would probably have the same reaction. Since such a young age, many fiddlers seem to be so socialized to the music that many techniques seem to come naturally.

MacIsaac also discusses tempo, and balancing tradition with commercializing the music in the following:

> Tempo is very important, traditionally and for dancing and listening to ... there are other times where I play around [home] or for a square dance circuit; I'm consistent.... Last week, at an alternative rock bar ... I was to play for teenagers ... I played a lot different there than in Glencoe ... up tempo ... there was no tradition in that.

This comment begs the question—was MacIsaac's intent to play traditional Cape Breton fiddle music or to put on an exciting alternative spectacle for an alternative crowd? His response, that there was "no tradition" in what he did, supports the latter. Nonetheless, he remains a superb traditional fiddle player. Is there danger for the tradition in such performances? In the local context, perhaps not, as long as young fiddlers continue to learn as those before them did—with a strong family and local influence with a focus on aural learning.

THE FIDDLING GREAT AND THE KITCHEN FIDDLER

There are players who have stood out in the scene as being community musical icons, representing and possessing musical abilities and qualities that separate them from other players, the latter of whom were often referred to as "fidhlear chuidsin," or kitchen fiddlers. Of late, the difference between the two has become more clouded than in previous years. Cape Breton communities certainly took and still take pride in knowing their music. Performers have always been aware that they have been playing for a knowledgeable local audience, one that respects the music and requires certain qualities to be displayed in musical performance. Those musical expectations have gone on locally for generations and they are more "known" through listening instead of through any form of written standardization. Expectations and analysis have occurred in the context of local aural transmission of the form, its maintenance occurring through ignoring a standardized approach. That has perhaps kept individual styles and expression intact in Cape Breton.

Certain things are "listened for" in a performance that are indicators of a player being anywhere from a "poor" to "great" traditional style player. However, there has been less risk of a "uni-style" forming in Cape Breton because its folk culture has virtually ignored an approach of written melodic standardization often found in piping or fiddling contests that de-emphasize oral learning of art forms. In essence, there has been an oral and aural standardization, passed through musical families and listeners that still allows for individualized expression, which is more visible in the Cape Breton folk music tradition than in others that have become more formalized.

What Kennedy describes below, with reference to traditional piping, is also true of Cape Breton fiddling. He notes that there is less chance of losing characteristic features of musical art forms when a less formal and bureaucratic approach is used in analyzing performance quality:

> Within the collective consciousness of a folk culture such a development is unlikely. Everyone, and not just the artists, is immersed in cultural art forms from the time of their birth to the time of their death. The society internalizes an enormous set of complex and often quite subtle standards regarding the presentation of these arts. Interaction between the musician and this well-informed community is constant and intimate. The community expects pipers to deliver a functional community service and to a very high standard and pipers know that their reputation will be won or lost based on how well they provide that service. Because there is no formal, standardized method of training, there is little emphasis on process, but because the audience is knowledgeable and actively engaged with the music (for example as dancers), a great deal of emphasis is placed on result. The power to set standards never rests with a small few but is invested in the larger cultural community.[143]

The last point is, I fear, becoming less visible over the last decade with regard to Cape Breton fiddling. I suggest that the views of a few are now getting out into the community and the less localized consciousness of "new" Cape Breton music fans from regions outside the island.

This collective few are more vocal about their views than many who are more qualified or experienced in the tradition. This new collective are often not musicians themselves (although there are some with decent ears that aren't players). In this group I also include "newcomers" to the tradition who have not been exposed to the tradition long enough to formulate completely informed opinions or analysis, or have been influenced by musicians or "experts" who are out of touch with the constantly progressing traditional music scene in Cape Breton. That is, many older spokespeople or players who are speaking out about the music and the playing of younger musicians today are rarely seen at pubs, festivals or fiddle music events throughout the island. These events are where younger players are often employed and are heard by "regular" followers and purveyors of the tradition—some of those younger players having become or blossoming into fiddling greats. It is a shame that some of the emerging and well-known younger players are chastised while they may actually exhibit more qualities of a fiddling great than other, less talented players who may be speaking negatively of them. I should also add there are recent Cape Breton music analysts whose input deserves to be noted. They include David Greenberg, Kate Dunlay and Liz Doherty, and I am comfortable with quoting their views because of their extensive knowledge of musical style development, analysis and applications as they are fine musicians themselves.

Liz Doherty refers to "fiddling greats" as "Master Cape Breton fiddlers" or "star fiddlers." They often reveal certain elements of style that stand out, such as left-handed embellishments, intonation, expanding techniques, tempo and timing and bowing. A fiddling great would generally exhibit a solid command of execution of all of these features with relative ease and with a manner of appeal to the audience. Also of importance, but now seemingly less emphasized, is that a fiddling great displays a high level of correctness in tune interpretations, although being receptive to innovation is not to be completely ignored. Correctness is difficult to define, but again, the element of result, as noted earlier in Kennedy's comments, is what helps the term to be realized. As Doherty puts it, "associated with the immigrants' disposition towards maintaining traditions of the old country, is the obligation to maintain authenticity. In music terms this translates to correctness."[144] In other words, correctness is the level of aural ability to absorb a tune as closely as possible to the locally accepted norm.

One of the survey questions asked: "Do you feel that being a 'correct' player is important?" Of the twelve respondents who answered the question, eight replied, "Yes" while four said "No." A couple of things stood out in their comments. In the group that felt that being a correct player wasn't important, two revealed the importance of individual style, which is still visible on the island, as mentioned throughout this work. For instance, one respondent said, "Everyone should play their own way and their own style, regardless of how society will take them in." This is interesting, although this person was defining correctness in a broader stylistic context. Someone else answered, "I think that having your own unique, but traditional style is important." Notably, these were the two youngest respondents in the survey and they were referring more to style than tune interpretation. Some who felt that correctness was important helped raise the points noted above. As stated earlier, correctness is difficult to define but there are idiomatic boundaries that must be acknowledged. As long as a player is within a certain "accepted norm" for a tune interpretation, his or her correctness will not usually be challenged by the listener. For example, Rodney MacDonald says that being correct is important, "but individual ways of playing a tune is what makes our music unique. There can be twenty ways of playing a tune 'correct' [sic]." Kinnon Beaton re-emphasizes the importance of staying true to the notes of a tune, but also of putting your own "stamp" on it:

> Note-wise I think it is important. I guess I'd say to a certain point. As far as bowing tunes the way they are in books, I don't really agree with—I think you should bow it in your own way to give the tune your own flavour. Otherwise, it will become too mechanical.

Another consideration in favour of correctness is the respect and adherence to the original intent of the tune's composer. Again, we could refer back to Liz Doherty's conjecture about the importance of authenticity and maintaining what was given by those of earlier generations. For example, Mary Elizabeth MacInnis felt that being a correct player was important: "Otherwise, we will lose the flavour of our music and the uniqueness of the music contributed by different composers." Music enthusiast/fiddler and Gaelic singer Danny Graham adds that, "I think it is important in terms of preserving the integrity of the tunes, but rigid adherence can inhibit creativity and individuality."

The noticeable level of difference in correctness between two players is often a distinguishing factor separating a fiddling great from a kitchen fiddler (though I do not mean to disparage or degrade the latter, who are important to the making and maintenance of the tradition). This observation illustrates why some fiddlers, although tasty enough in style, are regarded by aurally informed, experienced listeners and players with keen ears, as kitchen fiddlers. Although decent players, these fiddlers may not have the accepted correctness in their playing that some of their fiddling cohorts would favour. That is, their interpretation of a tune may be noticeably distant from the accepted local norm, indicating a weakness in "ear" learning, an important part of being considered a "great" player. It seems, however, that this notion is not as prominent anymore.

Kitchen fiddlers of the past, as some of their more established fiddling contemporaries have passed on, are perhaps now being considered "greats" in the tradition, although their level of aural interpretation (ear-learning ability), intonation (especially on harder keys), liveliness or "danceability" are questionable. In other words, their *blas* (taste) is there, but they are perhaps a bit too "scratchy" or "draggy" (slow tempo, poor for dancing) in their playing. They remain, to some observers (and those familiar with the above notion), nice players—good kitchen fiddlers, but not one of the great dance players with a good command of some "listening" tunes; or community musical icons similar to those from earlier times, distinguishable by exhibiting command of the elements of style covered above. This is not intended to mean that ear players cannot and have not been considered fiddling greats. In fact, many fiddling greats have not been music readers (Brenda Stubbert for instance) while many of them have had a good command of both oral and written interpretation. The key factor here is that fiddling greats have exceptional ears that display a high level of correctness in their playing. Kitchen fiddlers often do not have this ability and characteristic.

Kennedy's reference to traditional piping also applies to the fiddling in Cape Breton and the discussion of fiddling greats and kitchen fiddlers. He describes the importance of "the ability to please active participants in the culture, such as providing creative, functional dance music and tasty interpretations of traditional tunes while remaining within recognized idiomatic boundaries."[145] A kitchen fiddler often exemplifies one or two of the above criteria, but lacks another, that most often being the last requirement—remaining within recognized idiomatic boundaries. One such boundary consists of staying true to the locally accepted original "shell" of the tune, capably interpreting it and showing no weakness in ear/oral learning ability. If a player is not true to this, it is almost always because he or she lacks a good ear. A fiddling great or knowledgeable listener may say something like, "She's lively, but she's got the tunes all wrong," or "He's a nice player, but he's too 'draggy' for a dance and he's got different versions of the tunes." Since the 1990s, distinguishing the exact difference between a kitchen fiddler and a fiddling great is not as common a cultural practice as it used to be. Perhaps this is because some of the more talented fiddlers and regular listeners are less vocal in the last two decades and the views of other, less experienced listeners, have become more visible today.

"LISTENING-TO" FIDDLERS VS. DANCE FIDDLERS

Joey Beaton's interview with John Donald Cameron consists of opinions on a variety of subjects pertinent to the musical tradition of Cape Breton.

Again, the role of family and locals are important, especially in the formative years. Dan R. MacDonald's influence is easily recognized. Interestingly, Cameron comments on the trend of dance playing among the young musicians, as opposed to the "listening-to" players of earlier years such as Dan Hughie MacEachern and "Little" Jack MacDonald. Notably, Little Jack was a classically inclined player who often preferred to perform difficult pieces. MacEachern was a master of such difficult tunes as "Tullochgorm," a tune requiring great bow control. I agree that the tradition has embraced dance music as much or more now than ever. However, one should not underestimate the ability of some younger players to perform "listening" tunes and sessions. One need only listen to Natalie MacMaster's recording "My Roots Are Showing" or attend a live performance by Troy MacGillivray. There is also the possibility that, under the assumption that the music is generally a complement to the dance, the growth in dance playing may be more similar to trends of the late 18th and 19th centuries than those of the time frame and type of playing Cameron is lamenting. Doherty seems to agree when she suggests that "changes in tempo over the last half century have complemented developments in the dance." What Cameron did not point out is that the "listening-to" player of the 1950s that he laments, is a much newer addition to the Cape Breton music scene—which may be coming full circle in this regard. For instance, Doherty theorizes that the 1900s saw three types of players: first, dance players, then the "co-existing dance and listening" player and then the "syncretic" fiddle players. She notes the combining of the two:

> The style of playing and, as far as it allows, the repertory associated with both contexts, has become synthesized, with much of the tempo and rhythmic propulsion being maintained in contexts removed from the dance, supplemented by a technical dexterity previously associated with listening players.[146]

The technical dexterity and overall ability of the last couple of generations of Cape Breton fiddlers must not be underestimated. One older and well-known musician (whom I won't name) who has performed with many fiddlers over the last fifty years has told me that the overall performance abilities of today's younger players are generally greater than those of their predecessors.

The subject of increased tempo was mentioned in the Cameron interview. Also noteworthy were his remarks that some (though not all) who are listening to the music do not really understand it and that since the music has become more commercialized, there is a tendency to play it faster for the commercial audience. This could very well be true, though these statements could theoretically lead to a broader argument regarding art and its purveyors within cultures. The idea that art is understood only by the few, especially the artists, is still common. It implies that the uninformed and uneducated do not fully understand (which, I confess, I may have reinforced regarding the fiddling great and kitchen fiddler distinction); in other words, the central truth and value found in the art is dictated by the superior purveyors. John Shepherd says that in this view, one would discover:

> a disdain for the critical abilities of the "culturally untutored." Although such disdain is necessarily implicit in the very notion of a centrally defined culture, it is again interesting to note that the attitude became more deeply entrenched at the beginning of the 19th century.... Coupled with the belief that art reveals higher truths fathomable only by a minority of superior minds is the idea that these minds are responsible for preserving the cultural values of society. This idea is as prevalent in [the] 20th century as it was in the 19th.... It is further interesting to note that this elitist attitude towards culture is based on the questionable premise that society is divided between those who have inherently superior, and those who have inherently inferior, intellects.... Not surprisingly, the attitudes so far described are to be found in the musical as well as in the literary worlds.[147]

John Donald Cameron's remarks were not intended to be elitist and should not be taken as so. I can attest that as a personal acquaintance of mine, Cameron exhibits no such attitudes. The point is that a highly theoretical cultural viewpoint can be inferred from his previous comments, which applies to art forms and cultures throughout the world. A simplified conclusion would be that those who perform and those who listen will select what appeals to them. The winning formula would be the balance of both interests; therefore, the surviving music will be that which is embraced by a combination of both realms; that combination, at least into the early 2000s, seems to be the leaning of the audience and player toward the importance of having a "good swing" for dancing, as step-dancing continues to be integral to most local performance contexts, but also noteworthy technical abilities.

CAPE BRETON FIDDLING TECHNIQUES AND VIEWS ON TEMPO

A number of the fundamentally important techniques unique to the Cape Breton style will be described as simply as possible. One should note that the characteristics described are those generally practiced. Of course, these techniques are selectively applied by Cape Breton fiddlers; in other words, fiddlers choose to use them in instances of individual selection and taste. Although individual performances vary, "the basic Cape Breton 'sound' is unmistakable."[148]

Upstroke

To complement dancing, bowing is very rhythmic, often one bow stroke being applied in one direction for one note. Upstrokes are often as powerful as down strokes with a variety of pressures being exerted on the bow for dynamics and accents. A type of reel called the strathspey features "a characteristic stuttering rhythm" called the "Scotch Snap." The up-driven bow, supposedly developed in the 1700s by Niel Gow, can often be applied in strathspey playing. The tip of the bow takes the first sixteenth note, leaving the rest of the bow to take the next three notes staccato, or, all alone, in one bow direction. Pressure is forced upon the bow throughout the three notes until the last sixteenth note is heavily accented.[149] The Scotch snap provides an accent similar to that found in Gaelic song and pipe music.[150]

Cuts

Another standard feature of Cape Breton fiddling is "cuts." These are a sequence of notes of the same pitch applied by using the wrist to snap or shake the bow through the series. Cuts are

> usually employed at the discretion of the player in an attempt to add a degree of complexity to simpler aspects of the melody line. A three-note "cut" may be bowed in either of two methods: (1) with alternating up-and-down strokes of the bow, or (2) with one stroke in a single direction.[151]

Grace notes

Various embellishments are used with the fingers of the hand holding the fiddle. Grace notes are used by many fiddlers. These are usually quick notes applied above or below, and in conjunction with a melody note. They add a sort of chirping sound that mimics bagpipe playing. Vibrato, a pressure-release, pressure-release sequence done quickly by the fingers, is shorter than in classical music and is a relatively new addition to the tradition, becoming visible as late as the 1940s and gaining prominence in the 1970s.[152] A variation of this, where a finger is quickly pressed on the string and then released and returned back to the string is sometimes done to embellish the melody; this provides an "older" sound. This technique, combined with "doubling," where the fourth finger is placed on the next lower string to close an open string note (making the doubled note "beefier" in melodic texture), also helps to bring out an "older" sound.

Drones

Drones are a common feature of the fiddle style as well. These are played both above and below the melody. Open string notes are often hit in conjunction with equal, applied notes. For instance, a D string may often be applied simultaneously with a fingered D note on the next string. An open E string drone is often heard beside melodies played on the next string (A), too. The ornaments, drones and selected accents are all said to mimic the pipes and Gaelic accents in mouth music and songs. The total combination produces a haunting and complicated art form, rooted in Gaelic, dance and the old musical sounds of Cape Breton and Scotland.

Double-up

In older times, in the absence of accompaniment and/or electronic amplification, players would "double up," often simultaneously playing alternate octaves of tunes as well as playing in alternate tunings that would increase volume. Joey Beaton's interview with Alex Francis MacKay touches on double fiddling and modes of increasing volume, in order to satisfy the dancer/listener:

> JB: How did you get the volume?
>
> AFMK: It wasn't easy with one fiddle. I usually teamed up with John Willie, Dan Hughie, Dan R....
>
> JB: How much money would you make?
>
> AFMK: A couple of dollars ... they knew a lot of music ... they helped me, especially Dan R.

Bow stroke

The interview continues with Beaton asking about changes that MacKay may have seen in the music since 1937:

> AFMK: A big change in the timing ... faster ... when you play too fast, you can't bring the music out as well as at the correct timing.
>
> JB: And the bowing?
>
> AFMK: Some don't use the bow too much ... the long bows bring the volume out.

Here, MacKay is obviously referring to condensed bow strokes, visible in the playing of Winston Fitzgerald, and evident in the playing of Jerry Holland and Howie MacDonald, superb players who would readily admit Fitzgerald's influence on their playing. Arguably, though they often reveal shortened strokes, these players are quite powerful, providing ample volume for today's performance settings, and are very versatile in stylistic application.

Violin and bow-hold

Again, with regard to techniques, violin and bow-hold should be discussed. In the interview with Joey Beaton, Natalie MacMaster discusses how she holds the fiddle. At first, MacMaster held the fiddle with her wrist against its neck.

This is the way most Cape Breton fiddlers have held it and it is adequate for most tunes in the repertoire which are in the first position, the fingering position closest to the scroll (top) of the fiddle. The classical and "proper" method of holding the violin is to grip the neck with the wrist in the air, away from the instrument.

> NMM: I had just changed the way I play with regards to how I hold the fiddle. I played for ten years with my hand leaning on the fiddle. And my thumb on the bow was not bent, so I had to bend it…. Over the years I noticed that other fiddlers of different styles would hold it this way so I decided I'd give it a good try … make things easier for you … the best move I ever made…. I used to have quicker vibrato…. Now it's slower…. And I think it also helps the tone a bit…. There's a fellow coming up from Vancouver … Chalmers Doane [a music teacher]. [It was] through Mr. Doane that I learned more about the theory of music. Everything helps; even if you play another instrument, it will help the fiddle … awareness is one of the best things…. If you ever want to learn things the proper way and stuff, you can't afford to try and just say, "to heck with that …," because it takes so long to learn. Stan [Chapman] always told me I should be playing with my hand up…. If you ever want to play certain tunes or back up a band—It's in me and no matter what way I hold the fiddle it's not going to change my music; it's just an aid.

MacMaster reveals some interesting viewpoints. Many fiddlers and instructors of Cape Breton fiddle music generally recommend or are open to holding the fiddle and bow in a grip of self-preference and comfort. That view would reason that personal grips (most especially on the bow) may allow for individual style development and evolution.

One common Cape Breton method of holding the bow is with the stick against the upper index finger, thumb tucked under and possibly touching the index and often held by the next one or two fingers. Though not the correct classical manner, it may likely be a more suitable grip for certain bowing techniques and bow pressure variations inherent to the style.[153] The fiddle grip itself would not seem to make much difference either way, although a technique known as "doubling" (the fourth finger is placed on the string next to the open "melody" string, to produce a note of equal value to add volume and sound texture) may be easier with the non-classical, common Cape Breton grip. There are arguably strengths and weaknesses to both methods. What is worthy of note is that MacMaster's increasing contact with other styles and "experts" have "swayed" her view from the common view held by many in her tradition. Her word choice, (i.e., "the proper way") leaves one to believe that she has been open to views from outside the tradition. MacMaster has been able to better herself musically in her application; however, her natural talent and ability and firm rootedness in the tradition certainly have contributed to her transition without affecting her style. The results for a newcomer to the tradition with "proper" training, as opposed to aural learning, would most likely be different and not as effective.

Views on tempo

As we saw earlier in Alex Francis MacKay's interview, there are concerns among players and enthusiasts in the tradition that there has been an increase in playing tempo. He has since 1937. In fact, this notion of faster playing seems to be the most significant change noticed by MacKay in this interview. Why this has occurred (if it really has) may be in conjunction with changes in dancing—a possibility that Doherty surmised earlier in this chapter. One point I should make is that the Gaelicization (adding step-dancing to square dance figures) may have been a later development in the Cape Breton traditional music scene than some may figure. Elizabeth Beaton, who would have been attending these dances in the 1930s, has commented that the attendees didn't "step" through the sets in those early days. This could indicate that a slower tempo in the music may not have affected the applications of the sets in their early development. Perhaps, as stepping was integrated, a complementary increase in tempo may have occurred in the playing of some fiddlers to accommodate the step-dancing. Also, change in tempo could correlate to society itself—efficiency and speed of application in any task seems to be more valued now. Or perhaps it is that younger dancers, both as individual performers, and at dances, prefer a livelier tempo; this may have been a trend since as early as the 1930s. Dunlay concurs that

> [a]nother trend in Cape Breton which has also occurred in other traditions is the tendency to play faster. Some fiddlers suggest that faster playing is an Acadian trait, because a number of the faster players have been of French descent. However, it is more likely a matter of individual taste.[154]

John Donald Cameron agrees:

> Tempo-wise, I feel they play much faster now ... even dance music is played faster.... In general terms, it's better to keep the tempo down.... Perhaps because today the music is much more commercial than it was in the 50s and 60s. Perhaps that would dictate it to be played faster ... especially when the music becomes commercial, the people you're playing for.... As long as it's fast. A lot of the fiddlers, the way they play, reminds you of Don Messer.

> JB: What are the advantages of playing in the proper tempo?

> JDC: When you play the tune fast, you missed the point the com-
> poser is making; the accidentals, the expression that goes in certain
> phrases in the tunes.... It (composing) comes from the soul and all
> you really believe ... it comes from the soul.[155]

Maybe faster tempo is not a major issue. Possibly, dancers and fiddlers have
become more dexterous and equipped to perform their art forms acceptably
at a faster pace. The "speed" issue may never disappear or be fully explained.
One concern, however, is that a perceived increase in tempo is often attributed
to the current generation of younger fiddlers in the age range of nineteen to
the early forties. This suggestion, in my opinion, is not completely accurate;
these fiddlers have been influenced by those before them. The tempo increase
(if it is to be considered a significant change) can be noted in players of an earlier generation—players like Angus Chisholm, Winston Fitzgerald and those
after them:

> Angus Chisholm has already been identified as a progressive figure
> in terms of tempo increase, standing midway between the old stan-
> dards, and directing the path of the new. Thus while it is becom-
> ing habitual to chastise the current young generation of fiddlers for
> their inclination towards faster tempos, it should be remembered
> that again, the initial impetus in this direction can be traced back
> to fiddlers of an earlier generation, who now serve as the influence
> point for today's players.[156]

An observation by my father, Danny Graham, also promotes the idea that the
tempo concern existed with an earlier generation: "The first time Winston
came to a dance in Judique the dancers on the floor were complaining that
they couldn't keep up to him." He also suggests that tempo differed even between communities, saying that, "The Margaree area fiddlers were known for
a quicker tempo before those in any of the other areas."[157]

Additionally, some players may have readjusted their tempos at different stages of their playing careers. Referring to her father's (Donald Angus
Beaton's) playing—for dances, Mary Graham says, "In the late fifties, Daddy
picked up the pace." Again, this may have coincided with the increase in stepping throughout the sets. Meanwhile, she also notes that his tempo on home
session recordings (where he was playing a few tunes in the house) differed
from his playing for dances. The tempo, she noted, was quicker at dances.[158] I
have observed that livelier players, who play the music at a quicker tempo than
the draggy players, have better-attended dances and more people dancing at
their gigs. It is difficult to gauge how extreme any perceived change has been.
Perception of tempo could also be affected by someone's age—as one gets
older, the "danceability" of the music may become more difficult, although
perhaps it isn't played any faster than when that person danced years before.

In Dunlay and Greenberg's tune transcriptions in *Traditional Celtic Violin Music of Cape Breton: The DunGreen Collection* are provided as interpreted by various players from commercial and home recordings. What I find ironic is that the highest tempo strathspeys and reels in the collection were played by mostly "older" players. "Angus Allan and Dan J's Strathspey," played by Dan J. Campbell (b. 1895) and Angus Allan Gillis (b. 1897) had a tempo of 202 beats per minute. In contrast, "Miss Ann Moir's Birthday Strathspey," played by Natalie MacMaster (the second youngest fiddler featured in the publication, (b. 1972) clocked in at 177 bpm. The highest tempo reels featured were also performed by older players. Angus Chisholm (b. 1908) played "The Bird's Nest Reel" at 122-125 bpm. Following this was Angus Chisholm's interpretation of "Cottonwood Reel" at 116-121 bpm. The third-highest tempo reels (119 bpm) come in as a tie between Alex Gillis (b. 1900) who played "Pigeon on the Gate Reel" and Donald MacLellan (b. 1918), who played "Put me in the Big Chest Reel." In contrast, two of the youngest players, besides Natalie MacMaster, featured in the collection, Ashley MacIsaac (b. 1975) and Kinnon Beaton (b. 1956), whose reel interpretations were included in this publication, performed their reels at slower tempos. For instance, "Mary's Fancy" was played by MacIsaac at 113 bpm while Beaton performed "The Thunderbolt" at 116 bpm.

The tempos compiled were quite accurate as, Dunlay notes, "metronome timings were taken using a tape player with adjustable speed: the speed was adjusted to match 'A'= 440. Although the tuning was probably not always standard, on some of the older tapes especially, some assumption had to be made" while "the presence of piano accompaniment on most of the recordings makes this assumption more valid."[159] Perhaps there will always be people in the tradition saying that some young players are playing too fast. Similar arguments have most likely existed since the 1700s. For instance, in the introduction of the Skye Collection of the Best Strathpeys and Reels in 1887, Keith Norman MacDonald suggests that, "One word of caution may here be given against the tendency that exists at the present day to play this class of music a great deal too fast."[160] Although this comment was made after most Highland emigrations to Cape Breton occurred, it shows that the tempo issue has been argued for more than a century and is certainly not cut-and-dried. Ultimately, as long as step-dancing remains alive and a part of regular performances and gatherings, an overall balance in tempo should be maintained.

What does all of this mean? Younger Cape Breton fiddlers are not always playing at faster tempos than their forbears did, although at times they do. Variations in tempo seem to vary from individual to individual, as we have just noted, and situation to situation, whether that be a fiddler relaxing and playing a few tunes in the home for their own amusement or "drivin'er" at a square dance for a crew of youthful step-dancers. Tempo is more deserving of an individual analysis than a general or generational analysis—the debate will continue. One of Cape Breton's most revered players—now considered an older player—was once asked, "Do you think the younger players are playing too fast now?" His response at the time was, "That's what they [some of the fiddle music followers] used to say about me when I was young."[161]

OTHER MUSICAL INFLUENCES

As has been observed throughout, a large number of influences have contributed to the evolution of the Cape Breton fiddle tradition whether they be piping, Gaelic language, ethnicity, out-migration, family, clergy, revivals, or local players. Interviews have shown that even purveyors of other genres have influenced some musicians, whether they be Phillip Glass (Ashley MacIsaac), Chalmers Doane (Natalie MacMaster), the Clancy Brothers (John Morris Rankin), or Don Messer (Wilfred Prosper). Even travel has influenced some musicians, such as John Morris Rankin whose earlier travelling experiences with other fiddlers, like the 1976 trip to the Cultural Olympics in Montreal, got him "involved with other musicians which would serve as a good influence...." Diffusion and enculturation are undoubtedly experienced at such events.

We shall now take a more in-depth look at contemporary influences such as other styles—like the Irish—other influential players, composition, popular music, radio and the importance of old session recordings. Generally speaking, the Cape Breton fiddle tradition comprises old Scottish and locally composed tunes. However, some tunes have been "borrowed" from, or are shared with, other styles and forms of music. There is concern that there are too many tunes being absorbed from other traditions. I would point out, however, that although new tune introductions from other styles affect the tradition through providing freshness and "new sounds" (which may or may not be desirable, depending on the listener) they do not, conclusively cause any stylistic changes in Cape Breton fiddle playing (unless application and scales are noticeably different). Doherty supports this view:

> Often repertoire is picked up without stylistic change ... through the Cape Breton symphony, some of the tunes by major Cape Breton composers have been transmitted to Scotland, and Scottish and Shetland compositions have been transmitted back to Cape Breton.[162]

What is often overlooked or not understood is that many tunes, especially jigs, have been borrowed from the Irish tradition.[163] Melody Cameron notes that some Irish tunes have been added to Cape Breton musicians' repertoires and that a Cape Breton fiddler will take an Irish tune and play it in the Cape Breton style.

With reference to the Irish tradition, in the Beaton interview Natalie MacMaster discusses a trip to Ireland by a Cape Breton contingent of musicians. In her comments we can see the influence of older players and the possibilities of diffusion as the two traditions interact. Beaton begins by asking her about her impressions of Sean McGuire, one of the great influential Irish musicians (who has since passed on):

> NMM: He's getting old; 70s, maybe. He's past his prime. But the performance he put on was just fabulous; all the fancy goings on, you know.... The last night we were there we had some time to mess around with all the other musicians and we all got together in the lobby in the hotel ... we went all day from after church until the wee hours of the morning ... it was all ourselves, the Cape Breton fiddlers and the Irish musicians that had been with us for the weekend.... [T]he nice thing about it was that all the Cape Breton fiddlers were together and that doesn't happen too often when we can just sit down and enjoy one another's music ... but it was really nice to spend a weekend with your idols.

Composing tunes has been a vital part of the tradition. With regard to composition, the survey asks: "Do you think that composition (people composing tunes) is important to the tradition? If so, how?" All but one respondent answered and all answered that composition was important to the tradition. Generally, the musicians felt that composition keeps the tradition "fresh" and "alive" and gives the players more of a "variety" of tunes to play. Jackie Dunn-MacIsaac makes the point that the tunes themselves must have that certain "sound" or structure that fits within the tradition. The tradition, at least until now, seems to have been able to "weed out" the tunes that don't fit so well with the general sound: "It is important to have fresh new repertoire in the fiddle culture as long as the tunes continue in the same general style."

After covering composition, the survey continues by asking, "With regard to Cape Breton fiddling, who have been your greatest influences and why?" Many names were given and are too numerous to list here. What is worthy of note, however, is that all of the respondents seemed to have named earlier family members or players a bit older or a generation before them. Traditions continue, guided by family and those who came before. A couple of musicians, however, did refer to players younger than themselves. That shows a respect for capable young players, who are not necessarily as experienced as some older players, but have a "touch" or ability that is acknowledged by older players. For instance, Kinnon Beaton says:

> In earlier years when I was learning, you would look up to the older fiddlers—Donald Angus, Buddy, Winston, Dan R., Dan Hughie. Later on you watch a new wave of fiddlers coming on and pass you by.

I don't know if anyone is passing Kinnon Beaton by, but he does reveal that there are some experienced players with a respect for the playing of some younger ones and that there is, to a certain extent, support and camaraderie within and among the musical community in Cape Breton.

John Donald Cameron (in the Joey Beaton interview), who at this juncture would be considered an older fiddler, expressed a number of noteworthy views on playing influences. John Donald began playing at the age of thirteen and as early as the 1940s recalls that he and his family "were hearing recordings of Little Jack, Dan R., Angus Allan Gillis and Angus Chisholm on 78 recordings" on the CJFX radio station. He also recalled listening to Tena Campbell's fiddling on CJCB Sydney's Cotter's Saturday Night and Angus Chisholm's fifteen-minute program on the same station in the late 1940s and early 50s. Therefore, commercial recordings were affecting up-and-coming fiddlers then as they do today. Of course, home recordings have also been found to be significant.

Two questions in the survey ask, "Are commercial recordings valuable to the tradition? If so, how?" And "Are home recordings valuable to the tradition? If so, how?"

All of the respondents agreed that both types of recordings are valuable to the tradition. Below are the main points made. Commercial recordings provide:

- An avenue of exposure for more people and expatriate Cape Breton music fans to hear and appreciate the music.
- A way to expose different general and individual styles.
- Exposure and more recognition for younger artists and lesser known older artists.
- Good recording quality for present and future generation listeners.
- Practiced, polished, high-quality playing and accompaniment.
- A "goal" for many young musicians to keep them motivated.
- A tool for learning old and new tunes.
- Added income for professional artists.

+ An avenue for artists to explore their musical creativity with new "sounds" and approaches to the music.

Basically, respondents noted that old home recordings were valuable to the tradition for some of the same reasons; mainly numbers 1, 2 and 7 above. A few surmised that some recordings were more valuable to the tradition than the commercial recordings. Some reasons include the capturing of more authentic atmosphere of style; the less formal, more relaxed performance styles; and the obvious privilege of being able to hear older players who haven't recorded commercially or have since passed away. All of these reasons would in turn allow for a truer picture of the tradition and the players themselves.

In summary, home recordings are valuable to the tradition for at least a half-dozen reasons:

+ An avenue of exposure for more people and expatriate Cape Bretoners.

+ A way to expose general and individual styles.

+ A tool for learning old and new tunes.

+ Excellent examples of showing a true traditional atmosphere in which the music is played.

+ A way of capturing the music in a "free," relaxed manner.

+ Important tools for younger players to model their playing from that of older musicians who grew up closer to the Gaelic culture.

The subject of modelling styles from the playing of older fiddlers is important and is also raised in the John Morris Rankin interview. First, Joey Beaton details Rankin's "tremendous command of the bow," his "quick little sixteenth notes here and there," and some "quick little cuttings." He asks if Rankin learned these idiosyncrasies by listening to older tapes or through self-exploration. John Morris notes that both methods contributed. Beaton then goes on to discuss certain tunes common to the "Mabou Coal Mines" style of fiddling:

> JB: I've heard tapes of you and my mother [Elizabeth] and if you didn't know it was you playing, you'd say, 'Well, that's Donald Angus and Elizabeth playing…. It's so Mabou Coal Mines geared, the whole thing.

> JMR: Yeah. I think I remember making that particular tape you're talking about. Somebody was suggesting to play those tunes, eh. And it just seemed to come natural to play like that. 'Cause Donald Angus was a very big influence. And I think a lot of it was because we had those old reel to reels. And to me, if I could play like that or half as good as that, that would be … an accomplishment to me.

JB: You play that type of music, but you put your own stamp on it.

JMR: I hope that's the case, because you don't really want to be imitating somebody.... And you always have to have an influence, and I think that's a fact.... It's very hard to just grow up with a distinct style from somebody else; you have to have influences.

Other influential fiddlers were noted. They included Theresa MacLellan, Jerry Holland, Winston Fitzgerald, and in particular John Campbell, whose style was "very much a Mabou style too ... very oriented to rhythm, a consistent rhythm." The importance of rhythmic consistency arises again when Rankin is asked about his piano style: "I'd rather have a good rhythm ... but influences ... Maybelle Chisholm; I also had a couple of aunts that played piano, so again, a wide spectrum of influences." Rankin also states that he learned piano mostly by ear and by "listening to local players on tape and on records and stuff." From the above, it is obvious that local musicians from Cape Breton communities have been very influential in perpetuating the tradition by passing it on to new learners.

CAPE BRETON FIDDLE STYLE
AND THE MUSICAL COMMUNITY

Since we have discussed the Cape Breton fiddle style with regard to the Gaelic language, piping and other influences, it seems valuable to seek contemporary views on the style's status by players in the new millennium. The survey asks questions about the Cape Breton fiddle style and the musical community in general. Subjects covered include style, "separate spheres," business dealings and ethnicity.

The first question in this part of the survey asks, "Do you think Cape Breton fiddling is in a healthy state today or is it in a state of danger? Why?" Most respondents felt that the fiddle tradition was in a healthy state, many citing the sheer number of young fiddlers. Buddy MacMaster and Rodney MacDonald note that there are many good young musicians playing these days, with Buddy surmising "now more than ever in Cape Breton. So many young people are interested." Some respondents were concerned about the real health of the tradition, however:

I think that the Cape Breton style is disappearing. I believe that today's "new culture" is taking over and people want to reach a bigger audience, which makes them change their style.

Angus Beaton and Jackie Dunn-MacIsaac take a cautionary stance, believing it to be healthy, but worrying about the possibilities of it being a trend or fad. Dunn-MacIsaac states that the tradition is both healthy and in a state of danger:

> [T]here are many players who are carrying on the "tradition" and many others who are not playing for the tradition but the "fame" and money, and they really don't know enough about the culture.

The next question asks whether anything is being lost in Cape Breton fiddling in terms of style and feeling. Three respondents did not answer. Two older fiddlers felt that something was being lost, but did not elaborate on the notion. One of the fiddlers also suggested that perhaps something also was being gained but, again, did not elaborate. They may have (with regard to something being lost) been referring to the "older" style that exhibits a lot of "dirt" that Jackie Dunn-MacIsaac mentions. She feels that the "old" style—grace notes, phrasing, bowing, accent—is being lost. Perhaps a perceived loss in phrasing and accent can be seen in some individual cases; this could be seen in Rodney MacDonald's suggestion that, in terms of style and feeling, there is "some loss due to the loss of the language," that some "lose an understanding" of the way a tune should be phrased and accented. I tend to agree with Angus Beaton that, in a general sense, there is not anything being lost in terms of style and feeling and that there "could be a few individual cases." Such could have been the case through earlier generations as well.

With regard to an "older" sound being lost, Andrea Beaton says, "the rusty, scratchy sound is disappearing" while Kinnon Beaton notes that "the old rougher sound is going." This is an evolutionary feature of note for Cape Breton fiddling. As depicted earlier, certain applications were undertaken with the fiddling in the absence of sound systems. Droning and heavier, more forceful bowing for volume probably used to be of more importance for most settings, namely in dance situations; thus, a rougher sound could be heard. Now, with transducers and amplification and more refined and skilled players emerging (who can drone, apply grace notes, phrase and accent in an aesthetically pleasing manner), there is definitely an evolved sound.

This leads to the next question: "In terms of style and feeling, is anything being gained in Cape Breton fiddling?" Kinnon Beaton states that he sees a general move towards a "smother" style; his daughter Andrea adds that players are gaining more knowledge about technique. This coincides with earlier musings from Liz Doherty that, in general, Cape Breton fiddlers are showing more technical ability than they were in earlier times.

Dunn-MacIsaac notes how good quality and improving accompaniment has helped the tradition, stating that it actually makes the fiddling sound "livelier." Buddy MacMaster also makes an interesting point saying that it is important that the Cape Breton style stay "Cape Breton" and not become a musical hybrid—an absorption of other folk music styles, more especially

Irish styles. In his words, "If it becomes much like Irish or other folk music it will no longer sound like Cape Breton music."

The next survey question is more open-ended. It asks if anything else is being lost or gained with regard to Cape Breton fiddling in general. Answers here varied. The fiddle tunes, in general, were brought up in a couple of different ways. Dunn-MacIsaac and another younger respondent noted that a lot of older tunes are being lost. Kinnon Beaton laments, however, that, "some of the composers are dying and their compositions not getting recognized—like someone who maybe only wrote five or ten compositions." Another person reiterates that the loss of the Gaelic language is a loss for Cape Breton fiddling while Mary Elizabeth MacInnis, on another note, feels that a general appreciation of the music is being lost:

> I think, an appreciation of the music itself. Most people my age don't know much about or listen to Cape Breton fiddling. Also, I think people want or expect more than just to listen to the music. Often it seems that there needs to be a "big show" put on to attract people.

Angus Beaton points to media: "There's a loss in that we single out the stars (e.g.., Mario Lemieux and the Pittsburgh Penguins). So many let the media decide who's a good player." This is a valid point and it is important that more and continued awareness be created about unsung heroes of the tradition, past and present. Educating the media, casual listeners, Cape Breton youth, tourists and tourism operators, through such entities as the Judique Celtic Music Interpretive Centre and the Nova Scotia Highland Village, about the countless rarely mentioned talented musicians would be a start in expanding the already general awareness about the music scene. Of course that awareness was initiated by the popularity of such performers as Buddy and Natalie MacMaster, Ashley MacIsaac and the Rankins—all outstanding musicians. The more people gain knowledge of other excellent island musicians, the more vibrant the tradition will become, both on and off the island from both the listener knowledge and economic growth perspectives.

The survey then goes on to ask musicians if they feel that the Cape Breton fiddle tradition will stay alive. All but two respondents answered "Yes." One did not know but hoped so, while the other did not answer. One respondent went so far as to say that "It's good for another one hundred years or so." When asked what could be suggested that will keep the tradition alive, many of the respondents point to the young. For instance, Kenneth Joseph Mac-Donald says, "the young people" will keep it alive in conjunction with "the old recordings they have access to." Others feel that it is important for the youth to listen to older players and the older style through home recordings while other ways to keep the tradition alive include: promoting language and dance, keeping the youth at home in the cultural environment that promotes the tradition and continuing to pass the tradition on through the many musical families in a natural, traditional manner.

In response to the question, "Do you feel that Cape Breton fiddling has evolved since its origins? If so, must it continue to do so to stay alive?", three respondents did not answer. One respondent (Mary Elizabeth MacInnis) feels that it doesn't have to change any further when she says, "I don't know what the fiddling sounded like in its origins. I don't think it has to change what it sounds like now to stay alive." Everyone else noted that it has evolved, while some added that it will probably continue to do so. As described throughout this book, however, there is the concern that the balance must remain between staying true to tradition, and responding to change. Dunn-MacIsaac, for example, says that, "Yes, it has [evolved], and I guess it can't stay totally stagnant but the 'general' traditional sound has to be protected as well as the old tunes." Rodney MacDonald reiterates by saying that it has evolved "to some degree, but saying it has to change too much will do it harm." Let us hope that the balance between continuity and change will remain as effective as it has. From information and opinions collected for this chapter, it seems that most Cape Breton traditional musicians feel that the tradition is safe, that the influences of those before them and those in their communities have guided the tradition safely to where it is today.

CHAPTER 5

THE ECONOMICS AND BUSINESS
OF CAPE BRETON FIDDLING
AND THE STATE OF THE ART FORM

On September 15, 1773, Nova Scotia's first shipload of Highland Scottish immigrants arrived in Pictou aboard the *Hector*. By the mid-19th century, 12,000 of some 15,000 Scots adopted Cape Breton Island as their new home. After the famed, failed and final Jacobite battle at Culloden Moor, the Highland Scots were left to exist under the mercy of the British Crown and their own chiefs, who calculated more wealth in the grazing value of sheep than in their own people:

> The exploitation of their country during the next hundred years was within the same pattern of colonial development—new economies introduced for the greater wealth of the few, and the unproductive obstacle of a native population removed or reduced. In the beginning the men who imposed the change were of the same blood, tongue, and family as the people. They used the advantages given to them by the old society to profit from the new, but in the end they were gone with their clans ... and their tartan in a shroud.[164]

This mercantile stage of capitalism was again a reality to the Highlanders in the New World; however, a life of free subsistence was more attractive than was the experience in Scotland. The earliest Gaels who arrived in Cape Breton, North-Eastern Nova Scotia and PEI, basically escaped an economic system that was threatening their culture. Their emigration to a new localism brought and preserved a culture that included a unique style of fiddle music, steeped in Gaelic tradition. Familial and local cultural transmission also helped preserve the style and promote its healthy evolution. However, the ensuing times would witness a changing economic climate as Confederation and industrialization set in. Although some economists simply attribute the continuous woes of the Maritime economy to the social backwardness of its people, others, such as Michael Clow, contemplate that "politics" and "federal policies" throughout the Confederation and centralizing industrialization process favouring central Canadian capitalist interests played a part in the history of Maritime underdevelopment.[165] Regardless, certain factors have played a role in maintaining aspects of Cape Breton culture throughout its history of economic struggle; they have gone hand in hand, as described by Kenneth MacKinnon:

> Localism and islandness nurtured the distinctiveness of their music and the [economic] backwardness acted as a barrier against the outside world to help preserve traditional music, language, and culture. While a stagnant economy increased population pressure and out-migration, small-scale local industrial developments were not inconsistent with getting left behind a rapidly-expanding North American continent. For, if lobster canneries, sawmills, and coal mines were for a few generations able to co-exist with and maintain the rural localism associated with farming and fishing, they hardly lifted the population much above poverty and were never the engine of growth some hoped they would be. Indeed the export-orientation of these extractive industries led not just to better continental transportation links, but to greater out-migration; attempts to improve market access for Cape Breton coal and steel led eventually by the 1950s to a less-gradual, more-coercive penetration of the market economy when the Canso Causeway opened. By this time, rural electrification, television, chain stores, and the Postwar Welfare State began the 30 year process of transforming Cape Breton's urban and rural areas into the familiar state of affairs we are now accustomed to, where the de-industrialized urban county [Cape Breton County] tries to downsize into a subsistence service economy, and where the rest of the island is dependent upon a depleted resource sector and looks forward to its culture and music helping with tourism and developing a secure niche in a new global market for Celtic products.[166]

Through the 20th century, the music and culture of Cape Breton have not escaped the constant effects of the economy and the predominance of advancing capitalism. Cape Breton and Maritime culture have been increasingly influenced by economic perspectives carried by governments and capitalists throughout the last century and into the new century. Culture has become commodified and, like it or not, so has the art form of Cape Breton fiddling. This is not to say that the "evil" capitalists have wreaked havoc on a sacred traditional art form. On the contrary, strong familial and local influences have allowed Cape Breton fiddling to advance with the growth of capitalism in a balanced manner. Actually, the music has contributed to the financial well-being of Cape Breton's fiddlers, probably since their arrival. This should not be undervalued with a dismal and totally idealistic view of "destruction of the traditionally sacred." Instead, this chapter will point out the realities of cultural commodification in the Maritimes and Cape Breton. If a balance between a traditional integrity of continuity and evolution and commodification is established, the outlook can be considered positive for Cape Breton fiddling in general. In other words, if one could make a good living or supplemental income without "selling out" the intrinsic value of his/her art form, the results will be mostly positive.

THE COMMODIFICATION OF CULTURE

Since fiddlers have played for dances and received money in exchange, their music has been commodified. Sut Jhally notes:

> All commodities have two fundamental features: They have an exchange-value (that is they are worth something and can be exchanged in the market place) and they have a use-value (that is, they do something that makes them useful to human beings).

Cape Breton fiddling has always been exchanged in the marketplace, whether at local dances, promotional tourism venues, or on the international stage. Its "use-values" are obvious. It entertains, is enjoyed by the public and also contributes financially (directly or indirectly) to various individuals and organizations, whether they be community centres, promoters, festivals or even government departments. A critical question arises from this. When a culture reaches a point where it is materially produced, or is "industrialized" what happens to and within that culture? What happens when commodity production and artistic integrity come face to face and economic realities surface in the industrialized state of culture? Could activities of material production cause cultural components to be reinvented and then reinterpreted by even the original cultural group? Certainly, commodification can lead to invention or reinvention and subsequently, reinterpretation. This occurs when profit or economic prosperity is the bottom line, and examples of this have occurred in the Maritimes.

While commercialization and commodification of Cape Breton fiddling have been evident for years, however, there hasn't been enough to cause a significant "for-profit" reinterpretation of the form. Artistic integrity has been maintained through local and family influences and this will most likely continue into the future. In the larger scope of the international music scene, the profitability of the art form has not been significant enough to change its interpretation on a local level. There need be no worry about the fiddle style being lost to the perils of capitalist profitability. Although some performers will stretch their musical and artistic limits, style application remains safe. Jhally aptly puts this into perspective:

> Within a capitalist economy there is always an unequal balance between the twin features of the commodity in that exchange-value subordinates use-value. Producers of commodities are primarily concerned with the exchange-value of a product. The owner of a factory that makes tables and chairs does not produce them to use them, but produces them to sell them. If they cannot be sold, then they will not be produced. The use-values of things are affected by the dictates of exchange-value. This affects their use-value. Compare hand-crafted tables with mass-produced ones. The same is true in the realm of commodity culture.

Except in the cases of a few performers, the exchange-value of Cape Breton fiddling has not reached the point where economic decisions dictate that it must reinvent itself, in terms of style, for the buying public. However, one need only note that in the late 1990s, when Cape Breton fiddling was still considered "cool" to the general public, there was a predominance of fiddling in East Coast Music Award showcases and television broadcasts. Since then, it's safe to say that this has declined with a new leaning of the industry toward music with a larger mass appeal. That large companies and industry promotion trends can control the music we hear is accepted as an increasingly visible reality. An example of this is the continued existence and success of multi-conglomerate recorded-music distribution companies and the unfortunate financial failures in recent years of niche-friendly local and national distribution and record companies such as Tidemark Music and Distribution and Sam the Record Man stores. Corporate structure does have an effect on determining what cultures (or aspects therein) can be manipulated into economic gain. As exchange-value increasingly dominates the cultural realm (where alternate social visions exist), culture and economics become increasingly intertwined. Unfortunately, capital is moving toward removing the effective presence of any alternate social and cultural ideas and visions.[167] The countering force for Cape Breton fiddling is the strength of family and community presence in nurturing the art form and its purveyors.

GROWING COMMERCIALISM OF CAPE BRETON MUSIC: GROWTH WITH INTEGRITY

Through the 1950s and 60s, popular music, television and modern progressive values challenged and often took precedence over traditional pastimes, while the Gaelic language was quickly withering away.[168] Largely through the media of radio and television, pop culture was invading rural communities and their ways of life. However, while having a detrimental effect on local Gaelic culture, media influence did provide positive results. There was greater exposure for the music while the musicians themselves earned modest financial benefits. Additionally, the music scene was still popular and strong enough to keep many fiddlers employed playing at dances. Paul Cranford reveals the commercial opportunities that existed in those days for players such as Winston Fitzgerald (1914-1988), arguably the Island's most influential fiddler:

> After the war Winston formed his band, Winston Fitzgerald and the Radio Entertainers. This group, featuring Beatty Wallace on piano and Estwood Davidson on guitar, played live radio shows for years and made dozens of recordings (many 78s and four LPs). In the fifties, as Winston became more popular and was playing larger dances and places like the Venetian Gardens, he usually played with about six musicians in the band. This larger combination, the Winston Fitzgerald Orchestra, played a mixture of modern and traditional music—advertised as Round and Square Dances…. During his lifetime Winston played at dances throughout Cape Breton and Nova Scotia. He also played scores of weekends away in Toronto, Boston, Windsor, and Detroit. His television work on the John Allan Cameron Show as one of the members of the Cape Breton Symphony took him into homes across Canada and in later years he made a trip to Scotland as one of the featured performers in a National Film Board presentation.[169]

John Donald Cameron recalls that from the early 1940s to the early 1950s he was hearing '78 recordings of fiddlers "Little" Jack Macdonald, Angus Allan Gillis and Angus Chisholm. He also mentions that corporate-sponsored programs were heard on the radio stations in Sydney and Antigonish. Cameron also speaks about John Allan Cameron's and Don Messer's nationwide television shows as well as "a ceilidh show out of Halifax seen across Canada." He states that, "Cape Breton music got exposure long before now." He also discusses the Cape Breton Symphony, a fiddle group of which he was a member. Not only did the shows expose the group and the music across Canada, but they also created other travelling and recording opportunities. In the 1970s, the group issued four recordings and travelled to Scotland, Germany, Ireland, Shetland and Northern England.

Meanwhile, government policies were having an effect on Cape Breton Gaelic culture. While the most substantial aspect of that culture, the Gaelic language itself, was relatively ignored by government, increased commodification of tourism was accomplished through the manufactured pseudo-Scottish myth, emphasizing symbolism and commemoration, called tartanism by MacKay. The media, by contrast, discovered and exploited another substan-

Fig. 27. *The Cape Breton Fiddlers. Winston Fitzgerald, Wilfred Gillis, Jerry Holland and John Donald Cameron. Photo by: Cape Breton Post, c. 1980. Beaton Institute, Cape Breton University. 84-493-14593.*

tial element of Gaelic culture—the fiddling—which was managing to survive through a strong local and familial transmission, seemingly directly unaffected by tartanism. However, since this time, beginning in the late 1980s and gaining momentum through the 1990s and into the new century, Cape Breton fiddling (and its music in general) has been increasingly affected by commercialization. Various questions arise. Is it now just a commodity, having become totally altered and manipulated for profit-hungry capitalists and by governments interested in raising tourist numbers? Has Cape Breton culture, and culture in general, reached a point of total commodification through the dual workings of government and the corporate world? Is Cape Breton fiddling reaching a transition point where it will be completely absorbed into the cultural industry of music?

The United Nations Educational Scientific and Cultural Organization (UNESCO) study of cultural industries, offers the following definition:

> Generally speaking, a cultural industry is held to exist when cultural goods and services are produced, reproduced, stored or distributed on industrial and commercial lines, that is to say a large scale and in accordance with a strategy based on economic considerations rather than any concerns for cultural development.

Two crucial points are apparent. The music industry is obviously a cultural industry in that (1) it is large scale and (2) it follows strategies based upon economic factors rather than cultural development. We are referring here to such entities as record labels, management companies and booking agencies. If this is the case, Cape Breton fiddling is only at a very preliminary stage with regard to becoming a part of material production and distribution (as a product of large companies within the industry). This preliminary stage may remain just that—stagnation is just as possible as any significant growth at this level. Basically, only five Cape Breton fiddlers, who conservatively must number well over 200, have ever reached "big label" status; three of them were within bands performing other genres like pop and/or country. The five suggested musicians are Natalie MacMaster, John Morris Rankin (1959-2000), Kyle and Lucy MacNeil and Ashley MacIsaac.

There is of course always a possibility that an inherent artistic and stylistic integrity could be lost at a higher level of cultural production and exposure. After all, as Schiller suggests, "the cultural goods and services of modern cultural industries ... are not outputs of a historical, universalistic creative genius and talent."[170]

VIEWS FROM COMMERCIALLY-SUCCESSFUL CAPE BRETON FIDDLERS

Referring again to Joey Beaton's interviews with Natalie MacMaster, Ashley MacIsaac and John Morris Rankin, for all three players exposures to commercialization was a gradual process. Local concerts and dances eventually led to performances in urban centers, followed by folk festivals, recordings, awards, record label signings, etc. In the following, Natalie provides her chronology of commercialization:

> I remember playing for dances in Boston when I was twelve or thirteen ... but my first big adventure when I felt like the fiddle could take me places was when I got called to play at Expo '86 and I was fourteen years old.... After Expo I started getting calls to go ... to Ottawa ... Washington ... West Virginia ... a lot of them in the States .... Philadelphia.... I didn't realize then what contacts I was making, one festival leads to five more.... I was lucky to be at the right place at the right time. When I was sixteen I made my first album.

MacMaster also alludes to the abundance of festivals stretching geographically from New York to Japan. She has since travelled more extensively around the world. Notably, she did a "tourism gig" in Japan:

> JB: And how was Cape Breton fiddling received in Japan?

> NMM: It was great.... It wasn't open to the public; it was a tourism thing, tourist agents ... they told us that the Japanese may not respond to it; 'don't be upset if they don't freak out'.... By the end of the night their ties were off and their sports coats and they accepted it just as well as any response we could have received.

Since this interview, MacMaster has enjoyed much commercial success, signing with Warner Music Canada and with Rounder in the U.S. and completing and appearing on a number of recordings, videos, commercials and television programs, and even receiving a nomination for a Grammy award.

Ashley MacIsaac, the most flamboyant of the three, has been described (to me) on a number of occasions as a "marketing genius." For MacIsaac, it seems any publicity is good publicity. His comments reveal levels of commercial accomplishment and edge that many artists reach for and hold, pushing the limits required to make a good living. Joey Beaton's 1993 interview at MacIsaac's family home in Creignish reveals that MacIsaac's early commercial experiences were similar to MacMaster's. However, he mentions a very influential 1992 trip to New York where he acted and performed in a play and met composer Philip Glass: "I learned more about life and what's out there in the world than anyone would learn in fifty years of high school." Of his first recording, Ashley says, "It opened a lot of avenues. For one thing it opened a good financial avenue—got me sound gear, my fiddle repaired, led to the New York thing. The recording made my music more available."

As the interview continues, MacIsaac's views on innovation within cultures become evident:

> JB: Would you like to be labelled as a traditionalist, a new traditionalist, or a non-traditionalist?

> AMI: I'd like to be labeled as a traditionalist, but I want to get rich. I consider myself greedy, by becoming a new traditionalist.

MacIsaac goes on to discuss a Halifax band which was at that time signed to a record deal with a major label. He reasoned that his art form could be used to make money in the pop-culture world:

> This band ... they got a $25,000 advance from their record company. None of the musicians can play their instruments. A band like them will make their fortune; they can't even play their instruments. I'd like to go out there, being someone who can play an instrument and get rich off it 'cause if those pop bands, who can't play anything can go out and get rich, why can't we? So if I can play the fiddle the same way ... the packaging will be a little different.

> JB: If you have to segregate tradition from making money, you'd go the route of making money?

> AMI: Probably ... my decision was that I was going to make my living off music.

MacIsaac got involved with the music industry, whose mandate is described here by Schiller:

> Speech, dance, drama (ritual) music, and the visual and plastic arts have been vital, indeed necessary, features of human experience from the earliest times. What distinguishes their situation in the industrial capitalist era, and especially in its most recent development,

are the relentless and successful efforts to separate these elemental expressions of human creativity from their group and community [for the] purpose of selling them to those who can pay for them.[171]

Around that time, MacIsaac was signed to a major label and released a multi-platinum selling CD which largely contained pop- and grunge/alternative-flavoured arrangements around Cape Breton fiddle tunes. Yes, the "packaging was different," but one can safely say that MacIsaac's fiddle style (application of certain bow strokes, drones, double stops, ornamentation) did not change. The Cape Breton fiddle style was more popularized and exposed, but it didn't change because of MacIsaac's individualistic endeavours.

To a degree, as the music is recorded and brought away from Cape Breton for sale, a separation from the local culture occurs. Generally speaking, however, the strong sense of artistic and cultural awareness of these "commercialized" players, instilled with a sense of integrity by community and family, is most often, if not always, upheld as the music is brought back home intact. The strength of home and self/cultural awareness has kept the fiddle style cautious in its evolution. Well-marketed players realize the value in playing their music the way it has always been played—after all, it has survived for hundreds of years for good reason.

Joey Beaton asked the late John Morris Rankin how important it is to maintain one's roots in the face of commercial pressures:

> JMR: It's very important. It's something that comes natural too. If you're brought up listening to a certain type of music, I don't think you are going to try anything "that's too off the wall" and put your Celtic roots on the shelf.... You have a lot of pressure from the outside to change and conform to what's going on [out there] so it's not always the easiest thing.... I get asked that a lot.

> JB: How long do you think you'll go before you leave the traditional side of your performances ... and go another route?

> JMR: It's hard to answer that too, you know ... but up to this point, especially in concert situations, it's a very important part of what we're doing.

Besides reflecting past international performances and those at such prominent venues as Massey Hall in Toronto and the Royal Albert Hall in London, Rankin indicates that the music doesn't have to be reinvented when played elsewhere. One possible reason is that while many venues can draw on a substantial body of "Celtic music" fans, they also draw—especially in urban centres in Canada and Northeastern United States—audiences with large numbers who are either transplanted Maritimers or have some ancestral connection to the Maritimes or to a Celtic country:

JB: How much of the Cape Breton music are you incorporating into that type of performance or is [traditional performance] ... on the backburner at some of these things?

JMR: No ... especially if it's the further away that you go.... I find that especially the step dancing, without fail, it always goes over well ... we do fiddle numbers, the twin fiddle feature where Howie [MacDonald] and I double up ... play a medley that's eight minutes long or something ... the traditional side of it seems to be as strong as any other part of it, you know? ...We're really surprised and impressed when you sell a concert out and there's enough requests for tickets to put another concert on ... it's just good to see the fiddle, and the traditional side of it, goes over well. That not only happens in Canada ... it goes over quite well overseas and in the States.

It seems clear that ambassadors of Cape Breton music (and fiddling) have entered a more commercial scene without losing any sense of cultural integrity when the music is brought back to the originating cultural communities. Integrity of continuity and openness toward self-expression have been hallmarks inherently embedded in the psyches of these musicians. This is commendable at a time when corporate mergers create more competition in the industry, and governments use cultural industry rhetoric in their policy developments and departmental affairs.

THE POLITICAL ECONOMY OF CAPE BRETON FIDDLING

Where does Cape Breton fiddling fit within the larger scope of cultural industries, namely the music industry? First, both Cape Breton music and Celtic music have proven themselves to be a significant niche commodity internationally and perhaps even on as a national commodity of Canada. But aside from MacMaster, MacIsaac (who signed to smaller companies like Loggerhead Records, Decca and Linus), the Rankins and the Barra MacNeils, there is not much mention of Cape Breton fiddling in the industry. Considering how difficult it has been for Cape Breton artists to get a label signing, recent mergers of labels such as Universal and Polygram Records (late 1990s) will do nothing to help smaller bands, at least at that level. For instance, by the turn of the 21st century, conglomerate mergers and staff/act downsizing had become the norm. A December 1998 news report states:

> In an effort to create a lean company, Universal will fold the Geffen and A&M record labels under the umbrella of an expanded Interscope Music Group. The labels will release music under their own logos, but will operate with reduced staff and artist rosters. Sources estimate that 20 per cent of the 15,500 workers by Polygram and Universal could be let go.[172]

Mergers continue. Depleted artist rosters point to more uniformity of trendy pop and less room for Celtic artists to "cross over." While big bucks appear more difficult to attain for artists, perhaps more creative integrity is possible, and niche markets can be probed with and through formation of smaller labels that may or may not have to utilize distribution and marketing strategies by the larger companies. Such endeavours require hard-to-access capital and are deserving of government support—if the government is dedicated to the rhetoric of its policies for culture.

In Nova Scotia, principles guiding the government's role in culture suggest that "Cultural activities play a significant role in sustaining and developing the social, educational, economic, and spiritual life of our communities." While recognizing sustainability in the long term, government must "involve the community in decision-making through consultation and arms-length mechanisms." One such arms-length mechanism was the Nova Scotia Arts Council. Under then Minister Rodney MacDonald (who is now Premier of Nova Scotia), it has now become the Nova Scotia Arts and Culture Partnership Council, and now offers more fair geographical representation to individuals and groups (at least on paper), and will provide a better chance for funding to go into aspects of Cape Breton traditional music, as opposed to projects favoured by the old urban-centric, crony-based Council. Nova Scotia's Culture Sector Strategy also recommends an "increased investment in the culture sector to fuel viability and growth" while, in terms of community development, government should provide "an ability to create and respond to cultural opportunities in all communities."[173]

Cape Breton fiddling, a strong part of *true* Gaelic cultural identity in Cape Breton (no tartan needed), falls into this description. Notably, in terms of industry support, a recent survey by the Music Industry of Nova Scotia (MIANS) pointed to the need for continued or extended government assistance, and a lack of support for the region's music by local radio stations—the only artists receiving significant air play have been the ones within the Celtic genre. This has created some resentment in the industry, but the survey admits that "this trend is due in large part to the fact that much of the success in the music industry within Nova Scotia comes from the 'Celtic genre'." Perhaps this observation generalizes the financial success of a few musicians such as some of those mentioned above. When reality sets in, the survey points out that about 75 per cent of self-employed individuals (musicians most often fall in this category) report annual income below $10,000; this accounts for 60 per cent of the music industry population.[174] From an individual perspective this figure is quite dismal. It also reveals that music in Nova Scotia, though highly touted by government and media, is not highly profitable for most individual musicians—as in earlier years of Cape Breton fiddling, musical commodification serves as a supplemental income, at best, for individuals.

For those who mainly play for a living, teaching fiddle has served as an additional financial supplement. As Feintuch summarizes, "Historically, Cape Breton fiddle players have not supported themselves economically with their music. Until very recently nearly all these musicians held day jobs or worked the land."[175] With this in mind, commercialization and corporate activities (and absorption) with regard to Nova Scotia's music do not appear to be as threatening or relevant to Cape Breton fiddling as many seemed to have feared. Community-based cultures still have a chance to survive, although rationalization and centralizing policies favouring urban centres do nothing to improve rural situations.

Perhaps, though, improved technologies such as the Internet may increase awareness of Cape Breton Gaelic culture and fiddle music. For instance, the new website CapeBretonLive.com is providing live traditional music performances and artist CD sales to listeners from many countries while only being in its infancy at the time of this writing. Utilization of the Internet's huge communication powers may actually help Cape Breton fiddlers expand performance markets and sales potential. This type of "exporting" of the culture may also increase "imports" of cultural tourists to the area, thus boosting the Cape Breton economy. Hopefully, governments and their economic-development agencies will gain an increased awareness of economic growth possibilities that exist with relation to "living" exports (Cape Breton musicians) and imports (tourists who are attracted to Nova Scotia by the music culture and its live music events).

Some had valuable words with regard to this subject. The survey asks two questions: "Do you feel that Cape Breton fiddling, as an art form, is treated equally with other forms of art by governments?" and "Do you feel that governments can do anything to help Cape Breton fiddle music and anything associated with it? If so, what?" The first question garnered mixed views. Ten of eighteen respondents answered "No," Cape Breton fiddling is not treated equally with other forms of art. Three did not answer while two answered that they were not sure. Two respondents answered, "Yes." One simply answered that government "could do better."

A couple of respondents leaned towards the idea that the fiddling community and art form should be guarded from outside interference such as governments and pop culture and that we should have a bit of a protectionist approach to guarantee its maintenance. Buddy MacMaster notes that it is not government support that keeps fiddle music alive, but it is the love of it by its many listeners.

With regard to what government can do to aid Cape Breton fiddling, some respondents mentioned the connection between music and tourism and the need to provide grants for initiatives such as workshops, while others noted the need for community-level help with the language and with schools. Others saw tour financing as a way for governments to contribute (actually, government entities such as FACTOR, the Canada Council, the Nova Scotia Arts and Culture Partnership Council, and new initiatives in the NS Department of Tourism, Culture and Heritage and Music Nova Scotia do have some funding and programs available). Mary Elizabeth MacInnis suggests a more grassroots approach to funding the Gaelic culture as a whole:

> I think the whole culture needs to be supported, otherwise the music will become all "business" and eventually fizzle out....
>
> [I would like to see]—support for Gaelic in schools, business, etc.
>
> —more history of the Gaels in school, museums, etc.
>
> —I would like to see something in Inverness County that included a library of audio and video tapes of music, songs, stories, etc.

Her last suggestion has been realized with the opening of the government-supported, newly-constructed Celtic Music Interpretive Centre in Judique.

THE BUSINESS OF CAPE BRETON FIDDLING

The survey continues by asking a few questions about the "business" and commercialization of Cape Breton fiddling. First, respondents are asked, "Do you, have you, or would you play for money? (This assumes that you play for enjoyment as well)." All but two responded "yes." Of the other two, one young musician stated that she was not ready yet while the other said that he never has and probably never will play the fiddle for money. That fiddler, whom I know well, plays the fiddle as a hobby. The answers overwhelmingly support the assumption that the commercialization of music (service for payment) has gone on for a long time and will continue in the 21st century.

Playing for money (or some other service or product such as liquor, food, future paying engagements, gifts of monetary value, etc.) has been a general part of the tradition over the years. A few musicians agreed that a fiddler would get paid to play, but money wasn't the only reason for playing. For instance, Jackie Dunn-MacIsaac answers, "Yes, but all musicians 'pay their dues' by playing for fundraisers, social get-togethers, house parties, jam sessions totally for enjoyment and with no thought of being rewarded." Angus Beaton makes the point that playing music is a skill like any other skill such as sewing, driving, etc., noting that you can do it for pay, or play.

I feel that there is still a notion among some potential "employers" that professional musicians should play for pure enjoyment and "exposure." This idea must be challenged by people in the music community so that the musicians, besides the music itself, can stay healthy. After all, one can die of exposure in a world where some assume musicians should perform gratis. As mentioned earlier, pay for play has gone on for a long time. Buddy MacMaster gives an idea of how payment for playing might have evolved:

> In early years I don't think fiddlers got paid. They played for the love of playing and maybe a few drinks of liquor. Since over sixty years musicians get money for playing. Today fiddlers are usually well paid.

The survey expands on the above questions by asking, "Do you think that Cape Breton fiddling is becoming more business-oriented? If so, how? If so, is this "good," "bad" or "both" with regard to keeping the tradition healthy?" All answers (17) suggested that Cape Breton fiddling is becoming more business-oriented. Andrea Beaton noted from personal experience playing fiddle in another province (PEI) over the course of a year that, business-wise, the Cape Breton fiddle tradition may be further ahead than similar traditions in other provinces and areas.

Some of the other fiddlers who felt that Cape Breton fiddling is more business-oriented took the approach that it is beneficial for the tradition, but that keeping the tradition and making money must be kept in balance. Glen MacEachern observes that, "It has become more business oriented. It is good in the sense that it has made the music more popular. Bad that it seems to make it harder to find a session (kitchen party)." This is an indication that (1) many professional musicians are now too busy performing (especially during the summer) to play for a house session without pay; (2) house sessions are very rare now because they have been replaced by other social gatherings such as dances and pub sessions like those at The Red Shoe Pub in Mabou where the tradition continues, although the "original" setting may not; and (3) hosts may assume that professional musicians will not play free of charge at a house session, but this certainly is not the case, depending on the situation. This, however, points to the consensus that Cape Breton music is nowadays more of a business than it was in most of the 20th century.

Kinnon Beaton brings up the point that there is a fine line between the business demands and the social aspects of fiddling. The sharing between musicians must continue to keep the tradition healthy—although it's more commercial, we must not cross the line to the point where there's no longer a sharing of the music between musicians. In relation to a more business-oriented approach, tradition bearers also must be aware of "wannabe" stars, star-making parents and bandwagon Celtic music fans. Some of these people are not as grounded and attached in a familial way to the music as many other tradition-bearing musicians. Mary Elizabeth MacInnis elaborates on this and summarizes other business-related points when she deliberates:

> Being more business-oriented is both good and bad, in my opinion. It is good because it helps to bring the music to people all over, make it accessible and keep it in front of people here in Cape Breton so that the tradition is not forgotten about. I worry about fiddle music being more of a trend than part of our culture. Our music went over big for a while; even all the younger people were listening (at least to Ashley, the Rankin family) and going to dances, etc. Crowds have been getting steadily smaller at dances and some concerts the last few years…. I guess my point is that it's not all bad but we have to be cautious that "the business" is not the motivation for playing. I get the impression that some kids just want to be on stage, get awards, etc.

What I think is important here is that there are families and locals closely tied to and supporting the tradition. In keeping the tradition healthy, Danny Graham adds that, although the music is more business-oriented, "local people will always know and enjoy the tradition."

Fig. 28. *The Red Shoe Pub. Photo by: David Gillis, n.d.*

Fig. 29. *The Red Shoe Pub. Photo by: David Gillis, n.d.*

Musicians are asked if they think it is possible to make a living by playing and/or teaching Cape Breton fiddle music. Of the eighteen respondents, fourteen answered, "Yes." There were additional comments suggesting that it would be difficult to make a living playing the music, and could only be possible for a select few, established players, while a couple felt that Cape Breton fiddle playing can only be a supplemental income.

"Is it now more possible to make a living with the music than it used to be?" All respondents (one did not answer) to this question said, "Yes." Greater ease of travel and communication would probably be the main reasons here, as well as a more financially secure society in general and an increased global awareness of the music. MacInnis feels it is easier now to make a living at music than it used to be "because it is more business-oriented and people here are better off financially to support it today. Also, it is a much smaller world (ease of travel, communication, etc.)." Dunn-MacIsaac adds that making a living playing Cape Breton music is easier now because musicians are travelling more now than in the past. To make a good living playing the music, musicians should be prepared to tour because the population base on the island—and even in the Maritimes for that matter—is not large enough to support the music. The musicians have to be innovative by exploring other avenues besides performing such as recording and selling product, publishing and capitalizing on internet marketing.

To counter a volatile business climate, there must be cooperation among musicians to create a productive music community that can thrive in challenging times. One survey question addresses this by asking musicians if they've ever witnessed jealousy, unfair business practices, and/or a sense of competition in the tradition. Only two players (both of them older) answered "No." One answered "very little." One answered "to an extent" and the thirteen other musicians answered "Yes." The reason for jealousy and competition may be that there simply are not enough venues and events in Cape Breton to support all of its fiddlers and also because there seems to be a core group of players favoured to be hired by the local public and local venues. While there was very little elaboration on this question, Dunn-MacIsaac provides this insight:

> Difficult question ... I would say "yes," but [jealousy-competition]
> is almost unnoticeable and is unspoken. More so [it] happens with
> musicians who play full-time and tour a lot. It is very slight and
> may only occur because they need to stay on "top" to survive in their
> job. Sometimes audiences even appear to compare and/or favour
> certain musicians as well.

An instance of the favouritism occurred at a concert with a group of Cape Breton traditional musicians. One performance included a well-respected fiddler and piano player duo. The other main fiddling act was a younger player with more back-up musicians and more of a "show." Although the older fiddler and piano player performed much better musically, the fiddler with the showy, but poorer quality playing, received a standing ovation.[176] Of course, this could have to do with a "stacked" audience in a player's home town, but it does show that, even in Cape Breton, musical "coups" can happen whereby glittery presentations may be more valued or applauded over quality traditional music and that, at times, the balance between experienced, discerning listeners and good musicianship is disturbed.

SUMMARY

The political economy of the Maritimes has had direct and indirect influences on the Gaelic fiddle style transplanted to Cape Breton in the era of the High- land Clearances. The music itself has most likely always been commodified since its initial development. Cape Breton fiddling has an exchange-value and a use-value, and this has been utilized since pioneer days. Actually, the chance to make a supplemental income was readily taken by earlier generations as they willingly accepted offers of employment playing for dances. Economic realities produced migratory Gaelic communities in urban centers in Central Canada, the "Boston States" and the Maritimes, where dance scenes and ini- tial recordings abounded. Preservation of the fiddling style and community- based culture survived best in rural Cape Breton, where local and familial influences emphasizing integrity of continuity and self-expression was and is "enculturated."

A dominant ethnic population and island isolation also contributed to the style's "evolved preservation." A community cultural awareness on the is- land allowed it to escape the manufactured Scottishness that was promoted by the government of Angus L. Macdonald, and governments that followed. On a positive note, Macdonald's leadership brought infrastructure that con- tributed to (and still contributes to) the financial well-being of Cape Breton fiddlers (most especially during the tourist season). Radio, television and re- cordings brought Cape Breton music to the rest of Canada and the world. Increasing commercialization was depicted in the lives of Cape Breton's fa- mous innovator, fiddler Winston Fitzgerald, and fellow Cape Breton Sym- phony musician, John Donald Cameron. Although these individuals were well-travelled and witnessed an increase in commercialization of the music, they also lived through the 1950s and 1960s, when pop culture and capitalist values were taking their toll on the Gaelic language and traditional pastimes. The documentary The Vanishing Cape Breton Fiddler, for instance, though it took advantage of commodifying the music, helped spearhead a revitalization of Cape Breton fiddling.

The 1980s and 1990s witnessed the great commercial success of fiddlers John Morris Rankin, Natalie MacMaster and Ashley MacIsaac who proved that the music is capable of making money and contributing to the economy of the island. Moreover, musicians have not "sold out" their style (and need not feel it necessary to do so) through cultural industrialization. Actually, what makes the music different is probably what makes it more saleable in niche markets. Although the music has been commodified with the help of major record labels, stylistic and cultural integrity was essentially maintained and, when brought back to the originating culture, was not reinvented or interpreted negatively by these musicians or listeners. This has been possible because of an almost inherent sense of cultural integrity instilled in these musicians, and others less famous, by family and community in their formative years. Unfortunately, few in the Nova Scotia music industry have enjoyed the commercial or financial success these musicians have. The future holds even more challenge as corporate business decisions are being made with cost savings and profitability in mind, while governments rarely act on their rhetorical policies in a right-of-centre, conservative political climate.

However, the survival of an intact and thriving Cape Breton fiddle style—while commodification and commercialization grow apace—reveals it is possible for cultural awareness, integrity and identity to be maintained and continued in conjunction with (but in its own way against) today's tide of Anglo-centrism, Americanized pop-culture and globalization. This is a cultural victory and serves as an example to other cultures facing similar realities. It is good to see from the views of fiddlers in the new century that a positive attitude remains with regard to keeping the tradition vigorous: the island's fiddlers remain willing to adapt and take advantage of business prospects that arise, yet reveal that a strong sense of balance must remain between commercialism and art form continuance.

CHAPTER 6

IN CONCLUSION

Although there are a number of observers who see a danger in the fiddle style being lost because of the rapid decline of the Gaelic language, their fears could be premature. It is not the ability to speak the language, but the ability to *interpret* rhythm, intonation, bowing, accents and ornamentations—most often heard from earlier fiddlers—that give a style its sound; much of that sound is found in nuances of the language and its authentic purveyors. The Gaelic/older style remains and continues to be present in Cape Breton, and chronological age does not determine a Gaelic/older sound. A player does not have to be a Gaelic speaker to have a Gaelic/older sound and rhythm, accent, bowing and fingering-hand embellishments project the older sound (combined with *living* the culture), *not* necessarily an aged Gaelic-speaking player.

If it is true that the language is near extinction or lingers on only in a state of perpetual near-death, will the above criteria be enough to keep the older sound? The death of (or the lack of social life in) the language will probably have an effect on some aspects of the playing. Some songs and tunes played on the fiddle may eventually be lost, misinterpreted, or discarded if there are no Gaelic speakers singing or teaching them. Gaelic airs may take on a more classical sound, as some already have, if classical/theoretical interpretation takes precedence over rhythmic application and oral interpretation of these tunes. The aural nature of learning must remain in the new century if the Gaelic/older sound is to stay distinctive in Cape Breton music:

> People have to learn to listen again. We are constantly being bombarded by music of strict regular rhythm on radio and TV. I don't think we have anything near the listening capabilities of our grandparents who relied on memory skills developed through continuous sharing of traditional tales, poetry, and song. It will take patient, intelligent listening. It is crucial to remember that traditionally, Gaelic

song rhythms were led by the language more than by the music. Nowadays, music rhythms take precedence over the language.[177]

One must be careful when discussing the idea of Gaelic song rhythms. They will not always dictate a universally correct interpretation or version of a tune. First, Gaelic song words have not *always* come before the melody of a tune. In that instance, the composer of the words would require a keen ear to apply syllabic word patterns aptly to the melody in order for the compositional integrity of the melody to stay true. Also, there are some Gaelic songs that have two or more different rhythmic versions, although the words may be the same in each. For instance, I have heard the tune "Mo Dhachaidh" (My Home) sung with two different rhythmic approaches, in both instances by well-respected Gaelic singers. In a case like this, how does the musician decide which version is "correct?" The rhythm of the language does not always easily dictate how a tune should be played. The authenticity of a "Gaelic" interpretation of a tune can be more clouded than some may presume.

Also, to keep the music sounding authentic, Cape Breton musicians must not allow conventional music theory, sounds and rules to overtake the importance of their culture's "musical language." If the old sound is to remain in the island's traditional music, the musicians must be aware of and enforce the idea that what they are playing, with regard to scales, "non-standard" note placements and rhythms are *correct* with reference to the old style of music of their own culture:

> Contrary to popular belief, music is not a "universal language," but is culturally-specific. It can vary widely in form, content, style, and purpose in different societies. We must not blindly accept the aesthetics of Western Art music, the dominant musical tradition in Europe for several centuries, if we are to understand the music of other cultures with different musical traditions.[178]

What is vital now, at a time when we are almost overwhelmed with popular culture and popular music influences, is that learners in the tradition gain a better knowledge of how their music is different. Improved knowledge of its history may help them to ignore the "rules" of more dominant musical cultures. As areas like Cape Breton become de-Gaelicized, that historical knowledge is a main factor that will keep the old, Gaelic sound in the music.

Young people must be kept aware of the complexities of Cape Breton music. Ignoring its form and non-complying sounds in favour of Western Art music rules will cause a loss in flavour. But, Allan MacDonald argues,

> Not if musicians make the effort to learn where the music comes from and what makes it work. If they don't it could result in musicians playing to the standards being dictated by a more powerful

neighbouring culture. If this happens the creative spark of Gaelic music could be snuffed out, leaving us with a fossilized tradition.[179]

To elaborate further and to provide an example, a 2004 interview/discussion with Cape Breton-style musician Dave MacIsaac discusses note placements that are non-compliant with Western Art music:

> GG: Listening to the older players ... some of the notes they play ... you get some notes that people might call "neutral" notes, notes that don't necessarily follow the scales of classical music, I suppose.... Can you explain some of that?

> DMI: Maybe that comes from the pipes.... Do you think? It's almost like you'll hear a "g" note. It's not a "G" and it's not a "G" sharp. It's kind of in between there. It's almost like ... Eastern European music, like from Romania and Hungary.... Their fiddlers, they've got all these little "in-between" notes that they play.... How can I explain it ... if they were playing the guitar, instead of having twelve frets ... they'd have, like, twenty-four ... so there's always little "micro-notes," little "micro-tones" kind of thing.

> GG: I suppose my concern is—are there people from another style of music ... like a classical musician might see that as being "wrong," but really it's not wrong; it's just an expression of the culture that *you* come from....

> DMI: Exactly, yeah.

> GG: Do you think that our playing might move away from that? More towards the classical....

> DMI: Sometimes you get ... it's fine to take classical lessons.... You could learn to hold the instrument properly and get the bow straight and manipulate the bow and stuff, but maybe too much classical could be a negative thing too.

Dave MacIsaac is widely known as a prime example and exponent of the older style of playing found in Cape Breton, even though he is not a Gaelic speaker. Also, and in contrast to most players in the tradition, MacIsaac was raised in an urban setting. He grew up in Halifax, Nova Scotia, brought up by Cape Breton-born parents. Universal recognition of his old playing style again points to the influence of family and other musicians in perpetuating the tradition and style. MacIsaac says that he learned to play by listening to his father, Alex Dan MacIsaac who was brought up in St. Rose, Inverness County. Dave notes that Alex Dan learned tunes "from people like Ronald Kennedy, Johnny MacLellan, Angus Allan Gillis, people like that down in that area ... also 'Big' Ronald MacLellan" and "learned a lot of older music from these older fellows who were kind of forgotten over the years." Alex Dan "didn't read the note ... but he had a good ear and had a lot of stuff [tunes]." Dave MacIsaac mentions that "Carl MacKenzie would be around our place a lot in the sixties ... and he and my Dad played a lot together." MacIsaac's exposure to other players is clear, despite the urban upbringing. He also notes that:

> We had a lot of the old '78 records home and I learned tunes off that. I remember ... I think the first tune I learned when I was about six was "Donald MacLean's Farewell to Oban" off Joe MacLean's old record.

The following excerpt from the same MacIsaac interview describes the influence of the Gaelic language. Once again, being exposed to a Gaelic cultural setting is helpful in forging a Gaelic/older sound, but of equal or greater importance is being able to interpret the old style of the music through rhythmic (bowing) and digital (fingering) application (the most desirable being the combination of these factors).

Dave MacIsaac also indicates that *interpretation* produces the old sound, not necessarily a musician's ability to speak the language. Note here too the difficulty that musicians have in explaining how they apply ornamentation, bowing, rhythm, overall style and feeling. It seems that for the most capable musicians much of what they do is intuitive and is also based on having exceptional abilities to hear and apply many idiosyncrasies found in the music. *This* is what we hear in the music of those players who really "get it":

> DMI: I'm not a Gaelic speaker but heard lots of it growing up ... my parents spoke Gaelic fluently and my father was a Gaelic singer and all his brothers Gaelic singers ... but there are certain inflections that you try to put in with your fingers to put that kind of sound in it.... I can't quite explain it but ... little things you do, like you kind of don't hold the note down real tight. You just kind of hold it half and you ... it's a cross between a hammer-on and holding the note down. You're kind of choking the note to get the odd little guttural [Gaelic nuance].

> GG: That's a good word, guttural ... what about the bowing ... are there little things that you could do with the bowing that ... I know it's hard to explain....

> DMI: Yeah ... [motioning with his hands like he's bowing the fiddle and vocally "diddling"] "dee die de dum" ... [laughs] those kind of things.

> GG: Yeah. I've heard them called "didums" and "iterrums."

DMI: I can remember your ... grandfather Donald Angus doing things like ... doing one down-bow and three up-bows.... There are certain tunes [where] that's what you have to do to get the right phrasing and expression ... sometimes they'd do two downs and two ups too....

GG: So do you think that ... has to do with mimicking possibly Gaelic song and Gaelic; just the Gaelic?

DMI: I kind of think so, yeah.

GG: And some of that ... with the fingers ... do you think that that had something to do with the bagpipes as well—the influence of the pipes?

DMI: I think so, yeah.

In the third chapter, besides the challenges posed by the loss of Gaelic, the impact of other forms of change on fiddling was discussed. In the past, the preserve was instead of rural male Cape Breton Gaels; now the constituency of the music has evolved towards inclusiveness. With each passing decade of the 20th century, the tradition drew into its playing ranks women, Mi'kmaq, Acadians, out-migrants, ethnomusicologists and others. Interviews with Cape Breton fiddlers by Joey Beaton were explored and used to give a glimpse of diverse ethnicity within the fiddling tradition with views from Acadian fiddler Donnie LeBlanc and Mi'kmaq fiddlers Lee Cremo and Wilfred Prosper. The idea mentioned above about being able to interpret and apply applications for an older sound can help explain why players of other ethnicities on the island have been able to master the Cape Breton style—Acadian players like Arthur Muise, Donnie LeBlanc and Robert Deveaux. Because of their ability to apply learned rhythms and ornamentations to the violin, these players have taken the "Gaelic" influence from the Cape Breton style and made it part of their own playing. It is also here that I caution and question whether the style should still be called "Gaelic." Because of the abilities of other-ethnic and now non-Gaelic-speaking players to develop and exhibit this style that has been described, in the future it may be more inclusive and indeed correct to call the style/sound the "older sound," but still recognize it as being rooted in the influence of Gaelic language. There are people who say that you have to speak Gaelic to have an older sound or to be able to do some of this older way of playing that Dave MacIsaac was speaking about: "But you know, if you hear older players ... that play that style, it's going to, you know, you're going to pick it up if you listen to it."

Indeed then, why couldn't this apply to other-ethnic players like those previously mentioned? It would certainly be insulting and false to tell them that they cannot play the "Gaelic" style. Actually, the above players have as much or more "Gaelic" in their styles as some Gaelic-speaking players before them. Also, an overly "scratchy" sound indicative of a kitchen fiddler should not be mistakenly labelled as a "Gaelic" sound, but should only be noted for what it is: the sound of an amateur musician.

On the point that a style is based more on aural learning than a spoken language, it was fitting to ask Dave about learning blues guitar, his other mastered musical art form. The mode of learning that he used with the blues parallels his learning of the old Cape Breton fiddle style, supporting my notion that having a good ear and "feel" is the most important factor in learning folk music styles:

> GG: Besides playing Cape Breton music, what I find interesting about you as a musician, you play the blues. You're known as being a fine blues guitarist. Are their similarities in the way that you learned the blues?
>
> DMI: Well, I just listened to older players, you know....
>
> GG: And how were you exposed to it?
>
> DMI: ...there was a show on, I think it was 1966 ... it was on TV. It was a CBC blues special. And it had a bunch of Chicago blues guys on—Muddy Waters, Otis Spann, Little Walter Jacobs ... and I was just glued to the TV and I thought, gee, I like this music, you know? And it was a few years after that that I really heard some of the blues records through Scott MacMillan's brother ... my older brothers would be bringing home some of [the records of] the English bands like The Yardbirds, people like that—Eric Clapton and Jeff Beck. So that was a big influence too on my guitar playing. And I played in a band called The Acme Blues Band in the early 70s with a bunch of guys twice my age....
>
> GG: So was a lot of your playing self-taught, again, just by using your ear again?
>
> DMI: Yeah. I took a few lessons—a couple of years between [ages] ten and twelve I guess—and just learned, you know, your basic chords. But I didn't practice that stuff a lot. I was more interested in learning licks off the records.... I wasn't applying myself too much. I was in a way kind of wasting my parents' money because I wouldn't practice enough. But I learned basic chords and I think I could read music better for the guitar then than I can now ... and I was fortunate enough to play back up for John Lee Hooker, a famous blues man from the States ... in the late 70s, I guess ... and they asked me to play lead guitar ... and back John Lee up, which was great.

He was a real living legend of the Blues ... and he told me he liked my guitar playing so I must have been on the right track ... and I backed up Sonny Terry and Brownie McGhee, and a couple [of] old legendary blues guys ... and I jammed with each of them ... for the show ... and each of them said (joking, mimicking their accent), "Where'd a little white boy like you learn to play like that?" So that was a little bit of validation, I guess.

GG: So, I guess ... what I'm interested in seeing is that ... you didn't grow up in that area with them, but you were still able to capture their style.

DMI: I guess I had to have a kind of a feeling for it ... maybe came in the same place that I like the "Scotch" music from. They were both roots musics, you know? There's no bullshit with them. You either got to be able to play them or not.... You can't fool anybody (laughs).

GG: So it's a matter of being able to feel it and a matter of being able to interpret it by listening to it?

DMI: Mm hmm. And express it on the instrument, you know?

MacIsaac goes on to describe having that "feel" for the music, speaking about how he'll perform a guitar solo with relation to what's occurring with a singer's voice. He speaks of the musical term, "dynamics" (the use of soft and loud sounds to create mood and taste) and applying them to the instrument. Interpreting and applying, again, is paralleled between the blues and Cape Breton fiddling:

DMI: Playing a blues guitar solo I like to ... like when somebody's singing a song, they'll sing a few words, then I'll leave a little space, you know, just like playing sentences you know, the cadence of the voice will go up and down kind of thing and I like to do the same thing when I'm playing a guitar solo—I might start down on the low strings and just ... take my time, and just kind of build it, you know ... and kind of peak it when you're way up on the high notes ... build the intensity ... dynamically....

GG: And of course there are dynamics in Cape Breton fiddling as well.

DMI: Exactly, yeah. People like, listen to Buddy MacMaster. You can hear a lot of that in Buddy's playing. He'll lay off some notes and he'll *come on* to some other notes, you know, with the big up-bow ... and you can really hear a lot of that in Buddy's music.

Finally, we see the importance of aural learning and interpretation when it comes to learning tunes from sheet music. Players who mainly learn tunes from the written note or who mainly have classical training should heed this—it is vital in capturing the Gaelic/older Cape Breton sound:

> DMI: You play a tune out of the book with no ... grace notes or ... dynamics or anything, it's going to sound pretty flat ... you know, you play the notes, but then you've got to put your own stuff into it, put your own feeling into it, your own phrasing and expression, choose what grace notes to put in, maybe some ... different bowing things. But when you're learning a tune ... you should play it a lot just so you can really get into it so you can play it ... so you don't even have to think about it and *that's* when you start playing it.

Obviously folk musics, and in particular the traditional music of Scots-Gaelic Cape Breton, cannot only be thought of in terms of language alone. However, language is at the centre of all cultures, and its loss does affect the internal cohesion and thought processes of participants within those cultures. As a language disappears, it is up to the participants to decide the validity of maintaining other things which that language has influenced (e.g., fiddling, in the case of Gaelic). A continuing local effort to create family and community venues for Gaelic speaking, singing and listening should be helpful in maintaining the old style. Certainly, the lack of cultural space for Gaelic could be where a danger for loss of fiddle style could lie. If there are not as many youth being exposed to the speech, stories, humour, dancing, piping, song and fiddling of the older bearers of Gaelic tradition, then various aspects of narrative and musical style could be lost. If the rural population continues to decline, we will see not only the last of the Gaelic native speakers, but also fewer musicians staying on-island. I don't see this adversely affecting the fiddling though, for at least another generation or two, for Elizabeth Beaton has said to me that in her youth, the local people would have been excited to have enjoyed as many good fiddlers in Inverness County as they do today [2004].[180] This indicates that the fiddling tradition is still as strong in the first decade of the 21st century as it was in the 20th century.

This will remain so only if Cape Breton communities retain as much of their non-anglicized inheritance as possible. Cultural identity must be fostered in the early years of education for the island's youth. Although fiddling is the most popular of the Gaelic-influenced arts, language, dance, piping and song should all be recognized as important and intertwined. As the ceilidh house setting for learning fades, other venues such as schools, universities and private performance centres should try to foster all aspects of the culture. Acknowledgement of multiple learning realms by youth will strengthen identity and chances for growth and maintenance of all art forms. Young fiddlers, in turn, should be open to learning more about the language, dance, and piping to help improve their playing applications and style and increase their repertoires with added Gaelic-influenced tunes. New avenues of exposure to older players for learners could be explored. Perhaps, if government wanted to be involved, it could provide funding for apprenticeships and mentorship programs between older players and learners. One such initiative was spearheaded by Derrick and Melody Cameron of Mabou. They successfully held weekly gatherings at their home for young musicians beginning in the fall of 2005. Each week they'd be joined by a different older, mentoring musician who would be there for guidance, providing insights, demonstrating and of course jamming along with the younger players. Hopefully this and similar initiatives will continue. In addition, funding could be provided to bring traditional musicians into schools on a regular basis to keep young musicians interested and guided through the tradition, as opposed to them having to learn by only listening to commercial recordings, or attending formal lessons with just one teacher.

Fostering cultural identity will counteract the following of facile trends. For instance, the growing acceptance by some of a newer universal Celtic sound that's been generated through a non-family and homogenized Euro-classical fad will grow old quickly and be dismissed. Players steeped in the Cape Breton fiddle heritage understand what it's like to *live* a tradition, as opposed to live *off* of a tradition, whereas a pseudo-Celtic mentality is a weakly developed foundation that will likely disappear as quickly as a record label-promoted trend. Bandwagon followers and adopters of such music will see how quickly dismissed are their lack of musical application and interpretation of skills. Meanwhile, those who live their fiddle tradition will pass on their inherited knowledge, playing and listening skills as they always have—open to improvement and the realization that the music evolves through individuals who just "know and give." Indeed, the Gaelic/older mentality and essence of the culture must remain.

Individuals like Dave MacIsaac, Raymond Beaton, of Mabou, and David Gillis, of Scotsville, have amazing collections of audio and videotapes of older players and are often willing to share the music with eager young musicians. Also, from what I have witnessed, players like MacIsaac, Alex Francis MacKay, Buddy MacMaster, Kinnon Beaton, John Morris Rankin, Jackie Dunn, Stephanie Wills and Howie MacDonald, have been nothing but willing and proud to pass on to others tunes and compositions that they have learned. Younger players should be made aware of such learning tools as old tape recordings, and the need to respect player-predecessors and their importance in fostering the form. In general, a "back to basics" approach to maintaining our cultural art forms is what's needed. That family/community knowledge and guidance must continue in order to foster and support young musicians and keep them grounded in the "why" and "how" of the music, not the "how can I become a star" aspect that may be more evident in some learners since the 1990s.

Mike Kennedy notes the need for traditional learning modes to remain while others should be promoted. He also recognizes that it is not just the musicians' responsibility to maintain the Gaelic language and its influence on the music:

> If Gaelic is as important to Cape Breton fiddling as so many believe it to be, it will be more important to find ways to ensure that young fiddlers are given access to it. Since the traditional learning environment of the ceilidh house is being increasingly replaced by a more formalized educational environment, it would seem only logical that one of the focuses be on improving the representation of the Gaelic arts in the schools. In addition to teaching "Cape Breton" fiddling (Jackie Dunn-MacIsaac is currently the only teacher in Cape Breton schools teaching "Cape Breton" fiddling), better provision for Gaelic language and song in the schools, good local access to older recordings of a diverse number of local Gaelic singers, pipers, and fiddlers, and better educational opportunities for learning about what makes the Gaelic musical tradition distinctive would all help ensure that younger fiddlers are able to make well-informed decisions about the direction [in which] they would like to take the tradition in the future.[181]

Just looking to the past to keep a tradition healthy is not a safe thing to do, however. Although Dave MacIsaac mentions the importance of young people resorting to the old tune collections of such composers as Niel Gow, J. Scott Skinner and Robert MacIntosh, since they provided the "foundation" for our music, it is also vital that the tradition and musicians' repertoires be kept fresh with new compositions by younger players. Just as Dan R. MacDonald, Gordon MacQuarrie, Dan Hughie MacEachern and Donald Angus Beaton were recognized as great composers in the 20th century, so too should the tunes and new stylistic ideas of the next generations of writers and players be considered valid and important to the tradition. Also, excellent "drive" in dance playing and continued and increased proficiency in the playing of many young Cape Breton violinists in the 21st century indicate promise for the tradition for at least the next couple of decades. We must also look to the brilliance, innovation and knowledge of Cape Breton's new accompanists as a strengthening factor in the music's healthy continuance and appeal as well. Extensive coverage of Cape Breton accompaniment revealed that it has evolved over the years through various influences and that it has influenced the fiddle style too. As long as accompaniment evolution remains balanced and rooted in the playing of earlier musicians who followed the melody of the tunes, its future will remain promising.

During the premiership(s) of Angus L. Macdonald from 1933-1954, Cape Breton fiddling enjoyed a period of great players, composers and a healthy tradition as a whole (from around 1930-1965). While "Tartanism," promoted with good intentions by Angus L., helped create a romanticized Scottish view of Nova Scotia that promoted and aided symbolic representation far more than the protection of the Gaelic language and its Gaelic art forms, it did promote tourism and bolster the economy and infrastructure of Cape Breton, which contributed to the well-being of its fiddlers. The maintenance of traditional music was still left up to the local rural communities and families, which they ably undertook and kept healthy as the economy adjusted around them. Inverness County has always been and still remains rural. Depopulation threatens communities' survival. But even as schoolhouse dances, ceilidh houses and even the parish picnic have faded, replacements remain—whether they be Mabou's Red Shoe Pub, the West Mabou Hall, occasional party houses, performance and interpretive centres, or the parish halls on the island during the summer months—avenues for art form continuance remain; and thus, so will the thriving fiddle style. Amazingly, besides undergoing local social changes, the fiddle style has been able to withstand and respond to economic circumstances beyond local control.

A key economic factor, out-migration, significantly affected the Cape Breton fiddle tradition. Playing style and sound experienced an intermingling with other cultures in places like Massachusetts and Michigan which clearly affected its cautious evolution. In the Dudley Street area of the "Boston States," many Cape Bretoners continued living their culture in a new setting by establishing and attending dances, while some musicians were recording music for public sale with record labels. A similar, yet probably less prominent, scene was also occurring in Halifax in the 1960s.[182] While it became clear in Chapter 3 that although exchange and maintenance did occur in the migration destinations of the U.S. and Canada, the maintenance of Gaelic culture and fiddling in these areas did not match that of rural Cape Breton Island. This plainly indicates the strength of rural, close-knit communities in holding onto cultural expression that is otherwise more easily surrendered in economically thriving urban areas.

We also saw that influential people in the fiddling world, such as Dan R. MacDonald and certain members of the clergy, could have an effect on or even alter views and direction of the music. Such individuals have been important in administering the direction of revivals and revitalizations of cultural art forms. For instance, even as cultural revivals and revitalizations can occur, and the Cape Breton style over the years has "progressed," individualized styles may be less noticeable and "unistyles" may be becoming visible in Cape Breton and PEI. This trend could possibly result from both influential individuals *and* the direction of revivals and revitalizations. However, there may be style homogenizations occurring because of easier travel for musicians since around the 1950s. With ease of travel, fiddlers have been able to interact more and have gained more access to other styles of playing. Regional style variations have become less noticeable (this situation applies to Ireland too) although there is still a detectable "Mabou" sound.[183] Regardless of changes and possible style homogenization, however, the third chapter concluded that the 1970s revitalization, after the release of the *Vanishing Cape Breton Fiddler* documentary, was important in preserving the tradition and that the 1990s may even have witnessed a greater revitalization and interest in the music because of the commercial success of a few Cape Breton musicians.

Innovation has been a prominent force in Cape Breton traditional music. The Cape Breton community has been able to embrace changes such as the additions of the piano, guitar, electric transducers and even the sleeker, technically-proficient styles of influential musicians such as Angus Chisholm and Winston Fitzgerald. Influences that led individuals to take up playing, fiddling families and communities of fiddlers, differences between "fiddling greats," or "master fiddlers" and "kitchen fiddlers" have all influenced players' perceived ability and level of accomplishment as musicians. Cape Breton's folk culture has established, as we saw, a set of standards in musical analysis completely different from more standardized approaches, such as one would see in competition and less peripheral cultural settings. That openness for innovation and self-expression must remain. The fiddling community must stay undeterred by outside perceptions of what is considered Gaelic or Celtic. If, for instance, the competitive piping universe, Highland Societies, the Canadian fiddling competition world, and Maritime/Anglo-folk singing followers do not become more educated about Celtic history, and recognize their music realms as newly constructed versions of Gaelic and Celtic culture, the piping and fiddling of Cape Breton Island may continue to be minimalized, or at least less recognized, in today's predominantly pseudo-Celtic world. The maintenance of older-style fiddling (and older-style piping as purveyed by such players as Kevin Dugas, Barry Shears, Jamie MacInnis, John MacLean and Paul MacNeil) may only survive and counter pseudo-Celticism with continued personal pursuits, educated historical convictions and local perpetuation fostered by family and community.

With respect to the fiddling itself, I maintain (in agreement with Liz Doherty) that although on occasion it may be witnessed on an individual basis, most of the perceived tempo increases date back further than the present generation of Cape Breton fiddlers. In fact, the playing of some of the older generation has been timed at quicker tempos than some of those of the present generation. It must be realized that players may adjust their tempos intentionally or unintentionally from situation to situation. However, advice from experienced players should not be taken lightly. As Dave MacIsaac says, players should always watch their timing, utilize the old music collections and develop their own repertoires.

In the statements of fiddlers in the survey and the Beaton interviews, we saw some of the prospects for the tradition. These views also helped reveal the strong impact of family, locals and community on specific musicians. The interviews also helped display elements of innovation and enculturation present in the lives and the playing style of some of the Island's fiddlers. There was a consensus that the tradition had arrived safely into the present world of accelerated change.

Tied tightly to changes in cultures is the political economy and the economy in general. The same is especially true of Cape Breton's Gaelic culture. Both corporate and government influence stimulated changes in Cape Breton society and continue to do so. Purveyors of the art form have been resilient within economically challenged cultures, in this case the musical community of Cape Breton Island. Up until this point the art form has adjusted and survived through many challenges such as emigration and an increased bombardment of "Americanized" popular culture. The commodification of Cape Breton's traditional music has occurred since its arrival and the music has contributed to the financial well-being of its musicians, their families and their communities. The conviction that Cape Breton music should not be commercialized, but is becoming increasingly so, ignores the reality that it has always been commercialized in the form of "paid-for" entertainment.

Commodification and commercialization of Cape Breton fiddling were noted in interviews with local musicians. Through all of their travel and music business dealings, their sense of cultural maintenance, fostered by family and community, always remained evident in the work of John Donald Cameron, John Morris Rankin, Natalie MacMaster and Ashley MacIsaac. There are, however, few musicians who have only the music for their source of income. As a musical community, Cape Breton should be supportive and proud of its "musical exports" and not be too critical of musicians who may want to experiment a bit and repackage the music in order for it to be more exciting to foreign audiences, as long as style application remains. We may see a growth in "session" group-oriented bands such as Beolach and Slàinté Mhàth (now defunct) where there is a move away from solo playing toward a "bigger" sound with multiple lead instruments. This should be seen as both healthy and a good business move, allowing the island's musicians to "compete" with similar bigger-sounding groups from other Celtic realms on the festival circuit. The solo tradition will remain intact on the island, although we are seeing more duo-playing again on recordings and at sessions. Seeing that double violin playing was popular in the early 1900s, this revitalization of an old and exciting performance practice should also be considered a positive occurrence and resurgence.

It is clear that there is no real danger of "losing" our music as it is being exported. Actually, the extent of commercialization of the music is probably exaggerated; only a select few of the island's fiddlers have enjoyed any notable commercial success. Indeed, as a Music Industry of Nova Scotia survey on the state of the industry once revealed, the same is true of the music industry in the province as a whole. Even though for decades the economy in Cape Breton and most of Nova Scotia could be described as dismal, even though rural-based cultures continue to be challenged by centralizing policies, and even though corporate capitalism influences more and more of world culture, the fiddle music of Cape Breton has been able to survive and adjust to the changes. The resiliency of the music has been remarkable. The main battle for the future will be in preserving not only the fiddling, but also all related facets of the culture, such as the Gaelic language, bagpiping, storytelling and step-dancing, for it is the sum of the parts that make a machine work best. May they all continue to be fostered in their evolution through the strength of and perpetuation by family, local culture and communities. Cape Breton fiddling will live on ... at least while many of my musical peers and I walk on the island soil.

Notes on Chapter One

1. MacDonald, Hugh A., "Liner Notes." A Musical Legacy: Donald Angus Beaton.
2. MacGillivray, *The Cape Breton Fiddler.*
3. McKinnon, "Fiddling to Fortune" 8.
4. Shaw, "Language, Music, and Local Aesthetics," *Scottish Language,* 8.
5. MacEachen, "Cape Breton Fiddling," *Am Bràighe.*
6. Cockburn, "Article on Gaelic Puirt-a-Beul."
7. Newton, "An Introduction to the Gaelic Music."
8. Kennedy, *Gaelic Nova Scotia.*
9. Dunlay and Greenberg, *Traditional Celtic Violin Music,* 5.
10. Reid, (lecture, St. Mary's University, Halifax, NS, 10 September, 1999).

Notes on Chapter Two

11. Farmer, *History of Music in Scotland,* 204.
12. Johnson, *Music and Society,* 101
13. Carlin, *The Gow Collection,* 13
14. Farmer, 14.
15. Emmerson, *Rantin',* 5.
16. Carlin, 13.
17. Ibid., 14.
18. Bruford, "Highland Fiddle Music," in *Companion to Gaelic Scotland,* 74.
19. Ibid.
20. Farmer, 342.
21. Prebble, *Highland Clearances,* 9.
22. Ibid.
23. Bumsted, *The People Clearance,* 34.
24. Kennedy, *Myth Migration, and the Making of Memory,* 271-72, 278-94.
25. MacGillivray, *The Cape Breton Fiddler,* 6.
26. MacLeod, "Inverness County," *Mabou Pioneer* II, ix-x.
27. Hornsby, *Nineteenth-Century Cape Breton,* 31, 204.
28. MacGillivray, 1-4.
29. Dunlay and Greenberg, 5.
30. Lederman, "Fiddling," *Encyclopedia of Music in Canada.*
31. Perlman, *The Fiddle Music of Prince Edward Island,* 12, 20-21.
32. Dunlay, review of "Full Circle," 179-80, 188.
33. MacKinnon, in discussion with the author.
34. Lederman.
35. Campbell, *The Scotsman in Canada,* 154.
36. MacPherson, "Glengarry County."
37. Emmerson, "the Gaelic Tradition," in The Scottish Tradition, 240-41.
38. Lahey, Connell, in discussion with the author.
39. Jones and Steffenson.
40. Kennedy, *Gaelic Nova Scotia,* 174.
41. MacDonell, *Sketches Illustrating the Early Settlement of Glengarry.*

42. MacLeod, ix-x.
43. Bitterman, "On Remembering and Forgetting," in *Myth, Migration*, 260-61.
44. Scarff, "The Music of the Shetland and Orkney Island,"
45. Lederman.
46. Charles Dunn, *Highland Settler*, 34-58.
47. Macleod, viii-x, xii.
48. MacGillivray, 2.
49. Kennedy, 279.
50. Charles Dunn, 56-57.
51. Proctor and Miller, 325.
52. Caplan, Thompson and Schneider, "The Cape Breton Fiddler."
53. Bumsted, "John MacGregor," *Dictionary*, 547-49.
54. MacGregor, 70, 73.
55. MacQueen, Skye Pioneers, 31.
56. MacGregor, Historical and Descriptive Sketches, 259, 109, 261.
57. MacGillivray, 2.
58. Proctor and Miller, 325.
59. Charles Dunn, 55.
60. Qtd. in MacQueen, 69.
61. MacNeil, "On Living Celtic Culture."
62. P. J. MacKenzie Campbell, *Highland Community*, 68.
63. Feintuch, "The Conditions for Cape Breton Fiddle Music," 8.
64. MacGillivray, 2, 270, 269-72, 304, 3.
65. MacDougall, *History of Inverness*.
66. MacGillivray, 2-3.
67. Rhodes, "Dancing in Cape Breton," appendix in *Traditional Dancing in Scotland*, 269-70 and 304.
68. Charles Dunn, 74-90.
69. Allister and Bev MacGillivray, *A Cape Breton Ceilidh*, 24.
70. McKay, "Tartanism Triumphant," *Acadiensis*, 5-47.
71. Blaustein, "TraditionalMusic" (diss.), 32-27.
72. McKay, "Tartanism," 15.
73. MacInnis, "Scottish Music in Cape Breton," *The Canadian-American Gael*, 90.
74. Caplan, "With Winston 'Scotty'," *Cape Breton's Magazine*, 40.
75. MacGillivray, 3.
76. Kennedy, *Gaelic Nova Scotia*, 232.
77. Laidlaw, *The Campus and the Community*, 57-89.
78. Gerrits, "People of the Maritimes," 46-49.
79. MacGillivray, 3-4.
80. Elizabeth Beaton, qtd. in Feintuch, 12, 13.
81. Doherty, "Paradox of Periphery" (diss.), 267, 221.
82. Mary Graham, in discussion with the author.
83. Feintuch, "The Conditions," 15.

Notes on Chapter Three

84. Graham Survey, Appendix 1.

85. Finn Moore, in discussion with the author.

86. Dunlay, 188.

87. Doherty, 9.

88. Dunlay.

89. Kennedy, Gaelic, 203.

90. Dunlay, "the Playing of Traditional Scottish Dance Music," Celtic Languages, 173-74. 184, 180, 188-89.

91. MacEachen, "Dunlay and Greenberg," *Am Bhràighe*.

92. Gibson, "Traditional Piping," *Celtic Languages*, 160.

93. Jacqueline Ann Dunn, "Tha Blas no Gàidhlig" (thesis), 16.

94. Doherty, 306.

95. Allan MacDonald, "Reclaiming the Tradition," *Am Bhràighe*, 13.

96. MacGillivray, 6.

97. J. A. Dunn, 61.

98. Feintuch, 31.

99. Farmer, 285.

100. MacGillivray, 3.

101. Dunn, "Introduction," *MacEachern's Collection*.

102. Ferrel, "Boston Fiddle," Liner Notes, 6-8.

103. Ashley MacIsaac, interview by Joseph Beaton.

104. Dave MacIsaac, interview with the author.

105. Farmer, 280.

106. MacKinnon, comment to the author, 10 March 2004.

107. MacGillivray, 157.

108. Ibid., 112.

109. Dunlay, 186.

110. Smith, "Lee Cremo," *Canadian Music*, 544-47, 550.

111. Qtd. in MacGillivray, 100 and 161.

112. Smith, 549-50.

113. Donnie LeBlanc, interview by Joseph Beaton, 29 November 1993.

114. Cranford, "Introduction," Winston Fitzgerald.

115. McKay, "Tartanism," 5-47, 9, 105.

116. McKay, "History," 105.

117. Bitterman, 261.

118. Alex Francis MacKay, interview by Joseph Beaton, 1993.

119. Thornton, "The Problem of Out-migration," *Acadiensis*, 3, 10.

120. Nilsen, "The Nova Scotia Gael" (proceedings of Harvard Celtic Colloquium, 1986), 10, 32, 88, 83, 88.

121. Dunn, Introduction.

122. Jhally, "The Political Economy," in *Cultural Politics*, 71.

123. Ferrel, 23, 3, 5, 7.

124. Kennedy, Gaelic, 221, 199, 222.

125. Maggie Moore, "Scottish Step Dancing."

126. Elizabeth Beaton in discussion with the author, 2004.

127. John Donald Cameron, "Dan Rory" (unpublished manuscript).

128. J. D. Cameron, interview with John Allan Cameron, 28, 25.

129. Mary Graham, 2000.

130. J. D. Cameron, interview with J. A. Cameron, 30.

131. John Morris Rankin, interview by Joseph Beaton.

132. MacGillivray, 33, 69, 9, 62, 4.

133. Ibid., 4.

134. McGann, "Divine Intervention."

135. MacKenzie, interview by Allister MacGillivray.

Notes on Chapter Four

136. Natalie MacMaster, interview by J. Beaton.

137. A. MacIsaac, interviewed by J. Beaton.

138. H. A. MacDonald.

139. MacGillivray, 116-17.

140. MacGillivray, 119.

141. Qtd. in MacGillivray, 119.

142. J. D. Cameron, interview by J. Beaton.

143. Kennedy, *Gaelic*, 174.

144. Doherty, 300, 328, 271-72.

145. Kennedy, *Gaelic*, 181-82.

146. Doherty, 365, 225-26.

147. Shepherd, "Towards a Sociology," in *Lost in Music*, 60-61.

148. MacGillivray, 5.

149. Carlin, *The Gow Collection*, 14.

150. MacGillivray, 5.

151. Ibid.

152. Doherty, 338.

153. MacGillivray, 5.

154. Dunlay, 188.

155. J. D. Cameron, interview by J. Beaton.

156. Doherty, 359.

157. Danny Graham, in discussion with the author, 2003.

158. M. Graham, in discussion with the author, 2003.

159. Dunlay and Greenberg, 73, 91, 66, 81, 64, 47, 53, 140, 2.

160. Keith Norman MacDonald, *The Skye Collection*, iii.

161. Denny, in discussion with the author.

162. Doherty, 187.

163. J. D. Cameron, interview by J. Beaton.

Notes on Chapter Five

164. Prebble, 3, 4.

165. Clow, "Politics and Uneven Capitalist Development," *Studies in Political Economy*, 137.

166. MacKinnon, email correspondence with the author.

167. Jhally, 80, 7, 81.

168. MacGillivray, 4.

169. Cranford, ii.

170. Schiller, Culture, Inc., 30.

171. Ibid., 31.

172. Birn, "Massive Music Merger."

173. Nova Scotia Culture Sector.

174. Lyle Tilley Davidson [Chartered Accounts], 1999 Music Industry Survey, 10.

175. Feintuch, 27.

176. Name withheld, personal communication, 2000.

Notes on Chapter Six

177. Allan MacDonald, "Interview," *Am Bhràighe*.

178. Newton.

179. Allan MacDonald, "Interview."

180. Elizabeth Beaton, in discussion with the author, 2004.

181. Kennedy, Gaelic, 207.

182. D. MacIsaac.

183. Ibid.

SURVEY ON CAPE BRETON FIDDLING

Name (optional):

Age:

Gender:

Occupation:

Home: (You can mention where you are from and where you reside e.g., "I am from Mabou, but have been living in Halifax the last three years):

Marital Status:

Religion:

1. How much of (a) Cape Breton or "Scottish" music, (b) other violin music, (c) other kinds of music were you exposed to before taking up playing?

2. What was your attitude towards (a), (b) and (c) in the above question before getting involved with learning and playing?

3. Why did you learn to play the fiddle?

4. How old were you when you began to play the fiddle?

5. How did you learn to play the fiddle? (e.g., self-taught, from a relative, etc.)

6. Did you learn by ear, the written note, or both? Which way did you learn first? Did you take any formal lessons, either individual or group?

7. What, in your opinion, is more important in becoming a good Cape Breton fiddle player: having a "good ear," or being able to read the written note? Please pick one.

8. Do you feel that being a "correct" player is important?

9. Have you received any classical training? If so, how has it affected your playing?

10. Do you consider the fiddling art form that you play to be a family tradition? For example, has it been essentially passed down through family generations? Do you have close relatives who play as well?

11. If you do have relatives who play, do you notice a similar style or sound with reference to your playing and that of your relatives?

12. Do you feel that modes of teaching and learning Cape Breton fiddling have changed over the years? If so, do you feel that the results have been "good" or "bad" for the tradition? Explain.

13. Obviously, no two fiddlers play *exactly* the same. However, do you think that, generally speaking, there is a distinct "Cape Breton sound or style"?

14. Do you feel that Cape Breton fiddling differs from other traditional fiddling in North America and beyond that has roots in Scotland? If possible, please explain.

15. Do you feel that highland bagpiping has been an influence on Cape Breton fiddling? If so, how?

16. Do you think that Cape Breton fiddling is the same or at least similar to that played in the Scottish Highlands in the mid to late 1700s and into the early 1800s?

17. Do you think that fiddling found in Scotland has changed since the above time period? If so, what and/or who do you think may have contributed to this and how do you think it has it changed?

18. Do you think that fiddling found in Cape Breton since the above time period (or to be more concise, since the arrival of the first settlers) has changed since then? If so, what and/or who do you think may have contributed to this and how do you think it has changed?

19. Do you feel that the Gaelic language has had an influence on Cape Breton fiddling? If so, how?

20. Do you think that there is a Gaelic sound in Cape Breton fiddling? If so, what is it and what contributes to it? If not, what is a better way to describe this reference?

21. If you said "Yes" to the above question, do you feel that you have to be a Gaelic speaker to have the "Gaelic sound"?

22. Has interaction between Cape Breton fiddlers and fiddlers of other styles had an influence on Cape Breton fiddling? Please explain and/or provide examples.

23. Do you feel that interaction between Cape Breton fiddlers and fiddlers of other styles in the "Boston States" (e.g., the Dudley Street area of Boston) between the 1940s and 1960s had any impact on Cape Breton fiddling? If so, how?

24. Do you think that composition (people composing tunes) is important to the tradition? If so, how? Do you compose?

25. With regard to Cape Breton fiddling, who have been your greatest influences and why?

26. Do you, have you, or would you play for money? (this is with the understanding that obviously you play for enjoyment as well).

27. Has playing for money (or some other service or product such as liquor, food, future paying engagements, gifts of monetary value, etc.) been a general part of the tradition over the years? Feel free to comment.

28. Do you think that Cape Breton fiddling is becoming more business-oriented? If so, how? If so, is this "good," "bad" or both with regard to keeping the tradition healthy?

29. Are commercial recordings important to the tradition? If so, how?

30. Are home recordings valuable to the tradition? If so, how?

31. Do you feel that Cape Breton fiddling, as an art form, is treated equally with other forms of art by governments?

32. Do you feel that governments can do anything to help Cape Breton fiddle music and anything associated with it? If so, what?

33. Do you think it is possible to make a living by playing and/or teaching CapeBreton fiddle music?

34. Is it now more possible to make a living with the music than it used to be?

35. Do you think that Cape Breton fiddling is in a healthy state today or is it in a state of danger? Why?

36. In terms of style and feeling, is anything being lost in Cape Breton fiddling?

37. In terms of style and feeling, is anything being gained in Cape Breton fiddling?

38. Is anything else being lost or gained with regard to Cape Breton fiddling in general?

39. Do you feel that the Cape Breton fiddle tradition will stay alive?

40. What do you suggest will keep the tradition alive?

41. Do you feel that Cape Breton fiddling has evolved since its origins? If so, must it continue to do so to stay alive?

42. Do you feel that, generally speaking, there is a sense of camaraderie and friendship among Cape Breton musicians?

43. This question is for FEMALES ONLY.

    In earlier times in Cape Breton, it can safely be assumed that the fiddle players were predominantly male. Do you feel "equally accepted" in the tradition as males are or do you feel that it is still male-dominated (or possibly male-favoured)? If you do feel "equally accepted," has this always been the case for you?

44. Do you think attitudes toward female players have changed over time?

45. Have you ever witnessed jealousy, unfair business practices and/or a sense of competition in the tradition?

46. Have you witnessed, or do you feel that, some "older" players and/or listeners have revealed negative attitudes and opinions with regard to the playing of "younger" fiddlers? If so, is this justified or not justified?

47. Have you witnessed, or do you feel that some "younger" players and or listeners have revealed negative attitudes and opinions with regard to the playing of "older" fiddlers? If so, is this justified or not justified?

48. If you said, "yes" to the above two questions, which do you see happening to a greater extent, the first scenario or the second?

49. Do you feel that Acadian and/or Mi'kmaq players from Cape Breton have adopted the island's predominant general fiddle sound (or style, if you like) and absorbed it as a part of their own cultures or do they have a fiddling tradition/sound/style all their own?

50. Do you think that accompaniment for Cape Breton fiddle music has changed since it was first played on the island? If so, how?

51. Although there were earlier forms of accompaniment for Cape Breton fiddling than the piano, it can safely be stated that the piano has been the prevailing instrument of accompaniment over time. Generally speaking, and understanding that no two piano players play exactly the same, is there a distinctive Cape Breton piano sound or style? If possible, provide examples and/or contrasts with other piano styles.

52. Do you feel that Cape Breton piano playing has changed over time? If so, how?

53. If you answered "yes" to the above question, has the change been good, bad or both for the Cape Breton traditional music tradition?

54. Do you feel that piano accompaniment has had an affect, in terms of style on Cape Breton fiddling? If so, how?

55. This question is for PIANO PLAYERS ONLY. What musicians have influenced your piano style?

56. If you feel that Cape Breton piano playing has changed over time, what player(s) do you feel have been of greatest influence in this change?

57. It can safely be stated that the second most predominant form of instrumental Cape Breton accompaniment in the twentieth century is the guitar. Do you accept this instrument as a form of accompaniment?

58. Has guitar accompaniment changed over time? If so, how?

59. Do you think Cape Breton guitar accompaniment differs from other styles of guitar accompaniment (e.g., Irish or modern Scottish styles)?

60. If you feel that Cape Breton guitar accompaniment has changed over time, what player(s) do you think have been of greatest influence in this change?

61. This is for GUITAR PLAYERS ONLY. What musicians have influenced *your* guitar style?

62. Do you think it is okay to use other instruments, besides piano and guitar, as accompaniment for Cape Breton fiddle music? Why or why not?

63. Is it okay to mix other music genres like jazz, rock, blues, pop, dance (techno) music, flamenco, etc. with Cape Breton fiddle music? Why or why not?

64. Is it okay for experimentation (to back up the fiddle music with jazz, blues, rock, pop, and other styles) to occur *as long as the music and stylistic applications performed on the fiddle are played strictly the "Cape Breton way"*? Why or why not?

65. Do you agree, partially agree, or disagree with the following notion? Geographic isolation of Cape Breton Island is a primary contributing factor in the preservation, yet cautious evolution of its fiddling tradition. However, of at least equal importance is that Cape Breton fiddling has slowly and cautiously evolved with the careful guidance of family and the local community and a _general_ acceptance and support by local predominantly Catholic clergy.

66. Please feel free here to say anything you want about Cape Breton fiddling that you feel should be said... Now is your chance!

APPENDIX 2

Tamerack'er Down Reel

Donald Angus Beaton

(Some bars in part A contain more notes than required)

Tune Forms of Celtic Music and Celtic Dance

By Glenn Graham

Editor's Note: What follows is adapted from an evolving interpretive narrative written for and used by the Celtic Music Interpretive Centre in Judique, Cape Breton. Written by Glenn Graham, it is included here with the kind permission of the Centre.

CELTIC MUSIC

ADDRESSING SOME MISCONCEPTIONS

People with a passing interest in Celtic music may be viewing it in more "pseudo-Celtic" terms. They may see the music through common media presentations which seem to focus predominantly within an Irish context and on such recent commercially successful epic super-shows as *Riverdance*. When we take a closer look, Celtic musical artforms are found throughout all branches (besides the Irish) which would include Manx, Cornish, Welsh, Breton and, of course, Gaelic/Highland Scottish and its major diaspora, the Gaelteacht of northeastern Nova Scotia, Prince Edward Island and Cape Breton Island. Researchers are concluding that the music of the pre-emigration Gael is most closely reflected and seen now in Cape Breton than any other place because of various factors:

- The highest concentration of Scottish Gaelic emigration to Cape Breton and surrounding areas occurred as religious and economic pressures were causing cultural change in Scotland.
- Ethnic dominance in sheer numbers by the Gaels in Cape Breton allowed cultural continuance
- The geographic isolation of the island, especially up until the construction of the Canso Causeway in 1955
- Continued focus on family/community oral passage of the culture
- A general acceptance and "permissiveness" by Roman Catholic clergy of Gaelic musical artforms

Gaelic/Celtic music, as with other artforms within other cultures, can be affected changed, replaced and even lost because of various pressures, whether economic, political or religious. Such pressures were at work in Ireland and then Scotland over the previous few centuries. These influences were gaining momentum in Scotland during and after the time period that tens of thousands of Gaels arrived in Cape Breton. Essentially, the Gaels in Cape Breton were able to avoid and resist changes being enforced in the Old Country. Thus, Cape Breton traditional music should be seen as being "Highland" and "Gaelic" based. Also noteworthy is that there is a common misconception that the piping and dancing generally perceived and practiced worldwide as being Scottish, Highland and Celtic, represent older Gaelic culture. In fact, they are newer forms introduced by anglicizing forces such as those of elitist "improvers" from the Scottish Lowlands—occurring mostly during and after the emigrations. Cape Breton offers a picture closer to Gaelic Scotland. Let's check out the timeline that depicts this:

- 1603: Conquest by the English causes the collapse of the Gaelic socio-political system of Ireland; Scotland's socio-political Clan system lasts longer (about a century and a half longer), gradually disappearing until the modern era of emigration to Nova Scotia.

- 1746: English victory over outnumbered Jacobite forces at the Battle of Culloden seals the fate of increased assimilation of Gaelic Scotland
- Around 1750 to around 1830: Golden Age of Scottish Fiddling
- 1800-1850: Main Gaelic emigration to Nova Scotia/Cape Breton.
- 1843: Birth of J. Scott Skinner, the most prolific composer of Scottish music; influenced Scottish music by incorporating "modern" bowing and adding and emphasizing more Italian/classical technique
- 1850s: Highland games and competitive piping and dancing become prominent fixtures in Scottish culture, overtaking and replacing previous Gaelic customs and artforms

MUSICAL MOODS AND HOW THEY ARE EXPRESSED AS TUNES

The realm of Celtic music is large. At this point we will focus on the instrumental music. First of all, the traditional music that is played on our instruments—the compositions/melodies—are commonly called tunes, not songs. As the individual melodies are coming from the instruments, not vocal cords, they are called tunes, even though it is acknowledged that the occasional Gaelic song is transferred to the instruments.

All music is a form of human expression. At its best, it comes from the heart, expressing the deepest of emotions ranging from the depths of sorrow, to the utmost in happiness and joy. Celtic tunes are played for various occasions and place settings. Historically they would include battlefields, weddings, wakes, funerals, ballrooms, picnics, kitchens, dance halls, concert halls/theatres, pubs, etc. Certain tunes may more commonly be heard on a specific occasion or in a specific place setting. For instance, a reflective, slow-flowing tune would most likely be heard at a funeral while a lively, upbeat tune would be heard at a dance. A combination of the various tune types would probably be heard in a kitchen, concert, or pub setting as Celtic music is often played in a manner that conveys for the listener a change in emotional state throughout a performance. In other words, a group of tunes will create variations in mood, usually going from a reflective state to one of excitement and joy. The musician achieves this by beginning the performance with a slow melody and then gradually increasing tempo by changing tune types/forms.

CAPE BRETON TUNE TYPES/FORMS

There are many tune forms in Celtic Music. Some are found in multiple Celtic traditions while others may be exclusive to one. It seems that Cape Breton took longer to absorb other tune types, besides its core of Gaelic tune forms—Marches, Strathspeys and Reels—than other traditions such as Irish and post-emigration Highland Scottish. This is most likely because (1) Ireland was de-Gaelicized before the Scottish Highlands, (2) Ireland and Scotland were in closer proximity to continental Europe and its various cultural fashions (i.e., new tune types) and (3) emigration to Cape Breton was virtually complete before Anglo-lowland-elite-dictated changes affected the Scottish Gaelic musical tradition. Because of the above factors, other continental European tune forms almost certainly would have proliferated in the Highlands of Scotland and Cape Breton later than in places like Ireland and the Isle of Man.

Let us focus first on tune[1] types common to pre-emigration Highland Scotland and Cape Breton. We'll follow this with other tune types adopted into the Cape Breton tradition and forms found in other traditions.

---

[1] Let's also remember this about tunes: Tunes usually are made up of two parts; an "A" part and a "B" part. Each part is played twice and then the process is repeated again. Therefore, the tune is usually played twice, like this: AABBAABB, followed by the next tune. Remember, there are exceptions. For example, some marches and reels have four parts.

Slow air
- Slow, reflective sounding tune. Sometimes called a lament or pastoral, the lament would mourn love or death loss, the pastoral would simply be a slow melody pleasing to the ear.
- Sometimes free flowing, this type of tune could be found in common time or perhaps 6/8- or 3/4 time.
- Most often played at funerals, times of reflection, or special occasions during masses or other church services. A newer setting would be the Pastoral Airs Concert, held as a fundraising event in local churches in Cape Breton. Most often a slow air is heard as a first tune in a medley that changes in tune type and tempo (slow air through to eventually a reel—slow to eventually fast) in a concert, pub or home setting.

March
- Marches came primarily from the martial piping tradition in Scotland. Very old marches would surely have been played by Gaelic pipers leading their comrades into battle. To get the feel of a march, pretend you are marching; each time you take a step, feel your foot come down on the beat of the tune. March at a leisurely to an upbeat pace and say to yourself, "RIGHT and LEFT and RIGHT and LEFT."
- Most commonly played in Cape Breton in 2/4-time and adapted to the violin accordingly
- Also written for military piping in 6/8 and can be found in 4/4 common time as well
- Very often the first tune type played in a typical Cape Breton grouping of tunes
- Heard at funerals, weddings, pubs, concerts, house sessions, or as an interlude at a dance

Reel
- Fastest tempo tune in Cape Breton traditional music
- 4/4 common time
- Probably originated in France, but popularized and evolved to its recognized form in Scotland; its existence is usually attributed to the Scots.
- Travelled to Ireland from Scotland and became popular there, beginning in the late 1700s
- First and third beats in each measure are emphasized; thus, the foot is tapped twice in a measure. Say this in your head as you listen to a reel (the large letters are the stressed beat, where the foot would be tapped in these two measures): "THIS is how a RE-el goes// THIS is how a RE-el goes."
- The reel and the strathspey (see below) are the two main tune types for step-dancing in Cape Breton.
- Heard in almost any setting such as house session, pub, dance, concert, etc.
- Most often, the last tune type to be played in a medley, but reels can also be heard/played on their own in succession (i.e., for a third figure of a square set (see dancing))
- Cape Breton performance approach of the reel differs from modern Scottish and Irish playing. There are fewer slurs, more backbeat, occasional to fairly regular dotted notes and usually a slower tempo.

Strathspey
- Originated in the Highlands of Scotland in the strath (valley) of the River Spey and evolved from the reel
- In its early years was called the strathspey reel while the original reel was sometimes referred to as the Athol reel
- Also 4/4 common time, notes have a dotted (short long/long short) rhythm think jagged); foot is tapped on each beat (four times) in a measure. Say this in your head as you listen to a strathspey: "CocaCola Coca Cola//CocaCola CocaCola"
- Listened or step-danced to, followed by a reel or reels; often follows a slow air or march
- A newer performance approach exists in Scotland due to the decline in step-dancing, the influence of "improvers" such as J. Scott Skinner and cohesion of possible regional performance discrepancies between Lowland and Highland Scotland that wouldn't have taken effect during the time the immigrants arrived in Cape Breton.
- Strathspeys are also said to have been played and may still be occasionally heard in the northwest of Ireland (i.e., Donegal) probably because of the close proximity to western Scotland (travel, cultural exchange).

Slow strathspey
- For listening to; not for dancing
- 4/4-time, a reflective, smooth-flowing type of tune, it's faster than a slow air, but slower than a regular strathspey.
- Probably gained increasing popularity in the mid-19th century with purveyors/composers like William Marshall and, later, J. Scott Skinner

Jig
- Most likely English or German origin, but most often associated with Irish music
- Listen-to tune, but known as a dance tune type.
- 6/8-time jigs are the most common to Cape Breton, although one may occasionally hear some in 9/8 or 12/8. Slip jigs 9/8 are common in Irish tradition.
- For the most common 6/8 jig, think of the notes being divided into two groups of three in a measure. As you hear a jig, say this to yourself: "jiggidy jiggidy//jiggidy jiggiddy." The foot is tapped twice in a measure on "jig."
- Played less than strathspeys and reels until well after the migrations, jigs didn't become a staple in Cape Breton tradition until probably the late 1800s and into the early 1900s. This coincided with the introduction of lancers and quadrilles square sets to Cape Breton from the northeastern U.S.
- With the introduction of the new square sets came the need for more jigs; thus, many were locally composed and some came from Irish tradition.

Clog and hornpipe
- Most likely of English origin
- Absorbed into Irish, Scottish and probably Manx tradition from increasing English musical influence
- Both are 4/4 common time
- Clog is almost always considered the slower tempo of the two (think something like march tempo), although occasionally a hornpipe will be interchanged and played more as a clog.

- Hornpipes have been "smoothed out" in Cape Breton and sound more like (and are often played with) reels. They end with a "thump thump thump" sounding note combination in the last measure, as do usually clogs.
- Clogs are most often dotted on the first and third notes in a group of four
- As you listen to a clog, say to yourself, "CLOGyCLOGy CLOGyCLOGy // CLOGyCLOGy CLOGy CLOGy."
- As you listen to a hornpipe, think as you did above for a reel, but listen to the "thump thump thump" ending.
- The foot is tapped twice in a measure, on the first and third beats for both clogs and hornpipes.
- Hornpipes and clogs were probably not commonly found in Cape Breton until the early 1900s when Cape Breton fiddlers would have been migrating to the "Boston States" where they would have absorbed these tune forms from Irish and possibly Anglo-Scottish players. These tune forms aren't as popular in Cape Breton as the core Gaelic tune types.
- Played at house sessions, pubs, concerts and occasionally at dances
- Specific dances correspond to clogs and hornpipes in other traditions, but these tune types are mainly considered listening "performance" tunes in Cape Breton.
- Many popular clogs and hornpipes are played together in medleys in Cape Breton and are often associated with keys in the flats.

Waltz

- Originated in continental Europe, most likely the suburbs of Vienna and the alpine region of Austria
- 3/4 tune with focus on first beat, often played for slower, couples dancing
- When listening to a waltz, say to yourself, "ONE two three // ONE two three" Moved across Europe to France and by around 1816 found its way to England. After this found its way into Irish and Scottish tradition. A new addition to Cape Breton tradition
- Sometimes played fairly slowly in Cape Breton as a reflective piece

Polka

- 2/4-time, sometimes common time, couples dance-tune of likely Czech Bohemian or Polish origin; invented as late as 1834
- Made its way to the British Isles and the U.S. by the mid-1800s and probably didn't find its way into Cape Breton until the early 1900s
- When listening to a polka, say to yourself, "ONE and two and// ONE and two and." Imagine yourself doing the "Junior High Shuffle" (side to side with your feet on the beat) to this type of tune. Foot is tapped twice in each measure.
- Polkas are not common in Cape Breton, but were popular in Antigonish County.
  - Prominent purveyor: pioneering recording artist Hugh A. MacDonald
- Polkas and waltzes were added into social dance settings, arriving with immigrants to urban industrial areas like (most likely) Pictou and industrial Cape Breton and with migration between northeastern Nova Scotia, Cape Breton and northeastern U.S.

SOME TUNE TYPES IN OTHER CELTIC TRADITIONS

Highland
- Irish 4/4 tune type based on strathspeys, most prominent in Northwest of Ireland (i.e., Donegal)

Highland Scottische
- common time
- heard in Ireland and Scotland
- probably newer, but similar to a strathspey; sometimes played as a strathspey

Scotch measure
- Similar to a reel, but more "genteel"
- More sparse, note-wise, than reels with a "thump thump thump" ending like horn-pipes
- Played for the non-Gaelic dances found in Scottish country dancing

Slip Jig
- Irish-associated 9/8 jig

Slide
- 12/8 Irish jig-like tune type played briskly

Quickstep
- Scottish. Originally played as a quick tempo march, sometimes played as a reel

CELTIC DANCE

Although there are beautiful slow airs, marches and slow strathspeys found in Celtic music traditions, and this music is a pleasure to simply listen to, it is most often described as dance music. Indeed, the music has been danced to over centuries, but just as cultures evolve, so do the artforms within them. Perhaps some now think of Highland Games held all over the world with Highland dancers gracefully bouncing to the skirl of the bagpipes in hopes of earning top honours in the various games competitions. Yes, these are forms of dance within the Irish and Scottish traditions, but research shows that these are newly-evolved dance forms. There were/are earlier, more traditional dance forms found in Gaelic Scotland and Ireland— dance forms passed on in aural tradition that was, for many years, unaffected by the English and other cultures.

For various reasons, cultures change. In the case of Scotland and Ireland, one must look to formalization of piping and dancing artforms, especially prevalent since the mid-1800s, largely due to the influence of elites more closely tied to English culture than Gaelic. These "improvers" of tradition looked to appeal to the tastes of the upper class through a process of formalization and institutionalization, primarily associated with the Lowlands, in the case of Scotland. To better understand this, let's look at the evolution of Celtic dance, focusing on what is seen here on Cape Breton Island, beginning with the most popular dance type found in the island's rural/Gaelic districts: step-dancing.

STEP-DANCING

- A solo, individually expressive endeavour, the dancer steps out beats in time to the music, the feet often producing a percussive sound, although visual presentation and proficiency of performance is more important than feet sounds.
- Step-dancing is "close-to-the-floor," (done neatly within a couple of square feet of space), the best dancers moving mainly from the knees down to the feet, arms held in a relaxed manner to the sides of the torso, and head facing straight and parallel to the floor.
- Step-dancing is done primarily to strathspeys and reels, although stepping to jigs and reels in imported square sets (see social dancing) has been done in Cape Breton since around the mid 1900s.
- Research suggests that step-dancing is the oldest of Scotland's Gaelic solo dance traditions. For instance, in 1784, an Englishman observed Gaels in the Highlands "treepling" (beating out rhythms with the feet) to the music, which wasn't a part of the social dancing in the south of Scotland, again suggesting that step-dancing was an earlier artform in Scottish Gaelic, and therefore in Celtic, tradition.
- Evidence suggests that strathspey steps evolved from the Highland fling that previously incorporated close-to-the-floor, sideways movements (not to be confused with the modern Highland fling and dancing as described below).
- Step-dancing seems to be more similar to old-style Irish dancing than contemporary Highland dancing, suggesting the closer relationship between Scottish Gaelic and Irish Gaelic culture, than Scottish Gaelic and Lowland Scottish, at least until around the turn of the 19th century.
- There are also historical accounts of "stepping" observed in the Highlands around the time of emigration.
- The step-dancing in Cape Breton is most often done in hard-soled shoes and is a tradition passed from generation to generation since the arrival of the island's first Scottish Gaelic immigrants in a similar vein as the Gaelic singing and fiddling traditions.
- Step-dancing is generally considered a solo artform although in the last few decades, one may see two or more dancers put together prescribed routines, most often for formal performance situations.
- At various ceilidhs, weddings and picnics, Gaels step-danced through four and eight hand reels as well (see social dancing).

HIGHLAND DANCING
Old Highland dancing

- Historical accounts of Highland dancing suggest that these standardized dances were done in the Highlands with "stepping" throughout, not dainty, soft-shoed "bouncing" that we see now in Scotland, parts of Cape Breton and elsewhere. The dances had prescribed patterns and steps. In contrast, while the style of dancing was interchangeable with step-dancing, solo step-dancing didn't have prescribed steps.
- Some specific dances: Highland fling, The Flowers of Edinburgh, Seann Triubhas (Old Trousers) and Smaladh na Coinnle (Snuffing the Candle).
- Eventually, and especially after the Napoleonic wars, new dance forms were making their way northward in Scotland from continental Europe and England. Also, by the 1820s, religious fundamentalism and anglicizing forces were taking their toll on Gaelic culture and dancing did not go unaffected.

Contemporary/modern Highland dancing
- A genteel type of Scottish dance originating in the Scottish Lowlands, beginning around the end of the 18th century.
- Brought into popularity with efforts of dance masters and Lowland-based "improvers" who introduced more balletic and higher kicking steps, which were implemented into the movements of the older Highland dances such as the Highland fling and the Seann Triubhas. The newer dancing eventually made its way into the Highlands.
- As with the piping tradition, the popularity of dance competitions in the Highland games circuit (brought forth by urban elites) focused on formalization, romanticism and gentility—all pleasing to the tastes of the English and elites in the urban Lowland areas. Costumes were also invented and required for competition and performance. As scholar Mike Kennedy has noted, the Gaelic content and context at these events within the piping and Highland dancing realms, were virtually eliminated. Essentially they would take over their Gaelic precursors in the 19th century.
- By the 1900s, Highland dancing could be described more as "art" than "Gaelic" dancing.
- In 1939 contemporary Highland dancing and some country dances (see social dancing) were introduced to the Gaelic College of Arts and Crafts in St. Ann's Cape Breton. However, they were unfamiliar to most of the local Gaelic population and led some to question the authenticity of their own local dancing. Research by such scholars as Rhodes, Flett and Flett, Dunlay and Kennedy has since firmly established that step-dancing is rooted in Scottish Gaelic tradition and preceded modern Highland dancing and Scottish country dancing.
- Highland dancing is said to have undergone noticeable changes since the 1950s.

SOCIAL DANCING
Foursome reel/Scotch four
- Previously called the foursome, or four-hand reel, this dance has become known as the Scotch four in Cape Breton.
- In Cape Breton, this involves two couples doing a routine of stationary and travelling step-dancing moving into interchanging positions, in a figure-eight type formation.
- This was danced to reels in the Highlands, but may have also been danced to the strathspey and reels as the two terms were still used interchangeably up until around the primary migrations to Nova Scotia.
- Done on celebratory and ceremonial occasions in Gaelic society, the Scotch four was often performed at the commencement of wedding receptions in Cape Breton, Prince Edward Island and northeastern Nova Scotia to specific tunes commonly known as the wedding reels, featuring the bride and groom and best man and maid-of-honour. Sometimes the parents of the newly married couple would join in as a second Scotch four.

Eightsome reel
- Involved four couples step-dancing to reels through a prescribed routine.
- Sometimes referred to as the wild eight because of its liveliness, it is safe to guess that the excitement it provided was similar to the square set third figure (see below) danced now in Cape Breton.

Square dancing
  - Square dancing is considered by some to be a traditional social dance in Cape Breton. It was actually introduced from the northeastern U.S. in the late-1800 to early-1900s.
  - Square sets evolved from quadrilles and lancers, which came from England, France and continental Europe and infiltrated the Isle of Man, Ireland, Lowland Scotland, Highland Scotland, northeastern U.S., PEI and Cape Breton. Quadrilles and lancers were actually popular in urban capital areas like Halifax and Charlottetown by the 1830s and 40s but, as seen above, didn't reach the rural areas like Cape Breton until around the turn of that century.
  - Square sets involve four couples going through prescribed formations/routines. One set is often divided into three or more figures (parts) with different prescribed formations/routines. Jigs and reels are the most common tunes played for square sets in Cape Breton, with the occasional "Cape Bretonized" hornpipe thrown in. Evolution has led to a general allowance of more than four couples to a set since at least the 1980s.
  - There are different variations of the sets around Cape Breton. For instance, in Inverness County, sets are comprised of two jig figures and a reel figure while sets in the Christmas Island/Boisdale areas are made up of one jig figure and two reel figures.
  - Similar dances are "walked" through in other regions, but square sets were "Gaelicized," especially in Inverness County, by step-dancing throughout. However, a couple of accounts from local seniors indicate that step-dancing through the sets may not have become common until the 1940s or 50s.
  - The infiltration of square sets in Cape Breton contributed to players adding Irish jigs and locally-composed jigs to the Cape Breton repertoire.
  - Solo step-dancing is done as an interlude during square dances.

NON-GAELIC SOCIAL DANCING
Polka, waltz, round dancing
  - As mentioned earlier, people dance to these newer music forms as interludes at square dances. Polkas were favoured dance pieces in Antigonish County.
  - Polkas and waltzes may have been more common first in industrial areas such as Pictou County or Sydney/Glace Bay, etc., with arrival of continental European and English immigrants.
  - A fiddler may also occasionally play "songs" on the fiddle at a dance such as the occasional Anglo-Irish folk song, again, as an interlude.
  - Although fiddling and square dancing were "kings" in Cape Breton for the first half of the 20th century, round dancing to singing was implemented and round and square dances became common to the island for much of the second half of the century.

Scottish country dancing
  - A non-Gaelic dance form, Scottish country dancing was introduced from England to Scotland around 1700. Social, couples dancing, this genteel dance type involved couples going through various figures/specified dances in prescribed formations in "long-ways" sets. Dunlay's research tells us that country dancing became accepted in the Lowlands and then the nearby Highland areas by the 1800s, but didn't reach the Western Isles until the 1850s. This suggests strongly that these dances

would not have been familiar to the Scottish Gael as most migration to Cape Breton would have occurred by this time. The Lowland Scottish tradition eventually formed and broke away from English tradition after 1800, as the dance steps and figures were added to the point that a distinct style had emerged. Before this in England, however, dances were often done to the playing of Scottish tune types such as reels and their simpler, less rhythmic cousins, Scotch measures. Hence, even in England, some of these dances were known as Scottish country dances.

- Dance steps in the Lowlands are said to have been newer, having developed simultaneously with the balletic "new" Highland dancing while the dancing in the Highlands retained (for a longer time) its older Gaelic character.
- As step-dancing died in Scotland, the newer introductions to Scottish culture became accepted by later generations as "tradition." What was foreign to previous generations essentially became an accepted cultural truth to those that followed, even in the Highlands. Seemingly that trend of forgotten tradition has spread to Scottish descendants around the globe, partly because of influential authorities from various "tradition preserving" institutions.
- Scottish country dancing was brought to Cape Breton by Scottish authorities through the St. Ann's Gaelic College in 1939.

SOME OTHER CELTIC-INFLUENCED DANCE
Irish dance
- Evidence of dancing in Ireland appears as early as the 12th century when round dances were introduced by the Normans. These involved people dancing in a ring to the verse of a chanter/leader while the dancers sang back a refrain.
- Centuries later, we see the term "Hey" which was a type of round dance where women wove in and around their partners. Common dances included Pacing the Whip, Trotting the Hey and Skipping the Gort. These dances seem to have come from the country dances introduced by the English, which had in turn come from France. The dances were more popular in the Pale (an area of English settlement and rule) and weren't as lively as those found in the Irish areas outside the Pale.
- By 1750 and toward the end of the 18th century, Irish dance masters became prominent on the cultural landscape. They helped bring Irish step-dancing to higher status by inventing new steps and teaching the young through organized instruction. The advent of dance masters in Ireland paralleled their existence in Scotland and Cape Breton.
- Jigs were the most commonly danced tunes, and by the late 1700s, when the reel is thought to have been introduced to Ireland from Scotland, this tune type became the next most popular for dancing. At this point, Irish step-dancing may have been similar to and strongly related to Scottish Gaelic step-dancing that was now coming to Cape Breton with the migrations. Seeing that Ireland was de-Gaelicized around 150 years before Gaelic Scotland, the assumption can be made that step-dancing in Cape Breton may be our closest indicator of what may have commonly existed in Scotland and Ireland before the English conquest of Ireland in 1603.
- Country and figure dances remained popular throughout the 1800s while céilí dances, based on quadrilles were the most popular in that century and the 1900s. As with Cape Breton, they had localized forms.
- In 1893 Connradhna Gaeilge (the Gaelic League) was formed to revive Ireland's English-suppressed culture. Ironically, they pushed strongly for the advancement of céilí dances, dances not so definitively traditional.

- In 1929 An Coimisiun le Rinci Gaelacha (Irish Dancing Commission) was formed. It was responsible for standardizing dance competitions. Since then there has been an evolution in style, costumes, footwear, venues, etc. For instance, arms were once held more loosely than the rigid manner we see today. This reveals an earlier similarity to Cape Breton step-dancing. Also, larger performance areas (bigger stages) brought about more movement across larger areas and higher kicking movements, which came to be required in competition.
- Today, the main types of Irish dance are the jig, reel, hornpipe and set dances (dances to specific tunes).

Ottawa Valley and Metis step-dancing
- Step-dancing found in these areas of Canada is exuberant and lively, with more leg and arm movement than that found in Cape Breton step-dancing. Step-dance competitions are found in this area as well, another differing feature from Cape Breton step-dancing.
- Step-dancing in the Ottawa Valley is most likely a hybrid of Gaelic step-dancing and other forms from ethnicities such as French, German and Irish as they would mix and influence each other at lumber camps, creating a blending of fiddling and dance styles.
- Scottish, Native and French culture blending would have contributed to Metis fiddle and dance styles.

CAPE BRETON FIDDLE MUSIC:
MAKING AND MAINTAINING A TRADITION

COMPANION CD NOTES

by Glenn Graham

Editor's note: All selections were recorded live—mostly home recordings—because this best represents the "natural" setting by the tune types chosen. In other words, these are traditional tunes in traditional settings, rather than studio recordings. The use of home recordings (as opposed to commercial) emphasizes the author's views about the making and maintaining of this musical tradition. The home recordings presented here are from private collections kindly provided to assist the reader to understand and appreciate the tradition.

We are grateful to the performers, composers and those who hold the original recordings, for allowing their inclusion here. The CD is included with the book for the purpose expressed and not for commercial use—it is not to be sold or copied. All rights reserved.

If such a thing is possible, what follows is an analysis of the playing styles of various players in the Cape Breton tradition. There are many Cape Breton players that I could have chosen—I merely picked those whose music I had easy access to, were most prominent in the book and who, together, reveal a wide range of styles. Although there is a recognizable general style, individual performers can be distinguished from one another. These selections provide good examples of techniques used in traditional Cape Breton music. I do not claim to be an expert musical theorist, and my descriptions are meant to be accessible and understandable to readers with even a

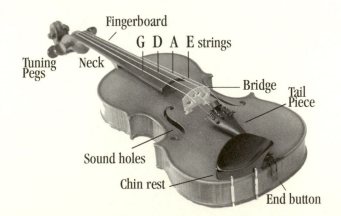

passing interest in the music. For a more in-depth theoretical analysis of Cape Breton Music techniques, I recommend that the reader seek out the various works of Kate Dunlay and David Greenberg.

1. Glenn Graham: Cape Breton fiddling techniques as described in the book.

2. Mary MacDonald with Mary Jessie MacDonald
Lady Ann Hope Strathspey, Allowa Kirk Strathspey, Sir Harry's Welcome Home Strathspey, Tullochgorm Strathspey, Lord MacDonald's Reel, Miss Johnstone's Reel

"Little" Mary MacDonald is playing strathspeys and reels in the key of G here. Mary used a lot of ornamentation and drones in her playing. Grace notes can be heard in the first strathspey. Also, when she plays on the D string, she simultaneously plays subtle, underlying G drones. The same can be heard in the second and third strathspeys which also seem to provide for more placements of grace notes.

She then goes on and plays one of her specialties—an older version of "Tullochorm" (most fiddlers who play the tune play the J. Scott Skinner version with his composed/arranged variations). Mary can be heard masterfully executing shakes of the bow, "cutting up" the strathspey. She also produces a "bigger" sound by playing two strings at once, often hitting notes on separate strings at harmony with each other, giving the sound of a chord. For instance, at the end of a tune-ending in G, she would also play a B note on the A string, beefing up the melody. This is a common feature of accomplished Cape Breton fiddlers. She then makes a smooth transition into the first reel, bringing the strathspey tempo into the beginning measures and then increasing the tempo to consistent timing. Again, one can hear her playing on two strings and implementing grace notes.

3. Angus Chisholm with Mary Jessie MacDonald
Moonlight Clog, The Cuckoo Clog, The Galway Hornpipe, The Western Clog (partial)

This clip is classic Angus Chisholm, one of the most technically proficient players ever in the Cape Breton tradition. Note that his style is somewhat cleaner than Mary MacDonald's. This is not to say that he's applying more difficult ornamentations and bowings, but his gracings are lightening fast while he plays with ease here tunes of notable difficulty. More attention is paid to purity on the melody notes as opposed to extensive droning in this instance. We also hear him masterfully bow quick, complex note combinations, ending his tunes with quick, pure vibrato.

On piano, is Mary Jessie MacDonald, daughter of Little Mary MacDonald. Her bass-hand playing has always been deep and strong while she masterfully played/plays the melody line along with the fiddler without being too dominant. She was also more exploratory with her chords than other players of her time, probably because of some background education in jazz.

4. Winston "Scotty" Fitzgerald with Mary Jessie MacDonald

Bovaglie's Plaid –Air (J. Scott Skinner), *The Red Shoes Reel* (Dan R. MacDonald), *The Snowplough* Reel (Dan Hughie MacEachern), *St. Kilda's Wedding Reel, Trip to Windsor Reel* (Dan R. MacDonald)

The late Winston Fitzgerald is another revered exponent of technical proficiency on the violin. His playing was clear and crisp, up-tempo with lightening-fast ornamentation. In this slow air we hear a free-flowing approach with controlled bowing, examples of staccato bowing, the rarely used in Cape Breton *slide* ornament and a pure, clean tone. In the reels we hear crisp grace notes with the slight drone of the open strings above and below those on which the melody is played—a classic performance feature of many Cape Breton fiddlers that gives the music a full textural sound. Open string drones can be heard applied above melody notes played on the A and D strings. Winston also graces the open E note in this instance. Strong cuttings and grace notes on the high D note can be heard in "St. Kilda's Wedding Reel." Open string drones and gracings on the high A melody notes can also be heard on his rendition here of Dan R. MacDonald's "Trip to Windsor Reel." The tempo builds in the reels towards Winston's recognizable lively swing. Mary Jessie MacDonald accompanies, again, with her powerful piano bass lines.

5. Donald Angus Beaton with Elizabeth Beaton

Maids of Islay Strathspey, Lucy Campbell Strathspey, Elizabeth's Big Coat Reel, MacKinnon's Other Rant Reel, John of Badenyon Reel, Hamish the Carpenter Reel

Donald Angus Beaton's specialties were the Gaelic dance tune types—strathspeys and reels. He was a popular dance player while both musicians and listeners describe his playing as having the Gaelic flavour. There was a noticeable rollicking and driving rhythm, in the Mabou Coal Mines fashion: a little extra force and accent on the beat of the tunes. His playing was thick and highly ornamented with various ornaments such as grace notes and "warbles" (a pressure-release-pressure of the finger applied to a note; another Greenberg and Dunlay term), as heard in the sample strathspey. Also, as the melody is played on the A string, a slight E string drone is heard throughout. As the melody is played on the E, a subtle A string drone can sometimes be heard. Both techniques mimic the Highland bagpipe. In the reel, Mabou Coal Mines-style wild notes can be heard—at the pick-up/first introductory note and at the beginning of the third measure (halfway through part one). He often utilized the driven bow. Also note double up-pushes on the bow, creating added accent for extra lilt, instead of a common smoother sounding up-bowed slur. His cuts/cuttings were prominent and emphasized in his playing while more "lift" was added to his reels by dotting ("strathspeying," as I've heard it termed by Kinnon Beaton) his reels. The result: extra snap and rhythm.

Accompanying Donald Angus is his wife Elizabeth. Her approach is in the old style, using a lot of lower bass keys with basic bass lines. In this cut, listen to a lot of right-hand syncopation on the strathspey with added matching force with the fiddle on emphasized beats, a lot of the time—those most often being the first and third beats (first and second foot tap in each measure) in the reels. This complemented the emphasis that Donald Angus often placed on the same beats, creating a driving Mabou Coal Mines sound.

6. Theresa MacLellan with Marie MacLellan

John McColl's Farewell March, Sportsman's Haunt Strathspey, Calum Crubach Strathspey, Kay Girroir's Reel (Joey Beaton), *Muileann Dubh Reel*

In this selection, we hear Theresa playing a march, the tune form for which she is most recognized. Theresa has also been noted by many as having a "Gaelic" sound to her music. She plays slight and quick vibrato throughout the march with various gracings. Listening closely, one can hear a drawn-out ornament common to the old style whereby a melody note is broken up into what sounds like three notes. The melody note is played, then quickly the finger above hits the string, then the melody note hits again, all keeping the same value of time as one melody note would hold in a written transcription. So, instead of the sound going like this: ___, it would be heard like this: _-_. The result is a tasty guttural sound. She can also be heard subtly playing two strings at the same time, creating a thick sound and, at times, harmonized undertones.

She's accompanied by her sister, the late Marie MacLellan. Again, as with most older-style Cape Breton pianists, Marie often used and stayed with the lower keys with the bass hand, and at times can be heard expertly playing the melody line with her right hand. She had a distinguishing "galloping" rhythm that she often used toward the further right upper keys on the piano with her right hand.

7. Buddy MacMaster with John Morris Rankin

Dusky Meadow Strathspey (Donald MacLellan), *Devil in the Kitchen Strathspey* (J. Scott Skinner), *Margaree Reel, Traditional Reel, Miss Stewart of Glentully Reel, Magnetic Hornpipe/Sean McGuire Reel, Put Me in the Box Reel*

As stated earlier in the book, Kate Dunlay has noted that Buddy is a great example of a player bridging the old and the new styles. He uses lots of quick grace notes, has a sweet (yet not overwhelming) vibrato and uses long, powerful and dynamic bow strokes. His playing is widely described as correct and precise. It has a lovely lilt and steady drive, while his tone is sweet, warm and thick. Buddy can be heard here playing strathspeys for a step-dancer. Note the rich tone and technical prowess as he plays the quick sixteenth notes in the last phrase of the first strathspey, "Dusky Meadow." He can be heard "doubling" with his pinky finger placed over the A string to create a closed E note—very important to the Cape Breton style. The beat is steady, exhilarating and builds into the second strathspey, "Devil in the Kitchen." Strong emphasis is placed on the cuts. Various gracings can be heard in this tune, for example, on the beat of the lower octave third part of the tune. In the "Margaree Reel," Buddy graces his high A notes and again can be heard "doubling" (closing with the pinky on the A) the open E notes. Grace notes are applied throughout "Traditional Reel" and can also be noted in the second part (turn) of "Miss Stewart of Glentully Reel."

Buddy is accompanied by the late John Morris Rankin, often noted as a leading figure in bringing Cape Breton piano accompaniment into a "newer" stylistic era. His style was busier than those of the older style, yet didn't distract from the leading instrument. As noted earlier in this book, John Morris was a leader in using more bass lines, "walking" up and down the keys with his left hand, adding more chords within the tune structures and being more creative with added right hand rhythmic variations. Note steady bursts of syncopation followed by flowing right hand rhythmic touches in the strathspeys.

8. Kinnon Beaton with John Morris Rankin

Celtic Ceilidh Reel (Dan R. MacDonald), *Miss Smallness House Reel, Leventine's Barrel Hornpipe, The Hughie and Allan Reel* (Kinnon Beaton), *Master McDermott's Reel, Derrick Beaton's Reel* (Donald Angus Beaton)

Kinnon Beaton is thought of today by many musicians and dancers in the Cape Breton tradition as the consummate dance player. Kinnon, like Buddy, is a fine example of combining the old and the new. His bowing is reminiscent of the Mabou Coal Mines style with varying pressures applied, the bow being dug into the strings in one instant, then let off the next—adding lilt and "danceability" to his music—as heard in these reels played in the 1980s. His tone is sweet and warm; his timing and application rock steady and smooth. Kinnon will occasionally add tasteful drones, vibrato, wild notes, bowing variations, gracings and dotted reel notes ("strathspeying" the reels) while he "cuts up" some strathspeys and has strong "up bow" pushes. He, too, is recognized as a correct player.

I want the listener to recognize the connection between the music and the dancing from this square set third figure of reels. You can hear the feet treepling of many well-known Mabou dancers in the background complementing Kinnon's steady driving dance playing. Again, John Morris Rankin provides the piano accompaniment with his moving bass, varying right-hand rhythms (syncopation, etc.), superb chord choice and impeccable timing. Also, listen closely for Kinnon's syncopated foot tap that gives a "thump-slap" sound—the heel (thump) rocks to the toe (slap). Like his father Donald Angus Beaton before him, Kinnon also does a toe tap in between each "thump-slap" for a one measure percussive sound that goes: Thump-Slap-ah/Thump-Slap-ah. It can be heard slightly near the end of the selection, complementing the feet of the dancers doing the "hop" (the main dance step for the reels).

9. Howie MacDonald with Mac Morin and Dave MacIsaac

Betty Matheson's Jig (Howie MacDonald), *Cherish the Ladies Jig, Tatter Jack Walsh Jig*

This selection is a fine example of the growth of jigs within the Cape Breton tradition since the introduction of square dancing. Here we see an example of Irish and locally-composed jigs added to the repertoire as Howie MacDonald starts with his own composition, followed by a tune that Howie learned from influential Irish fiddler

Sean McGuire and then finishing with another traditional Irish jig. Jackie Dunn-MacIsaac has described Howie's playing to me as "sassy," a good description. It is fun, in that he is open to using his technical proficiency adding personal variation to tunes and occasionally playing tunes not too common to the tradition. However, his interpretation as a traditional fiddler is also superb, employing the common ornamentations like grace notes, cuts, drones, etc.

One can also hear the influence of such players as Jerry Holland, Buddy Mac-Master and Winston Fitzgerald in Howie's clean tone and application. In the first jig, Howie can be heard playing the melody on the D string and playing an open A string in unison, especially in the last measure and a half of each part of the tune, producing a thicker, more melodic interpretation than if he had simply played on one string. One can also hear him employing grace notes. He tends to use his "pinky" finger for lightening fast gracings that sound "chirp-like," similar to those of Winston Fitzgerald. (My father tells me that Dan R. MacDonald noted that Winston's "pinky is like a snake's tongue," providing a mental picture of what this technique looks like when applied.) The same types of techniques can be heard in the next two jigs. While a bow stroke forming a cross-beat type of slur with a gracing occurs in the second jig, a down-bow is employed at the end of a measure/bar and the commencement of another. This bowing application is often heard in Mabou Coal Mines-playing as well. Howie's driving consistent timing is notable in these jigs.

Mac Morin, one of Cape Breton's most popular piano players is accompanying. His playing exhibits the influence of players like John Morris Rankin and Tracey Dares-MacNeil, employing wide rhythmic variation, extended chord use and knowledge, use of dynamics, and moving/climbing bass hand playing. Accompanying on guitar is Dave MacIsaac, well-known for his tasty use of bass lines on the guitar complemented by some percussive rhythmic strumming, dynamics and a sensitivity that avoids overriding the approach of the pianist and fiddler.

10. Ian MacDougall with Mac Morin
Heavy is My Fate – Air

Ian MacDougall is often described as having the old style. His first influential teacher was the great composer John MacDougall, who I'm sure enforced to Ian the importance of the fourth finger for "doubling" the open string notes. This, combined with extensive use of drones, grace notes and driving, consistent bowing, can be heard in Ian's performance of dance tunes. However, Ian's old style can be heard on this slow air known by some as "Heavy is My Fate" on the recording *From Foot Cape*. The tune begins with a tasty introduction by Mac Morin, one of the best examples of evolved, knowledgeable piano accompaniment and notably a top proponent on the "slow stuff." Mac's approach here is gentle, decorative and creative. The third note Ian plays is a doubled E. The first A note on the second beat is applied in true traditional fashion with Ian dragging a first finger (low E) note into the doubled A instead of just playing the melody A note. This creates a thicker, more expressive result. He then plays notes on the D string simultaneously with an underlying open G string drone. This is common to the old sound, giving it a bagpipe feel, very notable in the playing of the late Dan Joe MacInnis. Ian also subtly plays an open G drone with the G notes ending the first and second parts of the tune. On the repeat of part one, on the D note, very first beat, Ian in the old style breaks up the D into three sounds with a grace note above breaking up the D.

The similar type of ornament is used throughout, adding a guttural accentuation, similar perhaps to pipe gracings or the expression in a Gaelic singer's voice. Regular grace notes are also heard whereby the note above the melody note is employed just before the melody note. Slight vibrato is added as well, especially on his ending G notes. The drones and subtle playing on two strings are very noticeable on this cut, reinforcing the idea that the "bigger" sound gives Cape Breton fiddling added expression.

Beaton, Donald Angus. "Tamarack'er Down Reel." Port Hawkesbury, NS: Privately Published, 2000.

Beaton, Elizabeth. Discussion with the author. 2004.

Birn, Jennifer. "Massive Music Merger—Industry restructuring leaves signed Valley bands in limbo." December 1998. http://www.angelfire.com/az/lowwatts/wattsgetout.html

Bitterman, Rusty. "On Remembering and Forgetting: Highland Memories Within the Maritime Diaspora." In *Myth, Migration, and the Making of Memory: Scotia and Nova Scotia, c.1700-1900*, edited by Marjorie Harper and Michael E. Vance, 253-65. Halifax: Fernwood; Edinburgh: John Donald, 1999.

Blaustein, Richard. "Traditional Music and Social Change: The Old-Time Fiddlers Association Movement in the United States." Diss., U of Indiana, 1975.

Bruford, Alan. "Highland Fiddle Music." In *The Companion to Gaelic Scotland*, edited by Derick S. Thomson. Oxford: Blackwell, 1983.

Bruford, Alan and Ailie Munro. "The Fiddle in the Highlands." *Highland Information Series* 29. Inverness, Scotland: An Comunn Gàidhealach, 1973.

Bumsted, J. M. *The People's Clearance: Highland Emigration to British North America, 1770-1815*. Edinburgh: Edinburgh University Press; Winnipeg: University of Manitoba Press, 1982.

—. "John MacGregor." *Dictionary of Canadian Biography* 8. Toronto: University of Toronto Press, 1985.

Cameron, John Donald. Interview by Joseph Beaton. Judique, NS. 15 October, 1993.

Cameron, John Donald. "Dan Rory MacDonald: An Informal Biography." Unpublished typescript. Privately available from J. D. Cameron, Judique, NS.

Cameron, John Donald. Interview with John Allan Cameron. 31 July, 1995.

Campbell, P. J. MacKenzie. *Highland Community on the Bras D'Or*. Antigonish, NS: Casket Printing and Publishing, 1978.

Campbell, Wilfred. *The Scotsman in Canada*. Toronto: Musson, 1911.

Caplan, Ronald, Bonnie Thompson and Ruth Schneider. "The Cape Breton Fiddler: A Talk with Allister MacGillivray." *Cape Breton's Magazine*. No. 29. August 1981.

—. "With Winston 'Scotty' Fitzgerald." *Cape Breton's Magazine*. No. 46. November 1987.

Carlin, Richard, ed. *The Gow Collection of Scottish Dance Music*. New York: Oak Publications, 1986.

Carmichael, Alexander. *Charms of the Gaels: Hymns and Incantations [Translation of Carmina Gadelica, 1899]*. Edinburgh: Floris Books, 1992.

Clow, Michael. "Politics and Uneven Capitalist Development: The Maritime Challenge to the Study of Canadian Political Economy." *Studies in Political Economy* 14 (1984).

Cockburn, Craig. "Article on Gaelic *Puirt-a-Beul* (Mouth Music)." 30 April, 2004. http://www.siliconglen.com/culture/puirtabeul.html

Collinson, Francis. *The Traditional National Music of Scotland*. London: Routledge and Kegan Paul, 1966.

Cranford, Paul. "Introduction." *Winston Fitzgerald: A Collection of Fiddle Tunes*. Englishtown, NS: Cranford Publications, 1997.

Denny, Mike. Discussion with the author. August 2002.

Doherty, Elizabeth. "The Paradox of the Periphery: Evolution of the Cape Breton Fiddle Tradition, c. 1928-1995." Diss., University of Limerick, 1996.

Dunlay, Kate. Review of "Full Circle," by Bill Lamey, and "The Judique Flyer," by Buddy MacMaster. *Am Bràighe* no. 8, 2 (Autumn 2000): 15. http:www.ambraigh.ca/stories/story-content/judiqueFlyer.htm

Dunlay, Kate and David Greenberg, *Traditional Celtic Violin Music of Cape Breton: The Dungreen Collection.* Toronto: Dungreen Music, 1996.

Dunlay, Kathleen E., "The Playing of Traditional Scottish Dance Music: Old and New World Styles and Practices." In *Celtic Languages and Celtic Peoples: Proceedings from the Second North American Congress of Celtic Studies,* edited by Cyril J. Byrne, Margaret Harry, Pádraig Ó Siadhail. Halifax: D'Arcy McGee Chair of Irish Studies, St. Mary's University, 1992.

Dunn, Charles W. *Highland Settler: A Portrait of the Scottish Gael in Nova Scotia.* Toronto: University of Toronto Press, 1953.

Dunn, Jacqueline Ann. "'Tha Blas na Gàidhlig Air a h-Uile Fidhleir' (The Sound of Gaelic is in the Fiddler's Music)." BA thesis, St. Francis Xavier University, 1991.

Dunn, Margaret. "Introduction." *MacEachern's Collection.* Vol. 2. Antigonish, NS: Casket Printing and Publishing, 1993.

Emmerson, George S. *Rantin' and Trembling String: A History of Scottish Dance Music.* Kingston and Montreal: McGill-Queens University Press, 1991.

—. "The Gaelic Tradition in Canadian Culture." In *The Scottish Tradition in Canada,* edited by W. Stanford Reid, 232-47. Toronto: McClelland and Stewart, 1976.

Farmer, Henry George. *A History of Music in Scotland.* 1947. London: Hinrichsen, 1993.

Feintuch, Burt. "Introduction." *Cape Breton Fiddle and Piano Music: The Beaton Family of Mabou.* Liner Notes. SFW CD 40507. Washington: Smithsonian Folkways Recordings, 2004.

—. *The Conditions for Cape Breton Fiddle Music: The Social and Economic Setting of a Regional Soundscape.* University of New Hampshire. 2004.

Ferrel, Frank. "Boston Fiddle: The Dudley Street Tradition." Liner Notes for *ROUN7018.* 1996.

The Fiddlers of James Bay, directed by Bob Rodgers. National Film Board of Canada, 1980.

Foulds, Matthew. Discussion with author. Halifax, Nova Scotia, 2000.

Gerrits, G.H. *Dutch.* "Peoples of the Maritimes" series. Tantallon, NS: Four East Publications, 2000.

Gibson, John. "Traditional Piping in Nova Scotia." In *Celtic Languages and Celtic Peoples: Proceedings from the Second North American Congress of Celtic Studies,* edited by Cyril J.Byrne, Margaret Harry, Pádraig Ó Siadhail. Halifax: D'Arcy McGee Chair of Irish Studies, St. Mary's University, 1992.

Graham, Danny. Discussion with the author. 2002, 2003.

Graham, Mary. Discussion with author. 2003.

Graham Survey. A survey compiled and collected by Glenn Graham of fiddlers' views on the Cape Breton fiddle tradition. 2003.

Hornsby, Stephen J. *Nineteenth-Century Cape Breton: A Historical Geography.* Kingston and Montreal: McGill-Queen's University Press, 1992.

Jhally, Sut. "The Political Economy of Culture." In *Cultural Politics in Contemporary America,* edited by Ian Angus and Sut Jhally. New York: Routledge, 1989.

Johnson, David. *Music and Society in Lowland Scotland in the Eighteenth Century.* London: Oxford University Press, 1972.

Jones, Shanna and Ken Steffenson. "Local History and Information." Glengarry County Gen-Web, 9 January, 2004. http://www.rootsweb.com/~onglenga/history.htm

Kennedy, Michael. "Lochaber No More: A Critical Examination of Highland Emigration Mythology." *Myth, Migration, and the Making of Memory: Scotia and Nova Scotia, c.1700-1999*, edited by Marjorie Harper and Michael E. Vance, 267-97. Halifax: Fernwood; Edinburgh: John Donald, 1999.

—. *Gaelic Nova Scotia: An Economic, Cultural, and Social Impact Study*. Curatorial Report, no. 97. Halifax: Nova Scotia Museum, 2002. http://museum.gov.ns.ca/pubs/Gaelic-Report.pdf

Laidlaw, Alexander Fraser. *The Campus and the Community: the Global Impact of the Antigonish Movement*. Montreal: Harvest House, 1961.

LeBlanc, Donnie. Interview by Joseph Beaton. 29 November, 1993.

Lederman, Anne. "Fiddling." *Encyclopedia of Music in Canada*. 2nd ed., electronic version. 8 August, 2001. http://www.n/c-bnc.ca/music/17/index-e.html

Lyle Tilley Davidson [Chartered Accountants]. *1999 Music Industry Survey: Assessment of the Nova Scotia Music Industry*. Halifax: Music Industry Association of Nova Scotia, 2000. http://www.mians.ca/images/1999industrystudy.pdf

MacDonald, Allan (with Frances MacEachen). "Interview Piper Allan MacDonald, Glenuig. Part One." *Am Bràighe* 2, no. 1 (1994).

MacDonald, Allan. "Reclaiming the tradition: In conversation with Allan MacDonald, Glenuig, Scotland." Interview with Mike Kennedy. *Am Bràighe* (Spring 1994): 12-13.

MacDonald, Hugh A. Liner Notes for *A Musical Legacy: Donald Angus Beaton Cape Breton Violinist*. Mabou, NS: DAB Records, 1985.

MacDonald, Keith Norman. The Skye Collection of the Best Reels and Strathpeys Extant. 1887. St. Paul's Island, NS: [Paul Cranford] 1979; London, ON: Scott's Highland Services, 1986.

MacDonell, J. A. *Sketches Illustrating the Early Settlement and History of Glengarry (County) in Canada*. 1893. Milton, ON: Global Heritage Press, 2003.

MacDougall, J. L. *History of Inverness County, Nova Scotia*. 1922. Belleville, ON: Mika Publishing, 1972.

MacEachen, Frances. "Dunlay and Greenberg look at style and technique of 'fiddle signatures'." *Am Bràighe* (Autumn 1996): 9.

—. "Cape Breton Fiddling," 2003. http://www.ambraighe.ca/GaelicArts/fiddling.htm

MacGillivray, Allister. *The Cape Breton Fiddler*. Sydney: College of Cape Breton Press, 1981.

MacGillivray, Allister with Beverly MacGillivray. *A Cape Breton Ceilidh*. Sydney, NS: Sea Cape Music, 1988.

MacGregor, John. *Historical and Descriptive Sketches of the Maritime Colonies of British America*. 1828. New York: Johnson Reprint Corporation, 1968.

MacInnis, J. J. "Scottish Music in Cape Breton, Nova Scotia: 'Violin Players I Have Met'." *The Canadian American Gael* 1 (1943): 90.

MacIsaac, Ashley. Interview by Joseph Beaton. 21 December, 1993.

MacIsaac, Dave. Interview with the author. Halifax, NS. 22 April, 2004.

MacKay, Alex Francis. Interview by Joseph Beaton. Kingsville, NS. 1993.

MacKenzie, Carl. Interview by Allister MacGillivray. 14 August, 1995.

MacKinnon, Kenneth A. Discussion with the author. Halifax, NS. 2001.

—. E-mail to the author. 18 December, 2003.

—. Comment to the author. 10 March, 2004.

MacLeod, Alistair. "Inverness County: From Highland to Highland and Island to Island." *Mabou Pioneer II*. Mabou, NS: Mabou Pioneer Committee, 1977. vii-xvi.

MacMaster, Natalie. Interview by Joseph Beaton. 29 December, 1993.

MacNeil, Hector. "Our Living Celtic Culture." n.d. http://www.celtic-colours.com/culture.html

MacPherson, A. D. "Glengarry County, Ontario: A Visitor's Account in 1814." http://www.theclearances.org/clearances/articles.php?articleid=76

Macqueen, Malcolm A. *Skye Pioneers and "The Island."* Winnipeg: Privately printed, 1929.

McGann, J. Clifford. "Divine Intervention: Catholic Priests, Revival Movements, and Applied Folklore." n.d. http://www.tullochgorm.com/priests.html

McKay, Ian. "History and the Tourist Gaze: The Politics of Commemoration in Nova Scotia, 1935-1964." *Acadiensis* 22, no. 2 (1993): 105-38.

—. "Tartanism Triumphant: The Construction of Scottishness in Nova Scotia, 1933-1954." *Acadiensis* 21, no. 2 (1992): 5-47.

McKinnon, Ian F. "Fiddling to Fortune: The Role of Commercial Recordings Made by Cape Breton Fiddlers in the Fiddle Music Tradition of Cape Breton Island." MA thesis. Memorial University of Newfoundland, 1989.

Moore, Finn, Discussion with author. Mabou, NS. August, 2003.

Moore, Maggie, "Scottish Step Dancing." Scottish Arts Council, 1995. n.p. http://www.tullochgorm.com/scottish.html

Newton, Michael. "An Introduction to the Gaelic Music Tradition." 9 May, 2000. http://www.electricscotland.com/history/literat/GAELICTRAD.HTM

Nilsen, Kenneth. "The Nova Scotia Gael in Boston." In *Proceedings of the Harvard Celtic Colloquium*. V. IV. Cambridge, MA: The Department of Celtic Languages and Literatures, Faculty of Arts and Sciences, Harvard University, 1986.

Nova Scotia Culture Sector Strategy Management Committee. *The Nova Scotia Culture Sector Strategy: Culture in the New Millennium—Planning Our Future*. Halifax, NS: Department of Education and Culture, 1999. http://culturestrategy.ednet.ns.ca

Nova Scotia Department of Education and Culture. *Nova Scotia's Cultural Policy*. Halifax, NS: Department of Education and Culture, 1997.

Perlman, Ken. *The Fiddle Music of Prince Edward Island: Celtic and Acadian Tunes in Living Tradition*. Pacific, MO: Mel Bay Publications, 1996.

Prebble, John. *The Highland Clearances*. New York: Penguin Books, 1963.

Proctor, George A. and Mark Miller. "Fiddling." *Encyclopedia of Music in Canada*. Toronto: University of Toronto Press, 1981.

Rankin, John Morris. Interview by Joseph Beaton. 30 December, 1993.

Reid, John. Lecture. Saint Mary's University, Halifax, Nova Scotia. 10 December, 1999.

Rhodes, Frank. "Dancing in Cape Breton Island, Nova Scotia." Appendix to *Traditional Dancing in Scotland* by J. P. Flett and T. M. Flett, 267-85. London: Routledge and Kegan Paul, 1964.

Scarff, Jim. "The Music of the Shetland and Orkney Islands." Updated 13 November, 2002. http://www.sfcelticmusic.com/shetland/shetland.htm

Schiller, Herbert. *Culture, Inc.: The Corporate Takeover of Public Expression*. New York: Oxford University Press, 1989.

Shaw, John. "Language, Music, and Local Aesthetics: Views From Gaeldom and Beyond." *Scottish Language*. (1992-93): 11-12.

Shepherd, John. "Towards a Sociology of Musical Styles." In *Lost in Music: Culture, Style and the Musical Event*, edited by Avron Levinewhite. New York: Routlege and Kegan Paul, 1987.

Smith, Gordon E. "Lee Cremo: Narratives About a Micmac Fiddler." In *Canadian Music: Issues of Hegemony and Identity*, edited by Beverly Diamond and Robert Witmer. Toronto: Canadian Scholar's Press, 1994.

Thornton, Patricia A. "The Problem of Out-Migration from Atlantic Canada, 1871-1921: A New Look." *Acadiensis*. 15, no. 1 (1985): 3-34.

"Vanishing Cape Breton Fiddler." *30 From Halifax*. Narrated and written by Ron MacInnis. Directed by Charles Reynolds. Halifax, NS: Canadian Broadcasting Corporation (television). Recorded 17 November, 1971.